# For the Love of Learning

## A YEAR IN THE LIFE
## OF A SCHOOL PRINCIPAL

Kristin Phillips

Published by Simon & Schuster

NEW YORK   LONDON   TORONTO   SYDNEY   NEW DELHI

SIMON &
SCHUSTER
CANADA

Simon & Schuster Canada
A Division of Simon & Schuster, Inc.
166 King Street East, Suite 300
Toronto, Ontario M5A 1J3

This Simon & Schuster Canada edition August 2022

SIMON & SCHUSTER CANADA and colophon are trademarks of Simon & Schuster, Inc.
For information about special discounts for bulk purchases, please contact
Simon & Schuster Special Sales at 1-800-268-3216
or CustomerService@simonandschuster.ca.

Manufactured in the United States of America

1   3   5   7   9   10   8   6   4   2

Library and Archives Canada Cataloguing in Publication
Title: For the love of learning : a year in the life of a school principal / Kristin Phillips.
Names: Phillips, Kristin (Kristin A.), author.
Description: Simon & Schuster Canada edition.
Identifiers: Canadiana (print) 20210343524 | Canadiana (ebook) 20210343532
| ISBN 9781982170684 (softcover) | ISBN 9781982170707 (ebook)
Subjects: LCSH: Phillips, Kristin (Kristin A.) | LCSH: Elementary school principals—
Canada—Biography. | LCSH: Public schools—Canada. | LCGFT: Autobiographies.
Classification: LCC LA2325.P498 A3 2022 | DDC 371.10092—dc23

ISBN 978-1-9821-7068-4
ISBN 978-1-9821-7070-7 (ebook)

*For my three children*

# Contents

Author's Note                                                    ix

Introduction                                                     xi

## FALL

1. First Day                                                      3
2. Meet the Teachers                                             15
3. Becoming Learners                                             26
4. A Long Day                                                    37
5. Special Needs                                                 49
6. Being Present                                                 64
7. Try Something New; No One Will Die                            74
8. Bullying                                                      88

## WINTER

9. Bouncy Boundaries                                            107
10. "Bad Egg"                                                   119
11. Frankie                                                     129
12. Good Teachers Matter                                        135

13. Mom to the Whole School                              146
14. School Culture                                       152
15. Best-Teacher-Ever Feeling                            160
16. Starfish                                             169
17. Connecting Dots                                      176
18. Report Cards                                         182
19. Mental Health                                        195
20. Terrible, Horrible, No Good, Very Bad Day            203

# SPRING

21. Better Days                                          215
22. Downward Spiral                                      223
23. The Hard Stuff                                       235
24. Principal Wins Day                                   247
25. You Win Some . . .                                   256
26. Welcome to Kindergarten                              265
27. Last Day of School                                   275

# SUMMER

28. August Dreams                                        289

    Epilogue: Covid-19                                   293
    Acknowledgments                                      299

# Author's Note

THROUGHOUT THE BOOK I WILL TAKE YOU through a year in my life as a principal. I have taken the liberty to pull teachers, students, and families from a wide range of experiences, and have meshed characters together and changed names and details to protect people's privacy. Some time-lines have also been adjusted. But all of the stories are real, as are all of the decisions I made. Some I am proud of and others I would do differently if I could now.

# *Introduction*

IT'S A TUESDAY IN FEBRUARY, 2:45 P.M. Forty-five minutes left until the bell and I am stepping through slushy puddles in my high heels down the junior hallway. Boots are strewn all over the floor and student paintings decorate the walls. A few are hanging by one last piece of sticky tape. I absentmindedly try to tack them back to the wall, but they fall despite my efforts. I decide that isn't my problem right now.

I've had a call from room 4 to come and deal with Olivia, who is refusing to do any work and has rejected all requests to leave the classroom and come to the office. Peter, her teacher, has a heart of gold, but it has been like this all month and he is fed up. I open the door and sure enough, there is Olivia, her red hair a mess of tangles. She is wearing the same orange polyester skirt and green sweatshirt she wears every day. On her feet are high-top running shoes, laces undone. For grade 6, Olivia is a big girl, as tall as me and already developed. Room 4 is our class for learning-disabled students. Olivia has a diagnosed learning disability but also a whole host of other issues. No one can quite get a handle on her behaviours: anxiety, ADHD, autism? There is no diagnosis but right now that doesn't matter. Peter needs support. I go over to Olivia's desk and whisper, "Hey, Olivia, why don't you come to my office for a bit? You can colour."

"Lalalalalalala," she singsongs loudly.

I close my eyes briefly and take a breath. I do not want a confrontation this late in the day. My feet hurt; I might be getting too old for high heels, but I am not ready to admit defeat. I haven't eaten lunch. I don't think I've been to the bathroom since morning announcements. Due to frigid February winds, we have had three days of indoor recesses and nerves are frayed. There is a staff meeting tonight and although I'm tempted to cancel, I won't.

"Olivia, you need to come to my office. The day is almost done. It's almost home time."

"Fine!" And she rushes out the door and down the hall. Battle averted. I hope she is really headed towards my office. As I make my way down the hall, an announcement is made: "Mrs. Phillips, line one." Why do I only get calls when I am as far from my office as I can be? Just then my vice-principal, Adam, passes me at a clip, sopping wet.

"What's going on?" I ask, not breaking stride.

"Toilet in the boys' washroom is spurting water everywhere and Vince [the custodian] stepped out for coffee."

"Okay. Glad you've got it." And I smile. This is *definitely* not my problem. On my way back to my office to check on Olivia, there is another page for a phone call on line one, which means it must be Max, my superintendent, calling. My secretary, Joan, wouldn't have bothered to announce the call twice if it weren't. Sawyer, a grade 5 student, stops me and asks if we can play backgammon today.

"Sorry, kiddo, I know it is our day, but it will have to be another day." He frowns and stomps back to class. Sawyer needs some TLC and we play backgammon at the end of the day on Tuesdays. I hope this cancellation of our time together won't cause another outburst before the end of the day.

Close to my office now I see Kim, an educational assistant, following Myles down the hall. Myles, a kindergarten student with some anger management issues, is barreling away from her. We share a look of exasperation and camaraderie—Kim's got this. I get to my office and Joan says Max called.

"Wants you to call him back ASAP. I tried paging you twice, but I can see you were busy." And she glances towards my office with a knowing look. I gather Olivia has made it and I sneak a peek in. She is sitting at the table colouring. I let her be for the time being and take a moment to visit the washroom.

Some days I wonder—I chose this job? I could have stayed a teacher. I loved teaching. Why did I want to become a principal? Today I can't really remember. There are no plans when you are a principal. I remember the excitement of my first day as a vice-principal.

I was ready. My pencils were sharpened. I had new pink high heels and a suit—something I would never have worn as a grade 1 teacher. I was nervous but trying to hide it. Everyone around me seemed to have something important to do, while I had no idea what I was going to do all day. So I sat there at my desk, waiting. Nothing happened. I left my office and started wandering around. I walked into the staff room and the conversation stopped. I smiled awkwardly and reintroduced myself but there was silence. Whatever the topic of conversation had been, it quickly changed to the weather. I walked down the hall and a classroom door shut at the sound of my heels on the floor. The next classroom door was open and I entered. A hush fell over the room and all thirty pairs of eyes, teacher's and students', turned to stare at me. I smiled and left. I wasn't one of the gang anymore. I went back to my clean desk and sharpened pencils and wondered, now what? Since the age of five, for thirty-six years, my life had been organized into forty-minute blocks of time with clear objectives and tasks, whether I was the student or the teacher. I was in uncharted territory. I was scared.

By ten thirty I had figured it out. I didn't have to do anything. The job came to me in a never-ending flow of problems. Kids were sent to the office for misbehaving. Teachers' timetables didn't work and two classes ended up in the same English class for period 3. Parents were calling that their kids were unhappy about their class placement. The secretary wanted to know how we were going to spend the fundraising money. Human Resources called to ask about the teacher opening. The janitor came by to explain why the toilets weren't working and that I'd need to make an announcement that the boys' downstairs washroom was closed. The maintenance guy wanted to know where to plant the new tree! He made me traipse about the yard in my new heels. This was leadership? This is what I had signed up for?

The job of principal is complex and multifaceted. You take the courses about transformational versus transactional leadership and then you are called to the kindergarten room to deal with the kid who has had a rather disastrous accident, having not made it to the washroom in time, and you can't believe the mess. It's in between his toes! You take the courses about how to inspire teachers and then you are called to the muddy playground in November on the day that you only have heels and no boots because Shelly has got herself stuck in the mud of the soccer field and can't get out. You have read all the legislation on policies and procedures, but no one mentioned that you would have mittens drying on the heater in your office because you worked in a disadvantaged area and doled out mittens every recess.

Principals are responsible for the safety of up to 2,000 students in some larger high schools, although most elementary principals have 300–700 students. That's still a lot. It's also a principal's responsibility to ensure that the teachers are doing their jobs correctly and that the students are learning. The building is your responsibility. The budget is your responsibility. Responding to parents is your job. Just maintaining discipline in some schools can take two or three hours a day. Increasingly, interacting with outside agencies around student mental health is your job. Fundraising is your job. It is overwhelming at times. Principals typically work sixty-hour weeks. There is a high rate of burnout in the job. No day, no hour, no minute is the same. There is nothing more important than ensuring that the school experience for kids is exactly what they need to succeed. And I love it. Well, most days.

I head back to my office and it is now close to 3:30 p.m. I escort Olivia back to class, now that she's calmed down some, but a tantrum ensues when we arrive. I don't even know what happened. All of a sudden she is throwing books and overturning tables. Peter is able to get the rest of the kids out of the room quickly (we've done this before) and I back into a corner and let Olivia have the tantrum. I quickly call the office and ask Adam to call her mom and say that she can't go home on the bus. Olivia overhears and takes up the tantrum in earnest now. She isn't any danger to herself or me, so I do not instigate a restraint procedure. Hopefully she will tire herself out in a few minutes.

It's been a hard few days for her and she uses every bit of energy just trying to cope with a school system that can't meet her needs. She's a bright girl but the learning disabilities make mathematics and writing difficult. Socially, she can't make friends even though she wants them desperately. Her parents are worried as well but trying to access mental health supports is time consuming and the system works at a snail's pace. Olivia has been struggling for six years at school and we haven't made a difference yet. I don't know what to do.

Adam, now sporting a dry but slightly too small sweatshirt from the lost and found, shows up to take over watching Olivia, who is now huddled in a corner crying, but she doesn't want anyone near her. He will wait with her while I get to the staff meeting. It's been a day. Adam, bless his heart, says he remembered to grab donuts for the meeting this morning before everything fell to pieces.

Rushing into my office, Joan tells me Joey called. Joey is my fifteen-year-old son—tall, good-looking, charismatic, and into skateboarding and loud music. He is going to be a rock star, he says. I suggest a Plan B in case that doesn't work out. Joey could also be the poster child for the "Disengaged Boy in High School." I glance at my cell phone and see that there have been six missed calls from Joey and two texts. I sigh.

Is there a problem at home? I am the recently divorced mom of three teenagers.

I look at the first text:

MOM!!! Where are you? Can we have pizza for supper tonight?

I smile. I get that text almost every day from Joey. The second one says:

Frankie didn't get out of bed today. Just warning you.

Unfortunately, that one is not surprising, either. My eldest daughter, Frankie—eighteen, beautiful, smart, and musically talented—suffers from depression and anxiety. She has been spiraling down again lately. My heart clenches; I close my eyes for a few seconds, and breathe. Pizza is sounding like a good idea to me, too. I text Joey back quickly and then send a short encouraging text to Frankie. Lily, my middle child, has swim practice tonight and my ex is driving her there. I don't worry about her so much. Lily is the president of her school council, colour-codes her school agenda, and makes the honour roll. She and Frankie are close but so very different these days.

I put on my unflappable smile and walk into the library for the staff meeting. The teachers saunter in and grab a donut. They look as tired as I feel. I'd love to say, "Go home. We will postpone this meeting until next week." But in a highly unionized environment I am only allowed one seventy-five-minute staff meeting per month and it must be on this Tuesday. My time with the teachers is important and precious. We have learning to do, too.

This book is about my experiences as a principal: the good times, the bad times, the frustrations, and the joys. I was a classroom teacher for seventeen years and then a school administrator for fifteen years. I was an elementary school principal in three different schools in southern Ontario and I learned on the job, mostly by making mistakes! Despite the courses you take to become a principal, you learn as you go. There is no grace period or easing in. Within my first fifteen minutes of being a principal, starting mid-year in January, my vice-principal walked in and said, "So, boss, a parent just called and said that one of our educational assistants gave a student a pornographic website address to look at over the Christmas break. What do you want to do?" I didn't know. I closed my door and called a mentor. As it turns out, the name of a porn site and the name of a multiplication practice site differed by one letter and the problem was resolved. It was trial by fire.

It is also my story as a parent, because my two lives intertwine. As a parent of three children, I also experienced the school system from the outside looking in. Both Frankie and Joey have learning disabilities. Frankie suffered from mental health issues from grade 8 through her early twenties. We refer to it now as eight years in the dark ages. Navigating the school system and the mental health system was a challenge. I like to think that my personal experiences helped me to be more empathetic to the parents who faced similar problems. We were all doing the best we could.

A principal's job is about keeping everyone in the building safe, happy, and learning. That sounds simple enough, but it isn't. These are my stories as I learned to navigate the complexities of the education system. But it is also an intimate look at education: where it can excel, where it can flounder, and what we can perhaps do better. Our schools need to be places where the love of learning is at the core.

# Fall

# ONE

# First Day

I MET MYLES ON THE FIRST DAY of school. Five years old and starting kindergarten, he was cute as a button. Tousled bleached-blond hair, still a bit of baby fat, and a winning smile. That is, until he opened his mouth and swore a blue streak.

The call to come immediately to the kindergarten room was at about 10 a.m. It is unusual to deal with student behaviour on the first day of school and I was expecting a homesick child. As I began the walk down the long corridor, new shoes lined up in neat rows and lunch bags on hooks, a little boy came barreling down the hallway.

"Fuck. Double fuck. This place is garbage." Shoes were being kicked out of the way and lunch bags knocked off hooks. Anxious teachers were peering out of classroom doors and quietly shutting them.

I attempt to intercept.

"Hey. Are you having a bad day?" I ask. Myles runs past me and hides under a table at the other end of the hallway. At least we are closer to my office. I know the recess bell will ring in fifteen minutes and I want him in my office, door closed, by then. Thankful I have chosen a longer skirt this day, I sit down on the floor near but not too close to the table.

"My name is Mrs. Phillips. It looks like you are sad." Tears and wailing and swearing were the response. "First days can be hard," I continue. "I bet you miss your mom."

"I hate this place. People are dumb here."

"Hmm. School can be tricky." I pause and the wailing turns to sniffles. "See over there? That's my office. I have some books and toys in there. Do you want to come see? It's quiet in there and there aren't any other kids." Myles glances and scowls. He looks at me, wondering if he should trust me. "It's going to get noisy in the hallway in a few minutes. We could hang out in my office where it is quiet." Myles considers this possibility and starts to scoot his bottom towards my office. I get up and hold out my hand. I wait in silence as Myles sizes up the situation. He scrambles to his feet and shuffles towards my office. He ignores my hand.

I keep a variety of toys on the table in my office. I have a wand that has sparkles and gel, and some fancy egg timers. There are fidget toys and squishy balls. I find that both kids and anxious parents will pick them up and calm themselves. Myles sits down and picks up the wand. I sit down and say nothing. There's also a box of tissues, but it is my experience that young boys prefer their sleeves, so I don't offer one.

I engage him in conversation about mundane things. Does he have any brothers or sisters? A younger brother and a baby sister. What did he have for breakfast? Cereal. What games does he like to play outside? Soccer. He mumbles his answers without making eye contact.

I don't mention the swearing or the outburst. Early in my principal career a young kindergarten boy had been sent to my office for saying "motherfucker." I had told him that if he kept saying bad words he would have to go home. His eyes lit up and I could see his mind working—if only he'd known how easy it was to go home! I learned quickly that that was not an appropriate response to an out-of-control five-year-old.

Outside my window I can hear the kids playing at recess. Myles looks out my window but doesn't ask to go outside. He is content with the quiet. I offer him a snack and read him a story. He doesn't engage with me but he doesn't run away, either. The recess bell rings and the kids enter the building. Once I can hear that the hallway din has subsided I ask if he'd like to walk back down to his classroom and play there. He looks at me warily but agrees. This time he takes my hand and I walk him back to class. Sondra, his teacher, meets us at the door. Luckily Sondra is a very experienced kindergarten teacher and without batting an eye she welcomes him back as if nothing has happened. I thank my lucky stars for Sondra. Myles enters the room cautiously and heads towards the art centre, where he begins colouring. Sondra and I agree to touch base later and I let her know to call should things escalate again.

This pattern would continue on a daily basis for the first couple of months of school. He would enter the class and there would immediately be some sort of altercation: kicking, hitting, swearing, throwing. Every day was different and there didn't seem to be any one thing that would set him off. Almost every morning, shortly after nine, a call would come in to the principal's office from the kindergarten classroom. I'd answer and the directive was always the same: "Come and get Myles."

The kindergarten room was as far from my office as you could be. I'd start the walk down only to meet Myles running down the hallway at full speed. Sometimes I could catch him. Some days I jumped out of his path and quietly followed him where he was heading. If I was lucky we'd end up in my office with the door closed. Other days we could end up in a standoff in the playground or with him hiding in a corner or under a table. For two months that was my morning routine, and Myles's. Eventually he would calm down enough and return to class, where he usually settled down and enjoyed his day. Myles was a bright boy and was meeting all the kindergarten milestones, when he engaged in school. But he was so angry at the world and had no coping mechanisms.

Walking back down the hallway I heard wailing coming from a grade 1 classroom. The door was closed but I entered anyway. I bumped into Maggie, a teacher just two years from retirement but still totally present in her work, who was standing with her back to the door. She was calmly reading poems to the class while also trying to block a sobbing girl from leaving the room. I mouthed to Maggie, "What's her name?" Maggie came to the end of her poem and whispered to me, "Ana. She's a new Canadian and wants to go home, maybe. I think she thought recess time would be home time. She has been crying all morning, but it has escalated." I said I would take over with Ana and she gratefully gathered the rest of the students on the carpet. Maggie had lots of experience dealing with unhappy first-day students and students with limited language skills. I doubt she would have called for help but since I dropped by, she gratefully left Ana to me.

I quietly stood with my back against the door as Ana sobbed next to me. Her pretty pink back-to-school dress was twisted and crumpled as she bunched and unbunched the bottom of it wiping her tears. Her straight black hair had been in two neat ponytails but they were now askew. Using a quiet voice, I tried to engage her, but to no avail. She either had very little English or was too emotionally wrought to communicate.

It wasn't unusual for students in the early days of school to think recess was home time. Early in my teaching career I had taught grade 1 and I remembered how often I would have to say, "No, it is not home time yet." Little kids adapt to new routines fairly quickly, but we have to remember that their ability to process time is limited. After five minutes I determined that we were making no progress. So I held out my hand and said, "Let's call Mama." She looked up and took my hand, the word "mama" registering and offering salvation. We walked to my office and called her mom.

Ana's mom spoke little English but was able to understand the issue. I reassured her that Ana was fine, just homesick. Although Ana and her mom spoke on the phone in Spanish, Mom was unable to calm her down enough to stay. We agreed Mom would come and get her and we'd try again tomorrow.

We deal with many tears on the first day of school but usually they subside as the students become engaged in the activities. Our first course of action is to wait it out. But in Ana's case it was better to cut our losses and regroup. As it was impossible to engage Ana in at least some conversation to distract her and the crying had been going on for over two hours, my instincts were that we could try again tomorrow. When Mom came to get her, I suggested she give Ana a photograph of herself and the family to carry in her backpack. The next few days with Ana continued to be tenuous but Maggie kept her busy and they posted the picture of her family on Ana's desk. By the second week of school Ana was happy and participating and learning English.

Not all first-day hiccups are so quickly resolved. I settled down at my desk to call Myles's mother. It was the first of what became almost daily phone calls. Tiffany, at twenty-three, was a single mother of three. Myles was the oldest. There was no solid father figure and Tiffany was coping with a part-time job, subsidized housing, and no family support. I later learned she had not completed high school.

"Hi, Tiffany? This is Kristin Phillips, principal at Myles's school."

"What's he done?" Her voice was tired already.

"Myles was quite upset this morning and ran out of the room swearing. But he eventually came to my office and settled down. He's back in class now and everything is fine. I just wanted you to know."

"Yeah. He can get real angry. Someone probably bothered him. Do I have to come and get him?"

"No, no," I assured her. "We'll see how the rest of the day goes."

Clearly, Tiffany wasn't surprised there were problems. Already on the first day of school she sounded defeated. Myles had attended the

Catholic school down the road for junior kindergarten and I made a mental note to give the principal there a call.

Tiffany hated it when I called her. She didn't have any answers about what to do. On the worst days I'd ask her to come and get Myles but that didn't solve anything. Other days, in frustration, she'd blame the school system. I understood that. None of us really knew what to do.

Sondra, Myles's teacher, had a lot of tricks up her sleeve for dealing with 3–5-year-olds. But none of us had ever met anyone like Myles before. She tried stickers, rewards, timeouts—nothing seemed to work. Myles wanted to play with the other students but didn't know how. He interrupted the play by grabbing toys he wanted, didn't take turns, and lashed out when things didn't go his way. Sondra was constantly running interference and calming down the other students, who were beginning to keep their distance from Myles. Already a few parents were beginning to ask questions as they dropped their kids off in the morning. By the second week of school, I had assigned Kim to Myles's class and he was her main focus. Most days, however, the call still came at 9 a.m. and I would meet Myles in the hallway, now trailed by the educational assistant.

If you meet a kid on day one there is a good chance that kid is going to be a fixture in the principal's office. Most kids have a good three-week honeymoon period in September. Myles didn't.

There are also parents that you meet on the first day. It was a common practice to post the class lists before Labour Day so that kids and parents knew who their teacher was going to be on the first day of school. It makes the first day organization easier. Plus, as a parent I knew how agonizingly long Labour Day weekend could be for my own kids when they didn't know who their teacher or classmates would be. In my first year of being a principal I had posted the list at 4 p.m. and skedaddled out of the school as quickly as possible. That backfired when on the first day of school a long line of unhappy parents met me outside my office. Since then I had changed my practice to publish them on

Thursday so I could deal with as much of the unhappiness as possible before the long weekend.

Invariably, though, there would be a parent or two camped outside my office on the first day of school, nervous and crying child in tow. They had read the class list on Saturday and there was a problem: it was the wrong teacher, or the best friend was in a different class, or there was an archenemy in their class. Of course, the archenemy had been a best friend when we created the lists in June! Whatever the problem was didn't matter; the parent had spent the entire weekend assuring their child that they would fix this problem on Tuesday morning. Into my office we would go—the protective parent, the crying child, and me. Pretending to be oblivious, I would ask how I could help and listen to the issues all the way through. On occasion I would ask the child to wait in the office, depending on what the parent started to tell me. I was always surprised by what some parents were willing to say in front of their kid.

The parent's sole motivation is to make the crying stop, the unhappiness go away. It is a challenging navigation to help a parent see that rescuing their child from this situation is actually more harmful than good. I would begin by explaining that a change in classroom would not be possible. Making a change for one situation would open up the floodgates to an avalanche of parent requests, and I knew better. However, I would continue, this is an opportunity for your child to develop resilience by experiencing a challenging situation and learning that all would work out just fine. I would remind that parent that, of course, we, the grown-ups, faced this sort of thing on a regular basis in our adult lives—maybe when starting a new job, or a new course for ongoing education. If the child was there, I might remind them of a time when they were nervous to go to a birthday party, or summer camp, or swimming lessons. And through the sniveling, the child might remember that those things had turned out just fine. We would end the conversation with me visibly writing in my agenda to touch base with the student in two weeks to make sure things were going okay. This made both the parent and student feel there was still hope that I would change my mind. There was also a deadline to the perceived unhappiness. Almost without fail, when I checked in two weeks later, the kid could barely remember they'd been unhappy. On the very rare occasion when the classroom placement didn't resolve, I would quietly make the change, admonishing the parent to keep quiet and emphasizing that this was a once-in-a-lifetime occurrence. Schools provide numerous opportunities for children to experience "cope-able" problems. My job was to help parents recognize these as opportunities, not as catastrophes.

After lunch, Mandy's mom called. As we exchanged pleasantries I called up Mandy on my computer and discovered she was in grade 7 French Immersion. The issue: Mandy had not been chosen to be a bus monitor. All of Mandy's older sisters had been bus monitors and Mandy was devastated.

I hated bus monitors. Actually, I hated buses. It was the board's practice to assign older students to monitor the buses. In theory it was a great idea. Kids would get a bit of responsibility by ensuring that the younger kids had someone to go to if there was a problem on the bus. Bus monitors were not, theoretically, disciplinarians. That was the job of the bus driver.

Now, imagine being a bus driver. I can't think of a more impossible job. Not only do you need to drive a bus during rush hour in all types of weather, but you have to monitor the kids' behaviour. Bus drivers receive a quick one-day workshop to deal with the behaviour of sixty 5–13-year-olds. Kids get on that bus and it is often a free-for-all. And in any unsupervised setting, otherwise good kids can make poor decisions. Dealing with bus behaviour is the worst part of the job, since kids are very reluctant to tell the truth about what happens on the bus. Very early in the school year a bus hierarchy is established, and no one wants to be the snitch. As principal I used to invite my bus drivers in for coffee and a chat every few months and checked in with them regularly. I also had assigned seating on my buses, spreading out the older kids and behaviour problems, seating siblings together so that if they fought, the parents could figure it out, and putting the quietest kids at the back. But this solution worked only if the bus driver enforced the seating plan, and frequently the vice-principal or I would have to intervene.

My issue with bus monitors was that they often tended to add to the problems rather than help to solve them. They often took, with the bus driver's blessing, control of the discipline and would call out kids on their behaviour, threatening to tell on them. It gave those students a lot of power in an already tenuous situation. I couldn't dismiss having bus monitors, as it was a board initiative, but I could choose the bus monitors carefully and train them to be helpers, not tattlers. When the teachers and I had met in late August to choose the bus monitors, I had expressed my feelings and we had chosen students that we felt would not abuse their power. Mandy had not made the list and her mom wanted to make it better.

I didn't know Mandy or her mom or her situation. This call was very similar to the meetings in the morning about parents wanting their children to move classes. It really was more about Mandy's mom wanting her daughter to stop crying than anything else. With Mandy's siblings, there had been status attached to being a bus monitor and Mandy, and her mom, felt slighted. I launched into the same spiel about how important it was for kids to learn to deal with disappointment. Of course, I empathized, it would be tough for Mandy given that her sisters had all been bus monitors, but sometimes life wasn't fair. Mandy's mom was tenacious and we did this dance for a good thirty minutes before I offered a compromise. I'd put Mandy's name on a list in case one of the bus monitors didn't work out, and I certainly could provide her with leadership opportunities as a kindergarten lunchroom helper. I could tell that her mom was not appeased but we ended the conversation cordially.

Most parents do not come into contact with the school principal very often. Some, like Tiffany, have almost daily contact because their kids experience a lot of difficulty at school. There are always a few like

Mandy's mom, who will call every time their child comes home un-happy. I always welcome those calls since I don't ever want a kid to be unhappy at school. But often it is not about changing the situation—it is about supporting the parent. When parents overprotect their child from the disappointments and challenges that are necessary for growing up, children fail to develop resilience and coping strategies.

From my office I could hear the rustling that signaled kids were in the hallways. I glanced at the clock. It was 3:25. The bell would go off in five minutes and the first day would be over. Praying that no kinder-garten students would get lost on their way to the buses, I headed down that hallway. There is nothing like the first day of school. The students were all abuzz talking with old and new friends and saying goodbye to teachers. A young girl in her bright pink first-day-of-school dress, with matching light-up pink runners, was hugging Maggie, her grade 1 teacher.

"I love you."

Maggie smiled down at her and said, "Thank you. I like you too. See you tomorrow." The relationships that are so key to academic achieve-ment were beginning already. I continued down the hall greeting stu-dents and asking about their first day. Most of the kids had no idea who I was. For many students the principal is at best a shadowy figure in the distance. My goal would be to get to know most of their names and be present in the school, not just the office. I wouldn't be able to converse meaningfully with the teachers if I didn't know their students. But for today, it was smiles and hellos.

I spied Myles standing in line by the wall, getting ready for dis-missal. His shirt was untucked, his shoes untied, and there was a bright yellow splotch in the middle of his shirt. Paint? Mustard? I thanked the stars that Myles lived close enough to walk and wouldn't be riding the bus. There was a throng of anxious parents and strollers hovering out-side the kindergarten doors, craning their necks to get a glimpse of their children. We often forget that the first day of school is momentous for parents as much as for kids. Myles was looking around, not smiling but not, thankfully, scowling. Sondra hovered nearby. We made eye contact and she smiled wearily. We would catch up after school and I would learn that Myles spent the day on the edge of tantrums but had held it together with careful and timely interventions by Sondra. Myles glanced up and saw me. I smiled warmly but he turned his head. I left it at that.

I made my way to the school entrance to supervise the buses and greet parents. As I was new to the school, there wasn't as much interaction as there would be once everyone figured out who I was. As the last bus left at 3:40 p.m., Bryce, my new grade 6 teacher, sauntered out of the building, unencumbered by a briefcase or backpack. He greeted me with a winning smile. "Hey, Kristin. How was your day?"

"Great first day. You? Good group of kids?"

"Awesome," he replied jauntily. "So cool." And nonchalantly, he made his way to his car, done for the day. I could hear a bunch of boys calling out, "Hey, Mr. B! See you tomorrow!" Already Bryce had made some connections with his students. He was young and easygoing and would connect well with his grade 6 students.

I went back to my office. There was no lineup of teachers but I knew that as the school year progressed, that would change. I did a tour of the classrooms, checking in on the first day and listening to highlights and concerns. Sondra and I had a good chat and I assured her I'd be available for support with Myles if required; little did we know how much support that was going to be.

I sank into my office chair, exhausted, and began to check the fifty or so emails that had piled up throughout the day. The first day had gone reasonably well. The game had started and I was excited about the challenge of a new school. There were kids and parents to get to know but, more importantly, for me, there were the teachers. The teacher is the single most important factor in a school. Research has shown that with a good teacher, students can actually move ahead two years academically, not just one. With a poor teacher, a student's academic growth stagnates and that can cause students to lose up to half a year. I needed to get a grasp on the teaching practices of the school and start the magic of teacher learning. That was the fun part. I packed my bag, gathered up my half-eaten lunch, and pulled out an apple to eat on the way home, realizing I was starving. I grabbed my gym bag but knew I wouldn't be going today. I'd forgotten, like I did every year, how tiring the first day of school is. Netflix it would be. Tomorrow I'd go for sure.

On my way out I passed by Kate's classroom. Kate was a new grade 3 teacher who had just got a teaching contract after five years of supply teaching. New teachers have to "do their time" supply teaching before getting a contract, which is a permanent placement. There are simply not enough jobs available for new teachers to land one right out of teachers' college, unless, in Ontario, you speak French! New teachers tend to learn the job through supply teaching (covering for an absent teacher for a day or two), or, if lucky, with a long-term occasional (LTO) job that could last a few months. These are created when teachers take a leave of absence for any of a variety of reasons, the most common being maternity leave. In LTOs a new teacher can gain the experience of planning, teaching, and assessing over a longer period of time. But they are still not permanent positions and every year new teachers change their jobs, taking on a new grade at a new school.

Kate was hanging student work on the wall in the hallway. With a slight build and her curly hair cut short in a pixie cut, she didn't look much older than some of our grade 8 girls. I stopped to admire the pictures and she told me about her day, minute by minute. I listened and remembered the excitement of my own first days as a teacher. Then I reminded her to go home. Tomorrow would be another day. I knew she'd be there until at least 7 p.m. I would have been.

# TWO

# Meet the Teachers

BY THE THIRD WEEK OF SEPTEMBER THE weather was getting cooler and summer seemed a distant memory. Working in education is funny: it's the only job I can think of where you get a "do-over" every year. The experts say that the hard start in September and hard stop in June adds to the stress of the job. But it also adds to the excitement. In September the walls are clean and empty. The floors have been polished over the summer. The staff fridge is void of moldy leftover sandwiches. There is a renewed sense of adventure as students and teachers form new relationships. I remember a grade 1 student, with pigtails and big eyes, telling me after her first day, "You are my favourite teacher ever."

"Oh, yeah?" I responded. "Who was your teacher last year?"

"I don't remember!" and she bounded off to the playground.

Schools have rules and routines. They have events and assemblies. There are procedures and protocols. But the heart of a school is its culture and the relationships it forms with students and families, and those among the staff members. September sets the stage for the relationships that will make or break the year.

As a principal, throughout the course of the year I will form relationships with many of the students, but mostly those, like Myles, who struggle to cope in the classroom. I will work closely with a few parents while only meeting many others with a handshake at concerts or open houses.

But the teachers in the school are the ones with whom I form the strongest bonds. In some ways they become my new class. A principal's job isn't limited to administration and ultimate disciplinarian (as many students may believe). It is my job as the instructional leader in the school to determine how we can do even better as educators and to move us there. It is my job to develop a passion for learning about teaching.

In England the principal is called the "head teacher." I've always liked that title better than principal. It makes me feel like "one of the gang" still instead of some mysterious power figure hiding out in an air-conditioned office. Getting your teachers to accept you as one of them is another thing altogether. When I started as a principal I was blissfully, and tragically, it turns out, unaware of my position of power. After all, I was the same person that September that I had been the previous June, or so I thought. My new position became clear the first time I entered a music classroom as an administrator: every kid sat up straighter. I was in such awe of this new power that I immediately tried it out in five other classrooms. Sure enough, in every class the kids sat up straighter. Who knew?

That new power extends to the teachers. As a principal, I had to get used to the conversations in the staff room sometimes stopping when I entered. I learned early on that when I casually asked a teacher to pop by my office at the end of the day, it created anxiety and angst for that teacher for the whole day. And all I wanted was to let them know a parent had called. So I began going to teachers' classrooms when I needed to talk to them, or prefacing a desire to chat later with "you're not in trouble."

There are many aspects to forming relationships between the

principal and the teachers but part of it is being visible in classrooms. When I had first started this practice, a teacher called the union to ask if the principal was really allowed to come into classrooms whenever she wanted. The response is yes. If you ask most principals if they regularly get into classrooms, they will answer that there is simply no time, quickly followed by an acknowledgment that it is important to do so, but, you know, the job is just so busy. Early in my career my best intentions to visit classrooms had also been thwarted. Looking for a solution, and believing that one finds time to do the things in life that are important (I can say I am too busy to exercise or I can admit that I'd rather veg out in front of the TV), I'd begun a few years earlier to schedule time each week for these visits. So, I had blocked out in my agenda that I was going to pop into classrooms this morning.

Click-clacking in my heels, the sound of which has been known to worry students that I am coming to get them for some recess infraction or another, I started down the hallway, running shoes lined up outside classrooms. Kids' colourful backpacks hanging half-open on the coat hooks. A lone running shoe in the middle of the hallway. A half-eaten bologna sandwich that didn't quite make the wastebasket. A row of autumn-leaf tissue-paper art pieces hanging on the walls. Janet had posted her students' bar graphs. I remembered last week the parade of students coming to my office to ask for my favourite ice cream, which toppings I preferred on pizza, and if I owned a pet—all of the information was now colourfully documented in the bar graphs.

Bryce's door was open and I glanced inside. He was at his teacher desk and finished up sending a text before slipping his phone into his pocket and rising to greet me.

"Hey, Kristin," he said, venturing over to the door. "Who do you want?" He assumed I was looking for a student.

"Oh, I'm just wandering about today. Kids are working on the Chromebooks, I see."

"Yeah. They are doing an assignment about their worst day ever."

"Great. Those will be interesting to read."

"Yeah. My associate teacher when I was student teaching gave me his binder of activities. It's all laid out. The whole year. It's great."

"Hmmm." I wandered over and chatted with some students who explained to me that they had written their stories and were now typing them into the Chromebooks for their good copies.

Bryce was a new teacher. He'd been assigned to our school in the June hirings. Ministry of Education guidelines stated that new teachers will be placed according to seniority and qualifications. Although all the research states that the teacher in front of the kids is the single most important factor in academic achievement, principals' hands are increasingly tied in who is assigned to their staff. Last June I had been informed by the board office that I would get two new teachers, Bryce and Kate, through this process. I didn't interview them, so I didn't know very much about their experiences. Sarah was also new to staff; I had hired her over the summer when a teacher had decided to resign and move to Laos. Through the process I had to interview the top three senior internal applicants. I was thrilled Sarah had been one of them, as she and I had worked at a school together previously. But of the three new staff members, I'd chosen only one.

Leaving Bryce's room, I made a mental note about the cell phone. Would I address it with him or see if I noticed it again? He knew I'd seen it. By not saying anything I was perhaps giving tacit approval. On the other hand, I could let it go. Maybe it was an emergency and a one-time thing. I didn't know him very well. These are some of the little decisions you make every day as a leader. There is no manual. I decided to let it go for now as I made my way down to the primary wing. Probably earlier in my career I would have felt the need to say something right away—I was the principal, after all! But I'd mellowed some. Anything that was going to be a problem would surface again. I'd seen Bryce out at recess earlier in the week playing basketball with the grade 6 boys. The kids liked him.

I continued through the classrooms, noticing a lot of teachers talking. In others there were students working independently on worksheets, with the teacher sitting at the desk or wandering about the classroom. Sarah came out of her classroom as I was peeking in.

"See that boy over by the wall with his hood pulled up?" She gestured across the room. A pudgy boy of about ten sat slouched in his seat, curled into himself. His desk was against the wall, which he leaned into, looking like he wanted to disappear. His black hoodie was pulled up over his head despite a no-hats rule at school. Sarah had wisely decided to ignore the rule.

"I do. What's his story?"

"I don't know but he has been like that all morning. Not talking. Sulking. Name's Sawyer. All month he's been quiet like this but he seems more withdrawn today. He's new to the school and Maria, the special education teacher, doesn't have any notes on him." Sarah taught grade 5. She was a keen teacher with about eight years under her belt. There was a reason I'd wanted to hire her: I trusted her instincts. If she was concerned, there was probably a good reason for it.

"How about I join your math lesson and I will pay attention to him?"

I went in and joined a group of students at the table next to Sawyer's. Sarah presented a problem she wanted the groups of students to work on and I entered into the work with my group, keeping one eye on Sawyer.

"I think we need to add here."

"No. See, there are lots of groups. I think we can multiply." The students at my table were talking and working their way through the math. Sawyer's table was similarly involved but Sawyer was having none of it. His shoulders were scrunched up to his ears and he had pulled the hood of his sweatshirt down as far as it would go over his eyes. I glanced over and smiled but he wasn't making eye contact with me or anyone else.

Sarah stopped the discussion after about fifteen minutes and students began to present their thinking, with Sarah recording it on the board. It was a lively discussion. Sawyer was still not participating but I noted that he was following the lesson. At one point when an incorrect solution was presented he seemed agitated but still did not put up his hand. Curious. Maybe he wasn't so disengaged. He wasn't causing any disruptions so I left, making a note to follow up later.

I popped into a kindergarten class to play blocks for a bit and then joined Kate's class, which was involved in reading and writing activities. Kate, like Bryce, was a new contract teacher. Most of her previous occasional teacher work had been in the older grades; grade 3 was new to her. I could relate, as I had been a junior-intermediate teacher for years when my principal told me I was being transferred to grade 1. "Like with singing and printing?" I had asked. I was petrified that I would have to teach them to read! Changing grades is challenging and yet our system has our newest teachers doing it the most often. More experienced teachers tend to have first pick at the new jobs, and younger teachers who are often moving schools every few months get a lot of experience but never a chance to hone their skills in one grade for long.

Kate's classroom was bright and cheerful. The bins of learning materials were colour coded and labeled. There were posters and student artwork adorning the walls. Children's books were abundant and accessible. The classroom was a busy, busy place. I settled in with a group of students who were writing in their journals. Kate had a group of students reading with her. The others were occupied but off task. Managing a class of twenty eight-year-olds is not easy. I noted that Kate went over to redirect the boys at the listening centre and then the girls working with letter tiles on the carpet, but both groups shortly returned to off-task behaviour. The recess bell rang and Kate dismissed her students.

"I don't know how to get them to stay on task when I am not working with them. The grade sixes I had last year were so much more independent," Kate lamented as soon as the room was empty.

"Classroom management is tricky in grade three," I replied. And it was. And I was happy Kate had recognized there was a problem. Classroom management is key to effective teaching. A teacher can have strong classroom management and still be ineffective but no one can be effective without classroom management. Countless studies have shed light on effective classroom management and its correlation with high student achievement.

"What would you like to be different?" I asked.

"I want the kids to do what they are supposed to without fooling around. I want to be able to work with a small group without constantly being disrupted. I want to stop nagging."

I laughed. "That would be ideal. I think all teachers strive for that every day. The thing is, Kate, there is no perfect way to do it. All good teachers find the tricks that work for them to manage the class. You're a good teacher. You will find yours. I have a book in my office about establishing routines that you might like. I will stick it in your mailbox." I made sure to add, "Go grab a coffee and go to the bathroom before the break is over."

I had taught for seventeen years before becoming a principal. Plus I'd taught many of the grades K–10, including French and special education. I found that I relied heavily on my own teaching experiences, both successful and challenging, in supporting the teachers in my school. I distinctly remember the challenges in the early years of managing the class. My response had always been to change the furniture around on Fridays of bad weeks! I was sure an environmental change would make all the difference. It didn't. But over the first few years I learned what did work, which gave me some thoughts on how to help Kate. I could see that she worked hard and was reflective. She'd figure this out. She needed to know I believed she would.

The break ended and both Adam and I were busy dealing with the skirmishes that followed every recess in a large school. There had been some pushing and shoving over soccer and stolen cookies in the lunchroom. Three grade 8 girls had been discovered smoking behind the bushes at the far end of the playground and parents would need to be called. My secretary, Joan, needed to meet and discuss enrolment numbers and a parent committee met with me at noon to brainstorm fundraising options. At around 2 p.m. I realized I hadn't had a break for lunch so I grabbed my yogurt and apple and collapsed in the extra chair in Adam's office.

"Just getting to lunch?" he asked, also eating a sandwich at his desk.

"Busy day," I agreed. "Plus I don't feel all that welcome in the staff room sometimes." As a teacher I'd always loved meeting my colleagues in the staff room to talk about the day and get to know everyone. School staff members were often quite close. As principal I was always aware that I didn't quite fit in. Although most people don't believe it since I appear very confident, I am actually quite shy socially. Adam was the opposite—he kibitzed easily with everyone. In fact, it was his job to keep me informed about sporting news so that I could make conversation with our custodian!

"I think we should both make an effort to try and get into the staff room more frequently," Adam replied. "There's real value in 'being part of the gang,' as you say. You're good at being part of the gang when it comes to talking about teaching but you should get to know them all as people, too. And let them get to know you as a person, not just as a principal who knows a lot about teaching." Adam looked at me warily, wondering how I would take this suggestion. He was right; I knew it. I was letting the busyness of the day be an excuse for avoiding the staff room. I also knew that Adam had lunch in the staff room frequently and he was being nice by suggesting we both do it. I sighed.

"I guess you're right. Let's try that one of us will eat in the staff room every day, barring an emergency, and you can remind me when it is my turn," I conceded.

"Professional Development Day this Friday," I said, changing the topic to something more comfortable to me. "On my walkaround this morning I noticed lots of teachers lecturing in front of the class for long periods of time, and worksheets."

"I've noticed all that 'teacher talk,' too. Have you been in to watch Sarah teach? She's spectacular. Maybe we could get her involved somehow with the junior teachers."

"That's an idea," I said. "We could meet in grade groups and she could take the lead with the junior teachers. You and I could each work with a different division. I know you are more comfortable in grades seven and eight, but maybe this year you should work more with the primary team, particularly if you are going to apply for the principal's pool in the spring." Adam made a face but agreed. "I'd like to start the day with some thinking about how to move teaching practice into the twenty-first century. Except for the laptops, Chromebooks, and iPads, we could move our classrooms into 1950 and no one would bat an eye. I think we need to do some heavy thinking about critical thinking skills. It's just a matter of how to ignite the passion. Do you want to see how Sarah would feel about some leadership at the meeting?"

Schools in Ontario, Canada, are good. Ontario consistently scores high on international assessments. But we are stagnating. Standard test scores in the province in reading, writing, and mathematics are not stellar, with 30–55 percent of students province-wide falling below the provincial standard. While most teachers I know value professional development, school systems do a notoriously bad job at changing and improving teaching practices. Most experts agree that the best professional development is job- and site-embedded, but that can be hard to achieve at the school level. Boards hire educational consultants who have tremendous curriculum and pedagogical knowledge. They do great work with teachers, but they will be the first to acknowledge that their influence is limited to teachers who are extremely self-motivated. At the end of my career, I moved to work at the system level in the board office. There I had the responsibility to improve teaching in all schools and worked with a group of consultants to do so. The consultants would frequently complain that their hands were tied in schools where the principal was not engaged in the learning. Consultants, belonging to the same union as teachers, cannot be evaluative. However, the principal can go into any classroom at any time. Principals who make time to get involved in the teaching at the classroom level know what teaching practices are happening. Theoretically, principals using assessment data, standardized test scores, and classroom observations are equipped to direct the professional learning at the school level. But it is a daunting task. Nothing about the courses you take to become a principal really provides the knowledge and skills to be the instructional leader. Yet the principal is the only person in the system with clout. Principals are the only people in the educational system who can enter classrooms at will and make evaluations. A principal—not a consultant, not a lead teacher, not the superintendent—has constant access to what is going on inside classrooms and the power to evaluate. If the principal does not take on this role, it doesn't happen.

But the obstacles to making decisions that will impact professional development are many. As a new principal I was keen to get into classrooms and be visible. I wasn't going to be like some of the principals I had worked for who stayed in the office. That is, until I found out that leaving the office could be a challenging obstacle itself. There would always be another phone call, a bunch of emails, a kid misbehaving, or a system-level meeting to attend. It is easy to get caught up in the administrivia. Also, while principals have been teachers, they may or may not be comfortable with current pedagogical practices. Perhaps as a teacher you spent all your years in grade 8 science and now you are expected to lead primary teachers to improve their reading program. Principals aren't often hired for curriculum expertise, so that, too, needs to be learned on the job. Add in the union restrictions on how often and when you can meet with teachers, the revolving door of new teachers and maternity leaves (one year I had twelve teachers out on maternity leave!), and a lack of release time to support teacher learning, and being the instructional leader can be overwhelming. Within a unionized environment, all professional learning must be done during the school day, which requires supply teachers to come into the school while the teachers engage in the learning. This process is time consuming for all—administrators have to find the supply teachers and teachers have to plan the lessons for them. The only other time for professional learning was during the monthly staff meeting or during a Professional Development Day, when the students didn't come to school.

Friday would be our first time to meet for professional learning—it was a Professional Development Day. I would have the morning to work with the teachers and they would have the afternoon to watch mandatory health and safety videos. I wanted to plan my two and a half hours so that they would meet our needs and provide a springboard for staff learning for the remainder of the year. It was Tuesday. Surely I could find some time between now and then to plan something brilliant!

On the drive home my head was buzzing. What were our greatest staff needs and how would I get the teachers excited about learning and trying new practices? Our school's standardized testing data showed that we were about average in the board—but average meant only about half our students were reaching provincial benchmarks. That wasn't good enough. Pulling into the garage, I realized I'd completely driven past the gym without even thinking about it. I wasn't going back.

I opened the door to be assaulted by loud punk rock music and a dog that needed to be walked. "Hey, Mom. Is that you? Can we have pizza tonight? Can I get a drive to Chloe's after supper? Can you take me to swim practice?" And the other part of my life was starting. With three teenagers and a dog at home, life was chaotic. The problems of school were quickly replaced by the demands of family life. I'd pick up the train of thought tomorrow on the drive to school. "Sure, let's have pizza."

# THREE

# Becoming Learners

FRIDAY MORNING ARRIVED. THE SUMMERLIKE WEATHER OF earlier in the week had been replaced with a bitter wind and pelting rain. Juggling an umbrella, two bags of bagels and cookies, and a carafe of coffee, I made my way through the parking lot, avoiding puddles. My brain was racing trying to remember all the supplies I would need for this morning's session: whiteboards, chart paper, extra pencils, copies of the school data, the projector. Butterflies bounced around my stomach as I felt the familiar edge of excitement. This was a pivotal day for me: our first professional learning of the year.

My thoughts harked back to a conversation I had had last year with Constance, a colleague. Constance is about my age and is principal in a neighbouring school. We'd been discussing superintendent visits about our school improvement plans.

"You know, Kristin, we all know we are supposed to be the instructional leaders in our schools and make a difference. But you are the only one who believes she can."

I was dumbfounded. That was how my colleagues saw me? It might explain why I had found it so difficult to connect with my peers. While I loved teaching and being a principal (most days), I hadn't really connected with my principal colleagues over the years. There were a few that I chatted with at meetings but only two or three I would count as kindred spirits. In fact, for a number of years, I had questioned if being a principal was the job for me. I longed for deep conversations about educational change and innovation but instead sat through numerous sessions of rhetoric or complaining. I longed for peers who discussed the minutiae of educational change, not the exchange of information on where to buy the best school uniforms. Perhaps they found my enthusiasm for professional learning annoying. I hadn't realized everyone else was not as passionate about leading the teaching as I was. But I loved this part of the job. It was the energizing part. The part that would make the difference. It was about asking, "What if?"

By 8:30 a.m. we were gathered in the library, with bagels, donuts, cookies, and coffee available at the side. Teachers were relaxed, dressed more casually, getting reacquainted after the summer break.

"Good morning," I began. "I was recalling a conversation I had with my daughter Lily last year. We were driving in the car and she said, 'Mom, can I ask you something?' Oh, dear, I thought, here it is, the big sex conversation. I've got this. 'So, when you were younger . . . ,' she continued. Oh, dear, she is going to want to know about my own experiences. Was I ready to share? 'How did you talk to your friends?' Sex talk averted. We were going in a different direction. 'Well,' I said, 'on the phone.' 'Like one at a time?' she puzzled. Lily could not imagine how my social life could have functioned before texting and cell phones. That conversation got me thinking about how different today's world is from that of our students."

I scanned the group. They were engaged and amused. I could see the older teachers nodding their heads, remembering the good old days.

Bryce, I think, was also wondering how I had managed my social life; he wasn't more than twelve years older than my daughter.

"In my meeting at the board office last week, Siri started talking to me. Just out of the blue. I think we are getting close." Laughter. "As we think about our current students and where they will be as grown-ups, I think we have to recognize how the world is changing. How will our teaching change to reflect that unknown reality? So the question I have for you is, *What can't Siri do?* You could also think about what things could we be asking Siri that would just get her annoyed after a while. For example, I don't think Siri would mind solving 2,789 divided by 38. In fact, if I had to do that calculation I would certainly go and find my phone even if it was upstairs and under my bed. But I think Siri would get annoyed if I kept asking 2 times 2. There are some things it is just easier to know yourself, like times tables, the capital of Canada, and that Columbus sailed in 1492. It is good to know how to estimate the answer to 2,789 divided by 38 and have an understanding of what it means, but rarely would anyone do it with pencil and paper these days. In today's world there are facts that Siri can find out for you quickly and perhaps our students don't need to memorize all the important dates and battles of the War of 1812 or the names of all the rivers in Saskatchewan. In your table groups, use the chart paper to make a list of all the things Siri can't do. I wonder if that may be what we need to teach our students."

There was an immediate buzz as teachers started brainstorming. I went and sat with the intermediate teachers. I caught Adam's eye and he joined the kindergarten table. These were the conversations that excited me. Some principal colleagues argue that they don't sit with their teachers because it stops the conversation, as the teachers feel intimidated. I both agree and disagree. As I was new this year to the school, they were reluctant to speak. They felt that positional power. But I didn't let it deter me since I knew from past experience that they would relax as they saw that I wasn't going to be evaluative. I think the key is to join in as a teacher, not as a principal. As long as I join in as an equal, I've found the teachers to be honest and thoughtful. When I went to principal meetings and the superintendents all stood at the back while the principals worked solving issues at the table, I always thought it seemed a bit standoffish, like they thought this work was above them. I vowed I would have a different dynamic with my own staff.

I invited groups to add their words to a group chart: What can't Siri do?

*Analyze, synthesize, create, judge, compare, postulate, think critically, infer, apply, criticize, explain, justify, interpret, summarize, predict, contrast.*

I was pleased with the list they had generated. "If these are the skills that Siri can't do, maybe we should think about how often we concentrate on them as opposed to the straight memory tasks that Siri has a ready answer to."

"But Kristin, kids do need to know some stuff, like you said. Like their times tables."

"I agree," added Sarah, "but do we spend too much time on things like long division that kids don't need anymore?"

"But long division is in the curriculum," countered Mike, a grade 6 teacher.

"Agreed," I said. "But remember that as a teacher you know there is too much in the Ontario curriculum and you have a fair bit of flexibility in how much time you spend on any one aspect." This was a radical notion for some of the teachers. Not that it wasn't true or something they hadn't secretly thought to themselves, but some seemed shocked that I would state it publicly. In general, curriculum documents in Western countries are *way* too broad and every experienced teacher knows they won't get through them—and every new teacher panics about that. And yet the curriculum is sacrosanct. To suggest that professional judgement could relate to the curriculum was freeing to some, and scary to more. Teachers, for the most part, are more comfortable with strict rules. I was more comfortable with informed decision making. Working with my teachers over the course of the year to trust their own decision making would be an area of growth for everyone. Helping them to examine their own practices and try new ones. Developing a true sense of professionalism in a role that often relies on traditions and rules.

"Use the rest of the next hour in your grade teams to think about how you might change what you are teaching in the next few weeks to include more of the skills on our list. In doing so, what will you need to not do? You don't have time for it all."

My job was to plant seeds, not prescribe anything. Or at least this was my new plan. In my previous school I had been fairly prescriptive about the changes I had wanted to see in teacher practice. While there had been some uptake, I felt there had been a lot of lip service and not as much change as I had hoped for. In my last year at that school a grade 2 teacher had asked me about doing a new unit in science and I had responded, "I don't know. Why don't you try it? No one will die!" I had been in a rush somewhere but those words, that approach, had legs. The teacher put her heart and soul into the change in practice and it made a difference. She'd talked about it with other teachers. The words "Try something new; no one will die" were being bandied about. The teachers felt free to try new ideas and really examine their practices. Over the summer I'd given it a lot of thought and decided that I would see what would happen if I took a step back from prescription and tried to create an atmosphere of learning without judgement.

Adam and I spent the next hour sitting with teacher groups and listening to their plans. When the hour was over I asked each team to write down something they would try over the next month. Adam and I would use these plans to monitor whether anything was changing. Frankly, at this point I wasn't looking for large-scale change. That just wasn't realistic. But some accountability is important. I let them know that we would look at these goals again in October. It was gentle pressure. More important, though, was the excitement of the teachers as they tweaked plans for the coming month.

We finished up the morning by looking at our school data from the previous year. The teachers' unions do not support standardized testing and teachers have a love-hate relationship with the results. It is difficult when your students don't do well despite your best efforts. Our results had increased a few percentage points from the previous year in all areas except writing. On the whole, that was cause for celebration, although I knew that a one-year increase of 3 percentage points was not a trend.

I collected their interpretations and next steps, as I would include this information in our school improvement plan (SIP), the document I wrote and submitted each year to the superintendent. The problem with SIPs is that although they were required, and nerdy me actually liked writing them and we used them to guide our work, the superintendents tended to pay little attention to them. In fact, a good friend of mine was so fed up with the process that he wrote the phrase "fluffy blue bunnies" in the middle of his SIP every year. No one had ever questioned him. Another principal I knew just didn't write it. Also, nothing happened. Add this lack of system accountability to the obstacles that principals already faced in encouraging professional development and you can start to see why school improvement planning wasn't making the difference it could.

Professional Development Days are also times for staff to bond. My music teacher, Kimoni, had come to me with the idea of doing a drum circle with the staff. We gathered in the gym in a circle with plastic buckets and drumsticks. Kimoni had been very proactive this year in organizing staff activities. I'd been surprised, since my first impression had been that he was distant. He was tall, sporting long dreads and a clipped English accent. He was a strong union supporter, wearing the union T-shirt at least once a week. His classroom was a bit removed from the general traffic of the school and I rarely saw him in the staff room. His room, though, had kids in it at all breaks practicing their instruments. He organized a music festival and talent show every year. This year he had already petitioned me to rent a pinball machine for the staff room for a month.

"A pinball machine? Tell me why we need this."

"It would be fun. It's not that expensive. I know someone who would give us a deal. You know, with the job action a couple of years ago before you came, we kind of lost our sense of community. I think people are ready to have fun again."

In our district, teacher contracts are renewed every two to four years. The year before the contract is up, the unions begin to ramp up their influence on teachers. After all, if teachers are all happy, they will not vote for a strike during negotiations. Once the contract is up for renegotiation there is a year or more of unrest, usually accompanied by job action. Job action can be as mild as teachers refusing to participate in professional development, or more intense, such as not marking at home, not writing report cards, leaving the school at the bell, not participating in extracurricular activities, or not attending any meetings, including ones with parents. While all teachers belong to the union, they don't all feel the same way about the job action and tensions run high. Principals are not part of the union and that creates another level of angst.

Honestly, I wasn't sure this pinball machine was a good idea. I felt far more comfortable in the teaching realm than in social activity planning. It would never have dawned on me to rent a pinball machine. But I did want to encourage Kimoni, so I relented. It arrived the next week.

Now here we were laughing and cavorting as we all tried to follow his rhythmic patterns in the drum circle. Smiling and happy, everyone traipsed into the staff room to enjoy a catered lunch. I guess staff development was about more than a good meeting.

The teachers dispersed after lunch. Health and safety is also part of September chores and they are given the afternoon to watch a series of videos. I grabbed the pile of phone messages Joan had collected over the course of the morning.

"How was your meeting?" she asked, handing over the pile plus the daily red folder where she placed all the things needing a signature.

"I thought it went well."

"Sondra and Jim were in here afterwards and they said it was good."

Jim taught grade 7 English, geography, and history. Joan was often my ear on the staff. School secretaries straddle the staff and the office, which in some schools can be very divided. Joan had her pulse on the school and the staff liked her. Being a school secretary can often be a lonely job—she is integral to the smooth running of the school but isn't really part of the core business of education. Joan had found a way to be part of the staff. Plus, she kept me organized and knew when to interrupt me and what to handle on her own.

The first phone message was from a Mrs. MacDonald, with regards to her daughter Janine. I didn't know Janine and looked her up in the computer system. Grade 8, an A student; her picture showed a pretty young girl with straight chestnut hair. I remembered seeing her in the halls. She was popular and animated. I think she played volleyball last year. She was in Debra's homeroom but Debra had never mentioned any concerns. I pulled up her timetable and returned the call.

"Mrs. MacDonald. Kristin Phillips here. I'm returning your call. How can I help?"

"Thanks so much, Mrs. Phillips. I am not really a parent who calls the school. I don't think I've ever called the principal before. Really, I don't want to interfere." It was not uncommon for parents to apologize for calling me.

"No problem, Mrs. MacDonald. If you have concerns, we want to hear them. You are never bothering me."

"Well, then. It's about Mrs. Davis's class." That was Harriet. The outgoing principal had warned me about her in our transfer meeting. There had been numerous parent complaints before, and she had moved schools frequently in her long career. She was also up for a performance appraisal this year. "Janine's in her English class and says that all she does every day is read out loud. She's getting bored and feels like she isn't learning much. She had Ms. Morrow last year for English and just loved it. I told her there was probably a reason for her reading this book, but it has been three weeks now. Maybe she is exaggerating."

"Have you spoken to Mrs. Davis yet?" I always wanted parents to address concerns with the teacher first. Some parents were nervous to call out teachers, fearing that their children would end up being punished somehow. It wasn't my experience that that happened very often, but it was a common theme.

"I have called and left her a number of voicemail messages to call me back, but she hasn't returned my calls."

I hated these phone calls. I suspected Mrs. MacDonald's observations were correct. I had passed Harriet's classroom a number of times and she'd been reading aloud each time. I hadn't given it a lot of thought, assuming I was just missing the other parts of her instruction. I didn't think Mrs. MacDonald was exaggerating about leaving the messages. I had pulled Harriet's file from the drawer a few days before as I was preparing for the performance appraisals, and it was three times as thick as the others. I hadn't read it yet but I had the feeling I was about to.

"Let me follow through with Mrs. Davis and either she or I will give you a call back next week."

Sighing, I pulled the file out of the manila envelope. Teachers' files are housed with the current principal. They include contracts, teacher performance appraisals, and any disciplinary actions. Most teachers have slim files. I spent the next hour going through Harriet's trying to read between the lines of eduspeak.

She had three formal performance appraisals, all satisfactory. Performance appraisals only have satisfactory or unsatisfactory ratings. But, reading between the lines, it was clear there had been issues from the beginning. Harriet is encouraged to explore a variety of effective classroom management strategies. Harriet is encouraged to ensure she has adequate assessment data before assigning a final grade. Harriet is encouraged to investigate a variety of teaching strategies in order to engage her students. Harriet is encouraged to differentiate her instruction to meet the needs of all learners. There were problems.

Teachers in Ontario must be appraised once every five years. Although a principal can visit classrooms as often as required, many performance appraisals are completed with only one mandated classroom visit. I usually did four or five. While there was the occasional unsatisfactory appraisal given, principals agreed that it was hardly worth the trouble. Once you handed out an unsatisfactory, both Human Resources and the teachers' union became involved. You had to write a comprehensive improvement plan, which the union would often formally grieve. After sixty days, the principal had to reevaluate the teacher to see if changes had been made. If not, then you went through the whole process again, reevaluating after 120 days. All of this could take more than half a year. That was half a year of grievances and paperwork. Every interaction had to be documented. All on top of an already busy schedule. And in the end, the number of teachers who actually were dismissed was minuscule. Most principals I knew had a horror story to tell.

I wasn't surprised to see the satisfactory appraisals. She had been allowed to persist because the process to dismiss was too time consuming. There was also a disciplinary letter of expectation about classroom management. Sometimes in lieu of an unsatisfactory performance appraisal, superintendents would get involved and write a letter of expectations. That was last year. It was 3 p.m. and I went in search of Harriet. Her classroom door was closed. She'd left for the day.

I passed Kate on my way back to my office. She was standing on a chair hanging artwork in the hall outside her classroom.

"Ladder training," I reminded her.

"Oh, yeah. Sorry." Her cheeks flushed. Despite the annual training on using ladders, most teachers stood on desks and chairs. As the principal, I had to remind them. I knew she'd probably stand back up on the chair when I left.

"Hey, come and look at all the stickers I bought last night." I followed Kate into her classroom. A large table was covered in a pile of stickers. Sparkly stickers. Sports stickers. Fuzzy stickers. Smelly stickers. "I am going to use these to reward good behaviour."

"Okay. Good plan. Let me know how it goes." For effective class management, I knew it wouldn't work in the long run. Her students needed clear boundaries and expectations, not stickers as a bribe. Kate would discover that on her own. "Have a great weekend!"

# FOUR

# A Long Day

I HAD JUST SAT DOWN AT MY desk on Monday morning when my phone rang. I motioned for my secretary to answer it. "Myles," she mouthed, and no sooner had she hung up than he raced into my office.

"Fuck, fuck, fuck."

"Good morning, Myles. I see you are having a tough day." He went to hide behind my door. We waited in silence. I knew that I wasn't going to find out what was bothering him. You don't rationalize with a five-year-old. Eventually he went over to the children's bookshelf in my office and pulled out *Mortimer*, by Robert Munsch. It was his go-to book. I don't know why he liked it so much; a song was part of the narrative, although he never joined in. He sat at the round table in my office and put the book down. He didn't look at me. I rolled my chair over and picked up the book and we read it. Fifteen minutes later we walked hand in hand back to his classroom.

This was how most mornings went with Myles. We weren't making very much progress in getting him to settle into the routines of school.

Today was relatively calm, as I had not had to go and extract him from the classroom. More and more he was just turning up at the office on his own. Sondra said he was a bright kid. He loved drawing and stories. He didn't really interact with the other students very well. Tiffany, his mother, and I had come to an understanding. In the beginning I would call her every time he came to the office. Effectively it meant she received a phone call every morning sometime between 9 and 10 a.m. After a week she stopped answering—a perk of call display. I couldn't blame her.

"Tiffany, it's Kristin Phillips calling," I said one day when she picked up.

"Yeah. I know. What's he done? Do you want me to come and get him?" She often asked this.

"He had an outburst again this morning." Tiffany responded with silence. I could picture her, baby on her hip, shoulders slumped. Tiffany didn't have any better idea what to do with Myles than I did. I felt for her and my daily phone calls weren't helping. "Tiffany, would you be comfortable if I *didn't* call you every time he had an outburst? I'd only call if something out of the ordinary happened or if I needed you to take him home for the day. I know you care and I am happy to call every time if you'd like. But we can also do it the other way." Generally my rule is to call parents if their child is sent to the office. But I realized that in this case, it wasn't helping the situation. Tiffany sighed.

"Yeah. Okay. I guess." Tiffany didn't want to appear as an uncaring parent, but she had had it. Although she was quite guarded about sharing what went on at home, she had let enough slip that I knew Myles's outbursts were a regular occurrence there, too.

Myles was still having outbursts every morning, and I'd spent all weekend fussing about Harriet. While the excitement of our professional learning had been energizing, I just wanted this problem, and the others, to go away. Dealing with challenging teachers is, well, challenging. I don't think that any teacher wakes up in the morning and says to themselves, "I could do a better job, but I just don't think I will today." Really, who would say that? Therefore, Harriet was probably doing the best she could.

It would have been so much easier if I could've just told her to do a better job, and she would. Instead I needed to find a way to enforce accountability while supporting her in learning new strategies and pedagogies. Maintaining a positive working relationship would be key. She wouldn't make any gains at all if she thought I didn't have her back. I pulled up the teachers' timetables on my computer. Harriet was teaching Janine's class right now and then had a grade 7 class following that. After lunch she had a prep period.

The hallways were quiet. Making my way towards the intermediate wing of the school, I glanced out the window. Were those raindrops falling in the puddles? Please no; I sent a silent prayer to the weather gods. We didn't need a day of indoor recesses. If it was just sprinkling, I'd let the kids get outside, but my rule was if I could see the raindrops falling in the puddles then we would stay inside. On my way past I peeked into Sarah's room. Sawyer was in his usual spot hunched against the wall, hood up. Sarah made eye contact when she saw me and shrugged. No progress. Jim was sitting in his room alone. He must have a preparation period. He motioned me in.

"So, I've been thinking about Siri," he began. Jim was a slight man and impeccably dressed in a shirt and tie every day despite the more casual attire of the rest of the staff. The kids both respected and feared him. Nothing escaped his notice—nothing. He'd been teaching for about ten years and was confident in his practice. "The team was discussing and we'd like to get the kids talking more in small groups." Inwardly I smiled. Jim liked to lecture. He was entertaining but he often was center stage in his classroom.

"Sounds like a plan."

"We'd like some release time to plan. Could you arrange that for this Thursday?"

It was always better when teachers asked for release time to collaborate than when it was foisted upon them. Many teachers I knew disliked release time during the school day. First, they had to plan lessons for a supply teacher, and usually had to reteach those same plans the following day. And then, if the teachers' meeting didn't have a clear purpose and desire to collaborate, it was a wasted half day. Jim and his colleagues had a purpose for meeting. I knew that I was free on Thursday morning to join them.

"That would be fine. I'll ask Adam to arrange the supply teachers. I have Thursday morning open so I can join you. I'd love to hear your thinking."

I continued on. Rafi was sitting in the hall outside the math classroom, slouched against the wall, feet clad in untied running shoes sticking out into the hallway, baseball cap on.

"Hat," I said, stepping over his feet. Scowling, he removed it. I looked back in time to see him putting it back on and gave him the principal look I'd perfected over the years. He gave me a look back but removed it. A walk down the hall was never a straightforward exercise.

Harriet's classroom door was closed and I went to turn the knob. It was also locked. I always carried my keys, so I opened it. Had the door been locked on purpose or was it just a mistake?

Sure enough, Harriet was standing at the front of the class reading aloud. The book was *The Outsiders*, a perennial favourite in grade 8; it was such a favourite I remembered reading it myself in that grade. It was published in 1967. Was it still as relevant? Harriet had arranged her desks in rows, often an indication that the teacher wants to lecture and have the kids work quietly by themselves. She wasn't the only teacher in my school who chose this but I hoped that would change as teachers involved students in their own learning more. Backpacks were slung over the backs of chairs or shoved under desks. Add the long legs of grade 8 boys and many backpacks spilled out into the aisles. Most of the kids had their heads down. Some had eyes closed—was that small boy in the back corner drawing? Harriet looked up from the book but I just smiled to continue. I sat down at an empty desk towards the back. The kids around me sat up—I still had it, and smiled to myself. Harriet continued to drone on as I looked around. The bulletin boards were empty except for the odd store-purchased poster. Her desk was at the back of the room, littered with a few papers. There were three boxes half unpacked in a corner.

It was sixty minutes into the double English period. With twenty minutes to go Harriet stopped reading and started talking.

"Okay, 8B, who can tell us what is happening so far?" Crickets. Not one kid put up a hand. "Well, there was the rumble," Harriet continued. "Remember that? Who died then? No one? It was Johnny. That was a sad part of the story. How is Ponyboy feeling now? Who has an idea?" Silence again. Finally, a girl raised her hand. It looked like Janine.

"Sad."

"Right," Harriet confirmed. She then continued to expound on the plot of the novel. The students were quiet but disengaged. I left before the bell. As I was standing in the hall, the classes changed, with 8B exiting and a grade 7 class lining up outside the door. Harriet let them in and went to close the door but saw me standing in the hall and left it open.

I made my way down to the primary wing to pop into classes, joining in a discussion about pioneers in grade 3 and helping some grade 4 students to build equivalent fractions with coloured tiles. Getting into classrooms was calming; it brought me back to the reason I loved this job. On my way back to my office, I passed Harriet's room again, the door still open. She was standing in front of the class, reading aloud. The students were quiet, heads down, listening to her read *Where the Red Fern Grows*. It was a timeless novel. I'd read it in grade 7, too. The bell was about to go for recess. I squinted out the windows. There were definitely drops in the puddles—damn. Making my way back to the office to make the announcement, I heard the PA system ding.

"There will be an indoor recess today. It is raining. Students are reminded to stay in their own classrooms." Adam had reached the same conclusion and was calling it. Great, I thought, he can be the one everyone is angry with for calling it. Indoor recesses made for a long day and the forecast was calling for a week of rain. I grabbed my lunch and went into the staff room. The teachers who didn't have supervision duty were sitting around the table. Two were engaged in a competitive game of pinball. I could see that Kimoni had created a scoreboard on the whiteboard where players could list their high score.

"Kristin, you going to try pinball?" I had never played pinball in my life. I came from an academic family of high achievers. I'd spent most of university in the library and a fun night out was a glass of wine or cards. Despite my very public job, I was basically an introvert. Playing pinball in front of everyone would be showing the world my incredibly bad eye-hand coordination. The only thing I could think of that would be worse would be a staff volleyball game.

"Maybe later." I capitulated. Perhaps I could try out the game when the teachers were in class to see how difficult it would be? The conversation moved on to kids and families and Thanksgiving plans.

As I returned to the office, I noticed a man leaning against the wall across the hall. I looked quizzically at Joan. She shrugged her shoulders.

"Hi. I'm Mrs. Phillips, the principal. Can I help you?"

"No, I'm okay," he mumbled. I was puzzled. We didn't allow people to hang out in the hallways and if he was a parent then surely he was here for an appointment or to pick up his kids.

"Do you have kids that go to this school?"

"Yes, ma'am. Aimee and Carlton Byun." I knew who he was talking about. Nice kids; a bit rambunctious but not really a concern at school.

"Did you need to pick them up or talk to them?"

"No, ma'am." I could barely hear him, his voice was so soft.

"Did you have an appointment with one of their teachers?"

"No, ma'am." This was going nowhere. I couldn't just leave him hanging about in the hallway, though.

"Would you like to come in and chat with me a bit?"

"Mmm. No. Well, maybe. I don't know." I figured that was as much agreement as I was going to get.

"Come on in. Can I get you a coffee or tea on this rainy day?"

He sat down on the edge of my guest chair, hands folded in his lap. He was a slight man, no bigger than some of our grade 8 students. He was dressed in a worn white button-down and tie, and I wondered if he had dressed up for this visit or was coming from work.

"No, thank you, ma'am."

"So, tell me a bit about Aimee and Carlton."

"I'm a single father, you know. Their mom left when they were just little. She was from Korea, too. I came here about ten years ago. I think she just married me to be a landed immigrant. So now I take care of them."

"Being a single parent can be challenging," I said with empathy. My husband and I had just split up. Although it was an amicable split, our three teenagers were living with me most of the time. I was just learning about the joys of single parenthood. It wasn't always fun to be the only one dishing out the discipline.

"Yeah. They don't listen to me very well. They won't go to bed when I say so." He looked at me expectantly. Did he want me to tell his kids what time to go to bed? This was a little beyond the scope of my job. On the other hand, he was clearly struggling. Many of our new Canadians feel isolated in a community with no family or support systems. Were he back in Korea, he might have had extended family to help him raise these kids. Here he was on his own. I knew enough about Carlton and Aimee to know that they were kids with minds of their own. Mr. Byun was soft-spoken and out of his depth.

"So, what happens when you tell them it is bedtime?"

"They just keep watching TV. They don't go."

"Then what do you do?"

"I've tried getting angry, but they just laugh. Mostly I just leave it now. Then they are tired in the morning and won't get out of bed. It's just so hard." Mr. Byun looked to be at his wits' end.

"It does seem like a problem. We have a school social worker. I could make a referral and she could help support you with home routines."

"No, no. That's okay," he quickly said and got up to leave. A social worker wasn't the answer here, or at least not yet. It had taken all his courage to come and see me and I was passing the buck. He was obviously wary of getting involved in the social services system. Did I really want to get involved here? How much help could I be? I wasn't going to move in! Bedtime really did fall outside the school day.

"Let's just get Aimee and Carlton down to the office." Mr. Byun slumped in relief, wringing his hands in his lap. I looked up their classrooms on my computer and said I'd be right back. I always preferred to go get kids from their classrooms instead of calling them down, when possible. It got me out of the office and also gave me a chance to see what was going on, although lunchtime on a rainy day was sometimes best avoided! I gathered Carlton from grade 6 first.

"Hi, Carlton. Can you come down to my office for a few minutes? You have a visitor."

"Who?" He looked at me quizzically.

"Your dad is here."

"What? Why?" I let it go and told him to go on in. I was going to find Aimee. "Are we in trouble?"

"Nope," I replied. "Your dad just wants to talk to you and Aimee and my office is quiet." I collected Aimee from grade 4 and we all met in my office around the circular table. Mr. Byun looked visibly nervous and the kids were obviously confused. I didn't really know what to do, either, and we sat in silence for a few moments. It didn't look like anyone was going to start.

"Your dad says that you two aren't listening to him when he says it is bedtime," I ventured. The two kids quickly looked down at the table, guilt written all over their faces.

"You said you weren't going to tell Mrs. Phillips." Aimee addressed her dad. He was quiet. I think I was being invoked in the Byun household in the same manner of "Wait until your father gets home."

"What time does your dad ask you to go to bed?"

"Nine o'clock," Carlton replied sheepishly.

"Do you guys think that is reasonable?"

"Yeah," they mumbled. They knew it was. They knew they were being disobedient just because they could. Kids need boundaries. They don't like them but they need them. When my own children were younger they were not allowed to take their juice into the living room. So they drank their juice with their toes up against the edge of the living room carpet. Kids want to know where the boundaries are. It is comforting. It doesn't mean they won't push up against those boundaries—after all, it is important to know *exactly* where they are. Aimee and Carlton were pushing, probably just to see what would happen.

One of my first teaching assignments was at the Clarke Institute of Psychiatry, in Toronto. There was a day treatment program for kids who had reached the end of the line of their own school board's interventions. These kids almost always came from challenging home situations and suffered from a number of mental health diagnoses. The teaching was a mixture of academics and therapy. One boy, Viktor, came from a dysfunctional home. His parents were young, unemployed, and had their own mental health challenges. Viktor presented as a sweet and rather infantile kid. He often used a baby voice and liked to curl up under desks or in piles of pillows. He had a shock of messy black hair and round, dark eyes to match. He was a bit on the chubby side and had a slow way of moving. He shuffled and slouched more than he ran and jumped. He could also rage out of control at the least provocation. The first time I witnessed one of his tantrums I was amazed that such fury could emanate from such a small body. Viktor had two ways of coping: fury and tears.

One day my Child and Youth Worker and I were sitting doing puzzles with the five kids who made up my special education room and the question was asked, "What do you wish was different at home?" You might expect answers like more TV, more desserts, and fewer rules. Viktor piped up immediately and stated that he wished his parents would tell him what time to go to bed. There was a chorus of agreement around the table. Rules were missing for so many of these students. They didn't feel as if anyone was in charge in their households and, hence, they floundered.

"Do you think you are being fair to your dad by not listening to his rules?" I didn't expect an answer. Carlton and Aimee knew. I had to bring this conversation back to school in order to justify to myself why I was involved in the first place. "If you aren't getting enough sleep then you aren't going to be able to do as well at school, right?" They were nodding their heads, still looking at the table. "Starting tonight, I want you listening to your dad. He loves you. He cares about you. I'm going to ask you when I see you if you are getting enough sleep."

"Okay, Mrs. Phillips. Sorry, Dad," the kids chimed. They gave their dad a quick hug and returned to class.

"Thank you. Thank you, Mrs. Phillips. I didn't know what to do. I think they will listen to you." Mr. Byun was shaking my hand profusely. He left my office smiling and I was left wondering what my job really was! One of the most humbling aspects of being a principal is recognizing that your reality, your family situation, the way you were raised and how you raise your kids, is not everyone's reality. It is easy to judge: Mr. Byun should read a parenting book or be a better father. He shouldn't be wasting the school's time with home issues. Except, he is doing the best he can and it is not easy to ask for help. I wasn't sure my interjection into their family life would make a big difference but I did think that Mr. Byun, Carlton, and Aimee now felt supported. Safe, happy, and learning. That was my job, for the whole school community. Sometimes I likened the job to being mom to the whole school. And like any good mom, not all of the job was ice cream and picnics. It was time to chat with Harriet. She had a prep period so I walked down to her room.

On the way I ran into Rafi sprawled in the hallway again, this time outside the geography room. He took his hat off as he saw me coming. In response he received another well-practiced principal look. "You are having a bad day, I think." He mumbled under his breath. I left it for now but I thought I wouldn't be surprised if we saw him in the office before the end of the day.

Harriet's door was closed and I knocked before opening it. "Do you have a few minutes to chat?" I came in and perched on the edge of a student desk. Harriet was seated at her teacher's desk. "I need to have a principal chat," I began. I found that this opening helped teachers to realize that the conversation was not simply a drop-by conversation. Most of the time in talking to teachers I tried to be "one of the gang," chatting about school and teaching without any evaluation or judgement. But in those instances where I was wearing my principal hat I thought it was fair to let the teacher know from the outset. Harriet looked at me passively.

"Janine's mom called on Friday." I paused, giving her a chance to fill in the blanks. Her face revealed nothing. "She has left a number of voicemail messages for you and said you have not returned her calls."

"Oh. I guess I haven't really got onto my voicemail yet. I can listen to them today."

"Don't your voicemail messages also show up in your email? Mine do."

"Oh. I don't check my email that frequently. I'll look today."

"We communicate a lot through email at this school and encourage parents to phone if they have concerns."

"Sure, sure. I'll get to it."

"I'm going to give you a heads-up. Janine has been telling her that all they've done in English for three weeks is listen to you read aloud." I paused to give her a chance to respond. She didn't. "I've noticed that you are reading aloud every time I pass by." Still no response. "The first report cards will be here faster than you expect, late October. Are you going to have done enough reading, writing, and speaking to write the report card comments?"

"Well, I'm doing these read-alouds as mentor texts. That's what the other English teachers do, too. I heard them talking about it."

"Many teachers use a read-aloud at the beginning of the year to teach specific skills in reading. Do you have a list of the mini-lessons you are doing to teach reading with these texts?" Harriet started shuffling through the papers on her desk. "For example, are you using one chapter to teach about setting and another to teach about characterization?" I hinted, trying desperately to give her some support.

"A friend of mine from another school said she'd send me a binder of activities and I am just waiting on those."

"Oh," I replied. A binder of activities was not the same as a lesson, but I'd let that go for now. I was getting the picture. "How are you going to address Janine's mom?"

"You think I need to call her?"

"I do." I gritted my teeth. *Really?*

"Okay. Well, I will let her know that we are nearly finished with the book and will be doing some writing next week."

"I will leave it to you, then. Jim is arranging for all the English teachers to meet on Thursday. I think it would be great for you to join us. I will make sure we get you a supply teacher."

"Oh, yeah, sure. Great."

"I'll leave you to your prep now, Harriet. Maybe you could stop by and let me know when you've called Janine's mom back so I can check it off my list? I said you'd call today or tomorrow."

"Definitely," she assured me. "I'll be checking my email and voice-mail more often, too."

"Daily would be great," I responded on my way out.

FIVE

# Special Needs

"LET'S GO!" I YELLED AT MY KIDS. It was 7:35 a.m. I dropped the kids at high school on my way to work. "Joey, go brush your teeth quickly." He must not have a current girlfriend, I thought. His personal hygiene was always much improved when he was in love. "Where's Frankie?"

"In her room," responded Lily. "I'm not going in there. I did it last time."

"Not my turn," gurgled Joey mid teeth brushing. Living with Frankie was like walking on eggshells; all of us wary of her outbursts.

Just as I was about to climb the stairs, Frankie pushed past me. Dressed in black wrinkled clothes she'd picked up from her bedroom floor, she grabbed her backpack from the front hall. Despite the warmth of the day, she had on long sleeves. They covered the scars from cutting. Lily handed her a lunch that she probably wouldn't eat and her school books. She scowled and stomped out the front door. The rest of us got in the car, Frankie already slumped in the back seat. Joey sat in front and controlled the music. I decided to forgo a discussion on his choice of music and we listened to something loud and screaming. The ten-minute ride to school was silent except for the pounding bass.

We arrived two minutes before the bell. "Have a great day!" I said.

"Bye, Mom, you too! Love you," said ever-cheerful Joey.

"Remember I have swim practice tonight! Have a good day, too!" Lily chimed in.

Frankie said nothing and got out of the car like it was the hardest thing she had ever done. I knew the rest of the day would be just as hard for her. She often didn't get out of bed at all, although that was less likely on the days I drove them to school. If I had an early meeting and they had to walk, then she was likely not to go to school at all.

"Try to have a good day, sweetheart. I love you." Frankie didn't respond and shuffled off to school. I wondered if she would go in or turn around and go back home.

I switched the music and drove to my school, my mind on Frankie. For four years she had been suffering. I remembered clearly a June day when she was in grade 7. We had all been getting ready to go out for dinner. I called it QFBT: Quality Family Bonding Time. As the kids had moved into their teen years I felt it was important to do some family time every few weeks, so we had QFBT whether you liked it or not! It was stifling hot but we hadn't yet turned on the air-conditioning at home and the house was getting muggy. Frankie came down the stairs slowly and reluctantly. She had definitely been moodier and more distant lately, but I hadn't really thought too much of it. After all, I remembered the turmoil of my own teenage years and believing my parents knew nothing. I dealt with teens every day. This was normal.

"Aren't you going to be hot in that long-sleeved shirt?" I asked.

"No," she mumbled.

"Well, why don't you just push up the sleeves a bit," I replied, trying to compromise. I reached over and pushed up one sleeve. There on her lower inside arm were bright red scars. I looked carefully as the reality dawned on me. She looked at me, looked down, and started to cry. My daughter was cutting? How could this be?

How could I not have known? What do I say? Lily was looking sheepish. She knew. Joey was quiet for once, sensing that something had happened. I knew about self-harming behaviours. I'd even dealt with an instance or two by that time in my career. Statistics show that as many as 20 percent of teenage girls have self-harmed. It is not always an indication of suicidal thoughts, but it is an indication of some mental health issues. Stu, my husband, looked at her wrists and then at me. He didn't know what was going on. Except for Frankie's sniffling there was silence.

I gathered Frankie in my arms and held her tight. She struggled a bit and then relaxed. "We will figure this out. Do you want to talk now or still go for dinner?"

"Let's go for dinner," she said quietly.

We all got in the car like nothing had happened. I think we were in shock. But the response was also indicative of how we coped over the next few years: We didn't want to believe this was happening. We didn't tell anyone—not family or friends. This wasn't the kind of mother I was; I didn't have a child with mental illness. I was embarrassed and full of shame. I still felt that way four years later. Frankie's mental illness was a secret in our family.

As I arrived in the school parking lot, the day was beginning. Children were skipping and running into the parking lot greeting friends. Groups of mothers pushing strollers were gathered in the playground with an eye on their school-aged kids but happy for social time with other young mothers. The parking lot was full of teachers' cars and Bryce waved to me as I pulled in. I sat in my car and gathered my thoughts and feelings, pushing Frankie to the background for another day. The buses were arriving as I grabbed my bag and got out of my car.

I stood around outside as the buses arrived, chatting with kids and checking in with the bus drivers. Sam, an older man who had been driving school buses since he retired from his manufacturing manager position at a local plant, motioned me over. I'd learned already that year that Sam might appear a grumpy curmudgeon, but he cared about the kids.

"Hey, Sawyer," I said, passing him on the walkway as I made my way to the bus. Sawyer, still wearing his hoodie up over his head, looked up at me. Was there a bit of a smile? "See you later this afternoon for backgammon?"

"Yeah," he replied and shuffled off, his backpack dragging on the ground. Sawyer had not really warmed up to school yet, even though it was October. Sarah had tried everything to get him engaged and was worried about him. Last week he had ended up in my office for pushing kids in line after recess. Sarah said this was fairly common behaviour and she'd tried everything. He continued to be disengaged in class and nothing was working. I had tried to talk to him about the pushing and the disengagement but had gotten nowhere. He seemed like such a lost soul. He had eyed the backgammon game on my shelf and I asked if he knew how to play. It wasn't a game most students were familiar with.

"Yeah. My dad and I play." I'd quickly scanned his computer information and knew that his parents were divorced and he lived with his mom.

"We could play if you'd like." This kid didn't need discipline as much as he needed connection with someone at school. He looked up warily and agreed. We set up the board and he went first. I often played checkers or cards with kids in my office and usually tried to lose, at least at first. I didn't pay much attention to the game and tried to engage Sawyer in conversation.

"So, how is school going this year?"

"Okay."

"Is Mrs. Brennan nice?" I asked, referring to Sarah.

"Yeah."

"You live with your mom, right?"

"Yeah."

"But you see your dad, too?"

"Yeah."

"On weekends?"

"Yeah."

"Who are your friends at school?" No response. By now he had captured half my pieces and I had two of his.

"What do you like to do when you aren't at school?"

"Video games."

"Oh. Which is your favourite?"

"Mario Brothers."

And so continued our rather one-sided conversation. It was like pulling teeth. He was, however, engaged in the game.

"You win!" I exclaimed. "Good job. Would you like to come and play backgammon again sometime?"

Sawyer looked at me cautiously. This wasn't how visits to the principal usually went. "Okay, I guess."

"Here is a sticky note. It says come play backgammon with Mrs. Phillips on Tuesday at two thirty p.m. You can put it in your planner, okay?" He nodded and got up to leave.

"And Sawyer, no pushing in line after recess. If it happens again, you will miss a recess."

"But I can still come and play backgammon?"

"Yes. You can come and play backgammon even if you push in line. But I would rather you didn't push."

He left, clutching the sticky note, and I made another sticky note to tell Sarah about the backgammon plan and put it in her mailbox. That was a couple of weeks before and we'd been playing backgammon on Tuesday afternoons ever since.

Sam motioned to Sawyer and said, "That boy is not very happy. He is always pushing the other kids."

"That is a problem with him. He doesn't ride the bus, though, does he? How do you know him?"

"He's always hanging around waiting for my bus to park and stands right by the door, but for the life me I don't know why. He never seems to meet up with anyone. He just stands there and kids can't get by."

I told Sam I'd chat with Sawyer and that he should let me know if the behaviour continued. Sam thanked me and added, "I don't think he is a bad kid. He looks real sad." I didn't think he was a bad kid, either, but he was sad.

The entry bell rang and the kids lined up. Parents waved their good-byes and kids tramped into school. Another day begins. I made my way to my office, twenty minutes after arriving. The phone rang immediately and, of course, it was about Myles. Without taking off my jacket, I went to fetch him. Today he was refusing to come into the school. Kim, the educational assistant who had now been assigned to mornings in his kindergarten class, was watching him as he stood arms crossed against the school wall.

"He was lining up just fine and then before I knew it, he yelled 'fuck this,' threw his backpack, and ran over there. Every time I try to go over he yells at me and moves farther away," Kim related. "Tag team," she said, and smiled.

"Thanks." I grimaced. "Go on in and check on some other kids. I will let you know when he is in class." No point in two of us out there. I was fairly sure that Myles wouldn't run off at this point. We'd played this game before.

I stood against the wall about ten feet from Myles and said nothing. He scowled and said nothing. It was a standoff for about five minutes but he didn't inch away. I gave him time to calm down.

"Good morning, Myles," I finally ventured. "Tough morning." I waited but he didn't move farther along the wall. "You want to come to my office and play in your spaceship for a while?" The previous week I'd been unpacking new gym uniforms in my office when Myles had arrived. He'd asked if he could turn the big cardboard box into a space-ship. He'd decorated it with crayons and frequently sat in it when he came to my office.

He stomped past me and entered the school. I grabbed his back-pack (today was not the day to engage in a battle about Myles getting it himself) and I followed him down the hall. He was already crouched in the spaceship when I got to my office. Joan smiled sympathetically and Adam, who was standing in the office talking to her, chuckled.

"Good morning so far?" he asked smiling. I rolled my eyes and set-tled myself in my office. Myles seemed happy enough in his spaceship so I started my email. It was 9:15 a.m.

The morning passed relatively quietly. Myles went to class after fif-teen minutes of spaceship time and one reading of *Mortimer*. Adam had to rescue the soccer ball from the neighbor's backyard, and Amelia was sent down to the office because lice was suspected. Lice is part of the job and I was pretty good by now at checking for it. This was one of the things I had not expected to be part of my job as principal. However, union rules stated that you could not require a teacher or educational assistant to check for lice. Some schools had parent teams do it but at our school, for now, it was me. Adam and I had a deal: he would climb fences to retrieve soccer balls and I would check for lice. Sure enough, she had lice. They were easy to spot. Amelia was in grade 7. She had stringy blond hair with long bangs that hung over her glasses. She and I had already met, as she'd been back-talking to her teacher a few weeks ago. Amelia had not yet learned about graciousness.

"Amelia, you are going to have to go home and get a treatment for lice. It isn't a big—"

"I do not have lice!" she screamed. I could see them crawling across her glasses. It was quite the infestation. I was not mistaken.

"I'm sorry, but you do. As I was saying, it isn't a big deal—just a special shampoo. I will call home."

"You are lying. I don't have them."

I didn't respond and called home. Amelia's mother wasn't thrilled, as she had three other children and that meant a lot of shampooing and cleaning, but she came and got her. Joan was already preparing the letter we would send home to the rest of the class stating that a child had lice and encouraging parents to do a check. Adam laughed and said, "We're even today. One soccer ball and one case of lice." Relating how the lice had been crawling on her glasses, Adam agreed that he won today.

At the one o'clock break I had the weekly meeting with our special education team. Teachers who had concerns about students presented the issues to this meeting and decisions about how to support the children were discussed. Our board special education consultant and psychologist also attended. First up today was Olivia. Olivia was in grade 6 in the Learning Disabled classroom. While most students with learning disabilities manage in the regular classroom with extra support, our board still ran a few self-contained classrooms for kids who didn't fit in full-time in the regular classroom environment. More often than not, the students in the self-contained classrooms had a wide range of issues other than a learning disability. In that classroom we had students on the autism spectrum with a learning disability, a number of students with anxiety in conjunction with a learning disability, and then a few who were just quirky—there wasn't a firm diagnosis. The class had a limit of ten students. We had twelve. There was a great teacher, Peter, and a full-time educational assistant. Most of the students were integrated into regular classes when appropriate and with support.

We were gathered in the special education room. The walls were plastered with phonics charts, word charts, and mathematical formulas. Maria, the special education teacher, was dressed in running shoes, khaki pants, and a plaid shirt. She once told me that she dressed so she could run after kids and sit on the floor, not to be fashionable. She had a heart of gold and could talk knowledgeably about all the students in her caseload.

In any school, a solid special education teacher makes the difference. In a school of 600 students we had approximately 175 students on an Individual Education Plan (IEP). That was a little higher than the average of 15 percent and one of my goals was to address with teachers whether changing our teaching strategies might lessen the number of students on an IEP. But that might be an issue to tackle next year. And it might start to resolve itself as we changed some of the teaching practices.

The IEP states which grade level the student is working at and what the student will learn that year that is different from the regular grade-level work. Some teachers do a great job of adhering to the IEP but more often the student sits in class, is sometimes given easier work but not always, and then is given a C or B on report cards instead of a D or failing grade. It is not a good system, but it is the one we have.

The educational system is quick to use the IEP as a way to support students who are struggling. Typically, when a student isn't doing well, teachers try a few strategies, but in a classroom of twenty to thirty kids it is often challenging to meet all student needs and despite the attempts at differentiation, most teachers teach to the middle. I know that as a classroom teacher myself I struggled to meet the needs of students who were not meeting the grade-level standards. So after a few months to a few years of a student not doing well, the decision to implement an IEP is made. It means that many students on an IEP stay on it for their entire schooling, often getting pushed through the grades when they really aren't keeping up with the learning.

Ironically, once they reach secondary school this IEP changes and students are streamed into Essential, Applied, or Academic courses. Recently, Ontario de-streamed grade 9, but many of the issues of IEPs persist into high school. The IEP doesn't go away but now only lists accommodations such as access to a quiet spot for tests or use of technology. Thus students who end grade 8 with an IEP that says, for example, that they were working on grade 6 mathematics enter grade 9 applied-level math without having mastered the material required. It is a huge problem in the educational system. I didn't like it and could see the pitfalls but it was challenging as one principal in one school to change the system. Plus, we really didn't have a lot of other options. It isn't like I could just ask my superintendent for more money to hire more teachers to support the learning needs of the hundred-plus students in our school who were having academic difficulties! Also, Maria, as wonderful as she was, and her teaching partner Manny, good but new to special education, couldn't do it all.

Peter was still a hippie at forty-five. He had a ponytail and wore colourful pants, sandals, and tie-dyed T-shirts. He wore at least four friendship bracelets at a time and carried a big leather satchel for his schoolwork. Up through December he would ride his bike (through the cold and snow) to school. He'd worked in self-contained classrooms for the last ten years and had many ways to calm students and deal with the constant heightened emotions that could erupt at any time. It was unusual for him to bring a student's case to these meetings. For me it meant that the concerns were big.

"So, good day, all. Thanks for coming. Let's get started. Peter, you wanted to talk about Olivia. I see you have brought her file." It was a good inch and a half thick. It was passed around and everyone looked at the school pictures that were pasted inside. In kindergarten Olivia had been a tiny little girl with Pippi Longstocking pigtails, smiling into the camera. Last year's grade 5 picture showed a girl with messy hair going in all directions, her face set in a grimace. What had happened? Mary, our special education consultant, rooted through the file for a psychological report and skimmed it quickly.

"This is what I know about," Peter began. "Up to grade four she was in the regular classroom although there were frequent outbursts and violent incidents. In grade five she was transferred to a behaviour class that used a strict behaviour modification program. She failed miserably and was suspended fifteen times last year for violent incidents. The latest psychological test indicated significant learning disabilities in writing and math, so she was transferred here. She loves to read. In fact, if I let her she'd read all day. She refuses any writing or math work."

"She's been on my radar for years," Mary piped in. Mary, as an educational consultant, supported the special education needs in twenty schools, ours included. "She is a puzzle. Nothing seems to work. Her parents are at their wits' end."

"Any other diagnoses?" Maria asked.

"Attention-deficit disorder has been diagnosed. She currently takes Ritalin for that. She's also on clonidine for anxiety and Mom says she takes melatonin for sleeping disorders," Mary replied. No one said anything for a minute. That's a lot for an eleven-year-old.

"What are your biggest concerns?" I asked.

"Well, she isn't being integrated into anything right now. She refuses to do anything but read. She won't use the technology to help with writing and anytime I try to teach her math she crumples the paper and throws it across the room."

"Any friends?" Mary asked.

"Nope," Peter responded. "She's pretty much alienated everyone in the class so far and they are a pretty accepting bunch. A few times she has tried to join games but then gets frustrated easily and it all ends badly. Right now I've been keeping the peace by not expecting much but I don't think that is a great strategy."

"Do her parents think the medications are helping?" I asked.

"I talk to them about twice a week," Peter replied. "I feel guilty every time I call because I haven't been able to have a 'good news' phone call yet. They don't know what to do. She is refusing personal hygiene most days—not brushing her hair or teeth, wearing the same loose sweatpants and T-shirt. Unlike the other girls in the class, she doesn't seem to care what she looks like. I gather the tantrums at home are similar to what we see at school and they are tired of fighting."

"I get that," I said, thinking of my own battles with Frankie. "Anyone have any ideas?"

Stephanie, our Child and Youth Worker, had been quiet until this time. Stephanie was fresh out of school but had energy and a knack for reaching kids. Like Maria she dressed in running shoes most days.

"Maybe I could work with her a bit. We could start with some hygiene issues and she could brush her teeth and hair with me in the mornings. It would also give me an idea of what kind of mood she might be in before she goes off to class."

Stephanie tended to work with families and children around social and behavioural issues but didn't often get involved with the learning disabilities class, as they already had two full-time staff. I tried to keep her out of there, too, since we had limited resources. But Stephanie would be a new face for Olivia, who desperately needed a relationship at school that would never be disciplinary. Peter and Doris, the educational assistant, could form a relationship with her but they also would be the ones to call her out on the daily transgressions. Stephanie could work on building a relationship outside of schoolwork.

"What do people think?" I asked. There were nods around the table. "Okay, give it a go, Stephanie, and we will meet again in three weeks to see how it is going. In the meantime, Peter, we will have to figure out some ways to get her doing some schoolwork. I wonder if offering some choice might help. You could say she can do five minutes of writing or math and then she can read for twenty-five minutes. I know it isn't as much as you'd like but it could be a start."

"I'll try, but you might end up with a phone call before the five minutes of math are up!"

"Anytime." I smiled.

We discussed a few other students before I glanced at my watch. It was 2:35. I was late for backgammon with Sawyer. I excused myself and hurried to the office. I entered and Joan had just picked up the telephone. She saw me and put it down, motioning towards Sawyer, who was sitting in the office chair swinging his legs and watching the clock.

"Sawyer," I exclaimed. "So sorry I'm late. Ready for backgammon?" He followed me into my office and went to the shelf to get the board. As he set up the game, I looked longingly at my lunch that was still un-eaten, but I decided that it was rude to eat in front of him. I would eat later. This was our fifth game together and I wanted to see what Sawyer would do if I played a little bit harder. We began.

"How's your day been?"

"Okay."

"Do anything fun at recess today?"

"Nope."

"I think you like math. Do you?"

"It's okay." That was the most positive response I'd ever gotten to any question yet. I decided to go with it.

"What have you been learning lately in math?"

"Multiplication and division."

"How's that going?"

"It's easy." I was thrilled. We were actually having a conversation of sorts. As for the backgammon, I was paying more attention but he was actually a very strategic backgammon player. Very unlike your average ten-year-old, who tends to move pieces without much thought. Truth be told, it wasn't my favourite game, but maybe I wouldn't have to play so badly going forward. I wondered how he'd do if he lost but I decided I wasn't ready to find out yet. I moved my piece so he could move his to the centre bar.

"Mrs. Brennan has you working a lot in groups to solve math questions. Do you like that way of learning?"

"Nope."

"Can you tell me why?"

Silence. He moved his last two pieces off the home board. "I win." That conversation was over. As he packed up the pieces, I asked why he was hanging out by the buses in the morning.

"My friends are on the bus."

"Hmm. Which friends?" I asked. As far as I knew, Sawyer didn't have any friends at school.

"Just friends," he replied.

"I see. But you have to wait for them at the back of the school. The bus driver says you are pushing as they get off." Sawyer looked down and said nothing. "So, backgammon again next Tuesday? Maybe I will win," I joked. That got a sort-of smile. "See you then," I said. Sawyer didn't move. He stayed sitting, looking at me expectantly. I waited but he didn't move. I raised my eyebrows.

"Don't I get a sticky for my planner?" he asked.

"Of course you do!" Obviously this was an important piece to him. I wrote it out and handed it to him.

He clutched it close to his chest and started to walk out of my office, but then he turned and said, "Bye."

"Bye, Sawyer," I said steadily, but inside I was smiling. Joan came over to my office door.

"You just play backgammon?" she asked.

"Yup. I talk but he doesn't say much. We are forming a relationship." Joan was dubious about my methods. I think I was the first backgammon-playing, Lego-building principal she had worked for.

She shrugged and laughed. "Well, he seems to like it."

"By the way, Adam and I have a system meeting tomorrow morning so we won't be in until noon. Jim is the teacher-in-charge, but call if you need to. In fact, call me if a kid has a splinter or the tap is dripping," I said jokingly. Joan knew that I did not like going to system meetings and always wanted her to call me with an emergency so I could leave. However, I had faith that Jim and Joan would be fine.

It had been a good day. Or, if it hadn't, backgammon with Sawyer had made me forget all the other stuff. I spent thirty minutes after the bell rang talking to the teachers who lined up outside my door. The end of the day is time to touch base, answer questions, and hear the successes and challenges. Joan said goodbye and by four thirty I was done for the day. It was a perfect fall day with a brilliant blue sky against the leaves turning yellow and green and I needed a workout. If I rushed, I could make the 5:00 p.m. gym class. My phone pinged with a text. Joey wanting pizza. Not tonight, I wrote back. My thoughts returned to that morning and I wondered how Frankie's day had gone. Should I risk calling her on the way to the gym? I understood Olivia's parents more than anyone at work could imagine. It was sometimes easier to avoid the issue than cope with it.

I got in the car and decided I could be a good mother and called Frankie. She answered! Often these days she screened my calls. "Hey, Frankie, how was your day?"

"It was really good. How was yours?"

Was this the same sullen girl from the morning?

"I had a good day, too. Anything special make it good for you?" I asked.

"Yeah, I had lunch with Rebecca and we are going to a movie on the weekend."

"Great." Frankie's moods went up and down like a roller coaster. I'd learned not to question it and to be thankful for the good days. "See you for supper. I'm going to the gym."

"Okay, Mom. Have fun. See you when you get home." She hung up. I grabbed my gym bag and went to work out. All in all, it was a good day, for now.

# SIX

# Being Present

THE SMELL OF PUMPKIN PIE WAFTED THROUGH the hallways on the Friday before the Thanksgiving weekend. The pies were mine. We would head to my parents' house north of the city for the holiday and my contribution was the pumpkin pies, but I had simply run out of hours in the day to get them done at home. I'd brought them to school to bake in the staff room oven before we left that afternoon, but knowing that the aroma was a teaser, I'd brought some store-bought pies to share. Both staff and students were eager for a three-day weekend. Thanksgiving is the first break in the routine of the school year. The day had dawned with the crispness of a perfect fall weekend. I wanted to leave school early enough to enjoy the drive with the fall colours. I'd reminded my kids to get home right after school.

I was roaming the halls after escorting Myles back to class. I was making notes in my mind the whole time, as the school environment could give me insight into what was happening in classrooms and what teachers valued. If it was my job to lead the learning in the school, then I needed to always be assessing what was going on. I had learned, though, to observe but not take notes as I went. Taking notes led to teachers feeling that they were always being evaluated. They were, but they didn't need to know it. There were orange, red, and brown cutout turkeys decorating the primary hallway. Were the teachers paying attention to the diversity of cultures in the school? And if every turkey looked the same, was this really encouraging artistic development? The junior teachers had been working on environmental issues and their students had hung posters expounding on the virtues of recycling, the dangers of climate change, and endangered animals. This was better. I made a mental note to ask how the students had chosen their topics and if the teachers had been working together to think about what Siri couldn't do. The intermediate hall was void of student work. For some reason once kids entered grade 7, teachers stopped decorating the halls and bulletin boards. School became serious business, all in the name of preparing the kids for high school. Perhaps some positive comments in the staff room over lunch to the junior teachers would help. There were brown crumpled leaves gathered in corners; it was impossible to keep them from blowing in with the kids. Vince passed me with his broom. We stopped to chat about the latest sporting event—or rather Vince talked, and I tried to seem interested.

Peeking into classrooms, I noticed that Kate had a smiley-face chart up on her front blackboard. The week before, she'd confided that stickers weren't really working that well to improve class management. She was spending all her time giving out stickers.

"Well, that is certainly problematic with stickers as a reward system," I said, nodding. I remembered trying something similar in my early teaching days.

"I have a new idea!" she replied enthusiastically. "A friend of mine teaches grade three at a different school and she uses a smiley-face chart. Every day, kids who have been good get a smiley face. When we have a hundred smiley faces, we get a class activity of their choice!"

"You think that will be easier to manage?"

"Definitely! I only have to reward them at the end of every day. I made this great poster and all," she exclaimed, showing me a poster of glittery smiley faces and the kids' names printed along one side of a poster-sized grid.

"How will you determine who gets a smiley face?"

"Oh, you know, the kids who are getting their work done and listening," she replied, her brows furrowing a bit.

"Do you think you will have any kids who never get a smiley face?" I asked.

Kate's brow furrowed deeper as she thought about this. "Well . . . Ahmed doesn't listen well at all so I'd be thrilled if he got a smiley face. I think this will motivate him to listen when the other kids are getting their smiley faces."

"I'm glad you are trying new ideas. Have you had a chance to read the book I left in your mailbox?" Kate glanced down and I guessed the answer was no. "It is so busy at the beginning of the year but maybe if you have time one weekend have a glance through, particularly chapter five, about developing routines and structures. I think you will find it helpful."

Today as I entered her room, it was busy but didn't really seem any more productive than it had a few weeks ago. Kate looked up from her work with a small group of students; I smiled and indicated I was just visiting. As I looked at the smiley chart, Angelina came up to show me her story: I LK MI MOM. WE GO TO THE PK. IT IS FUN. I SEE A BRON DOG.

"Great story, Angelina. Do you go to the park with your mom every day?" Most people could probably figure out what she was trying to write, but ever since I taught grade 1, I was fluent in early spelling attempts. That spelling would be perfectly acceptable in October of grade 1. I was concerned about a student in grade 3 spelling like that and made a note to follow up with Maria to see if Angelina was on her special education radar.

"Yup. With my baby brother. He is two," she said, holding up two fingers.

"Tell me about this chart," I asked.

"Oh, that's the smiley-face chart. All the kids that are good get a smiley face before home time."

"What does good mean?"

"Ah, ya know, stuff like doing your work and not pushing. Some boys are never good. And Chelsea, see, she is never good." She pointed to the chart. Sure enough, there were three boys and Chelsea who had received not one smiley face. Angelina had a solid row of smiley faces.

"Hmm. I see. Do you like getting smiley faces?" I asked.

"Yeah. I guess. It's all right," she answered, and she scampered off to the listening centre. I wondered how long Kate would persist with this chart. I would see if she would come to the conclusion on her own and begin to introduce some more effective strategies of classroom management. Her first teacher performance appraisal (TPA) was coming up in November and I would have to decide how to handle it. Classroom management was clearly an issue, but she was working on it. On the other hand, if I gave her a satisfactory the first time around and she didn't figure this piece out, then I'd have issues with the union if I had to give her unsatisfactory on the second appraisal. New contract teachers were appraised twice in their first year. Their contract wasn't permanent unless the final appraisal was Satisfactory. Thereafter teachers were appraised every five years. This year we had Kate and Bryce, who were new, and then eight other teachers to appraise, including Harriet. I would do the appraisals for Kate, Bryce, and Harriet, plus two more, and Adam would do the other five.

Thinking of TPAs, I glanced into Bryce's room. He was giving a history lesson. There was a note on the board and the kids were copying it—a contrast to Mike's class, which was also learning about the Canadian explorers. His students had been working in groups, each learning about one explorer. I stood at the back for a minute. I could see Bryce's cell phone perched on the edge of the desk where he was standing. I only hoped he had some notes he was checking. Was he chewing gum? No, he couldn't be. The kids were not allowed to chew gum (I didn't care much, but the custodian didn't like gum stuck to the insides of desks, and many teachers were hard-line no gum chewing, so it was a school rule). I looked again. He was definitely chewing gum. Just then the bell rang. Bryce finished the lesson and the kids filed out. I didn't see any other kids entering and assumed he had a prep period.

"Hey, Kristin. How's it going? Doing one of your little walkthroughs?"

"Hi, Bryce. Yes, just wandering about, seeing what people are teaching. I notice both you and Mike are doing the Early Canadian Explorers unit. Are you collaborating at all?" Bryce was only a few years younger than Mike and I had hoped they would work together. Mike seemed to be a great teacher and he and I had already had some good discussions about the "What Can't Siri Do" theme. He was having the students work in groups, with the final task of having the groups debate why their explorer was the most important to Canadian history.

"Oh, yeah, Kristin. We talk about it all the time. He has great ideas. I've been sharing the worksheets out of my binder—I told you about that—with him, too." Perhaps I needed to arrange some more formal and guided collaboration time.

"His kids were really engaged in the explorers project when I was in there today," I responded, hoping he would pick up on the nudge. He smiled. I ventured forward with my second point, since talking to him face-to-face I had no doubts about the gum.

"Bryce, you are chewing gum in class. We have a rule about kids not chewing gum, so I think we teachers need to adhere to and model that rule. You can't chew gum in school."

"Oh, yeah, yeah, Kristin. You know, some onion pizza for a snack at recess and I didn't know what else to do . . ."

"I understand. Maybe mints would help. You can't chew gum in school. Thanks. Have a great rest of your day," I replied, and with an outward smile and an inward sigh I left.

"Mrs. Phillips, please come to the main office." It was Joan's voice over the PA system. I glanced at my watch: 10:35. I was meeting with Cathy Simpson, the parent council chair, at ten thirty. I picked up my pace. Cathy, mother to three school-aged boys and a successful business-woman, was the returning parent council chair. Cathy was a stay-at-home mom, ran her own part-time marketing business out of her home, volunteered for Meals on Wheels, and was involved in the school. We had first met the previous July, when I officially began as principal at this school. Principals assigned to a new school start on the last day of June, a Professional Development Day. You have a staff meeting, wander about, and answer questions you don't know the answer to. You also call the current parent council chair and arrange a meeting for either early July or late August. Cathy had been adamant that we meet soon.

I had inklings of tensions between school and community. Max, my superintendent, had alluded to the need for the school community to have a fresh start with a new principal and hoped that I could mend some bridges (and stop all the parent calls to him). In my first few days at the school, I had noted some signs on doors stating: "Parents wait outside" and "Staff-only washroom." I had removed them. On my first day at the staff meeting, we had done a get-to-know-you exercise where groups of teachers made "Top Ten" lists for the new principal. I had gleaned a lot of pride in their school and that they loved their jobs, but I also heard that there were problems with parents: interfering parents, helicopter parents, and more. When Cathy and I met in July, I became aware of the height of the wall that had been built over the years between the school and the community.

On that warm day, when the school was already cluttered with piles of desks and chairs in the hallways as classrooms were cleaned, Cathy had arrived at my office with two coffees. After the customary pleasantries, she got down to business.

"The community is thrilled to have a new principal and we hope that we can work together. The last few years have been very challenging. Many parents have not felt welcome," she began.

"I'm sorry to hear that. Certainly, I would like to work with the parent community. I have always found that a supportive and strong parent council only adds to the strength of the school." I was treading on perilous territory already. The incoming principal cannot be critical of the outgoing principal. Although it is not true, there is a time-honoured code that all principals are the same and that a new principal provides continuity and not necessarily a new direction. "Can you tell me how the parents would like to be involved?"

"We have not been allowed to be part of fundraising efforts and we don't know how the money is being spent. Parent council meetings were very tense," she added, "and sometimes erupted into arguments. More and more parents stopped coming. We would like to help organize some school events, like a fun fair." Cathy consulted her notes. "I have been president for two years now and I just get more and more phone calls from parents saying that they aren't invited to volunteer for school trips and that teachers don't want them to volunteer in the classrooms. Before, we used to organize all the special lunches but that was taken away from us and the teachers do it now."

I was confused by the last part. Special lunches were part of every school as a fundraiser and provided a nice break in the week from the monotony of bologna sandwiches. As a mother, I loved pizza days, but as a principal and teacher I did not. Why wouldn't you let the parents deal with organizing them?

Cathy continued: "We think that the school raises a lot of money and I guess that all goes to buying school supplies because anytime the parent council suggests an idea to buy something we have been told there is not enough money." I had already had a look at the books and I

knew that the school fundraising generated more than $8,000 a year—
and most of it for the last five years had not been spent.

"I understand your concerns," I replied. It was a bland response, but
I was on shaky ground. "The school has a budget for school supplies.
We don't use fundraising money for that. I'd like to work with both
parents and teachers to determine how we use fundraising dollars. That
should be a transparent process." Cathy looked at me in astonishment.

"Oh, we thought the money was for pencils and notebooks and
such. Do you know how much there is?" I did, but I needed more time
to think about how to handle this situation.

"I would like a bit more time to look into the school budgets. I just
got here! Perhaps we could meet again in August to plan the first school
council meeting in September and I will have a better sense of things
then?" Cathy agreed and we set the date.

Our first parent council meeting had gone well. Cathy had been
acclaimed council chair again and I had led the parents through an
exercise to gather information about how they wanted to contribute
to the school. More than fifty parents had shown up to see what this
new principal was about. I had noticed that the majority of the parents
were white, which was surprising to me, as the school population was
ethnically diverse.

As I arrived at my office, Cathy was there, two coffees again, chatting with Joan. We settled into my office. I looked around to see if
Adam could join us, but his door was closed and Joan mouthed that he
had Rafi in there. Again.

"How did you feel the parent council meeting went?" I asked.

"Great. It had such a different feel from the last few years. I heard
lots of positives from parents after the meeting. They thought you were
up front and funny." I hadn't tried to be funny, but I did tell stories—I
guess they went over well. "They really appreciated a breakdown of the
fundraising money and an opportunity to give input. They also liked
how you explained the EQAO results and took them through some of

the questions." EQAO is the standardized testing in Ontario given to grade 3 and 6 students in Reading, Writing, and Mathematics.

"They were a very keen group of parents, very engaged. And there were a lot of them!"

"Yes. Last year we would only have had about five, but I think everyone wanted a look at you."

"Probably." I laughed. I decided to bring up what I'd noticed about who was there and who wasn't. "I noticed that most of the parents who attended were white even though this is an ethnically diverse school. Is that typical?"

Cathy paused. "Yeah, I guess. I don't think I'd ever thought about it before." Most school councils are small and are often made up of a small group of mothers, with the occasional father, all of whom are already friends. Last year the participation had been so low and the meetings so contentious that it was no wonder Cathy hadn't really thought about the makeup of the council. The school pulled from two distinct neighbourhoods. About half the children came from an economically depressed area of town with lots of subsidized housing. Many were recent immigrants to Canada. The other half of the school population came from a new subdivision of middle- to upper-middle-class homes and they were bussed to our school.

"I wonder how we could get a more diverse parent council that might be more representative of our school population," I said. "Do you think that's important?"

"For sure," Cathy responded. "Truth be told, I knew lots of the parents at the meeting. They live in my neighbourhood. I don't know very many parents from the neighbourhood closer to the school." I knew from other school experiences that many immigrant parents did not feel as comfortable coming into the school and joining the parent council. Parents who had had negative school experiences themselves were also less likely to feel connected to the school. Many a parent had come to visit my office saying something like, "Oh, I'm in the principal's office again." I'd always reply, "It's okay. You are a grown-up now." But you could tell that the memories lingered.

"Let's put it on the agenda for the next meeting of the whole council," I suggested. I liked Cathy. She was smart and dedicated to the school. We went on to talk about plans to move the pizza days over to the parents. I'd discussed the issue with the teachers at our last staff meeting. There was definitely a wariness for having parents in the school. I countered with the fact that managing pizza days was an added burden for teachers and how this was an easy way to let the parents feel part of the school. I couldn't believe the issue was so contentious, but it was. I would have to get a handle on why the teachers felt so threatened by the parents. Reluctantly, they agreed, but I got the distinct feeling that they were doing this to show me how awful it was going to be. *She'll see*, I could hear them thinking.

The end of the day arrived without mishap. I had another parent call about Harriet's class and made a note to deal with it on Tuesday. The pies were ready and I carefully packed them into the car and went home to pick up the kids. Lily had everything ready to go. I worried about her, too, as she was sometimes Frankie's caretaker. Frankie was sullen today, but moving. Joey was chatty and excited to be heading north. He loved the outdoors and was happiest helping his grandfather cut wood and clear paths in the forest. I was looking forward to a three-day weekend and put the worries of school out of my head as we headed north in the weekend traffic with stunning views of the fall colours.

# SEVEN

# Try Something New; No One Will Die

TUESDAY NIGHTS I THROW POTS, NOT AT people but on a wheel. It is my creative outlet. It has also taught me a lot about leading change. When I first started, I imagined I'd be a version of Demi Moore in the movie *Ghost*. The thing was, it wasn't that easy to throw pots, nor did anyone remotely like Patrick Swayze appear. Week after week I would go and try to center the clay on the wheel and my instructor, Louis, would make helpful comments like "adjust your hand position," "pull your elbows in," "relax your shoulders," "get the clay off the bottom," and "keep your gaze to the inside." Week after week I could not center the clay and my feeble attempts to make a bowl ended in lopsided pots that never resembled what I had set out to make. I would concentrate on one of his suggestions but ignore the others. I could do only so much. The question I hated the most was "What are you trying to make?" It assumed I had vision, that I knew what the end would look like. My answer was always "Whatever the clay wants to be." I did not have enough control of the clay to make a specific shape. Any shape would do.

With perseverance it slowly got better and after six months I could make something that you could eat ice cream out of. Mug handles were the next hurdle. After a few years I got reasonably good, although I still needed Louis's guidance when attempting a new shape. Then he'd offer some helpful suggestion that made all the difference in the world.

"Why didn't you tell me that before!" I'd exclaim.

And with great patience, he'd always tell me, "I have, Kristin. Many times." I hadn't been ready to hear the new information yet. I could only assimilate so much at once. As I was learning I could only add a little bit of information at a time. I had to be ready for it.

As I began to reflect upon my efforts to learn to throw pots, I became a much better leader with the teachers at school. In my first years as a principal, I would make suggestions or introduce a new teaching idea and then wonder why no one followed through. I'd ask if they thought the ideas were good and they would say they were, but then nothing. I'd been a good teacher. I read the current books on pedagogy. I went to conferences. Why was this instructional leadership stuff so hard?

It is only in the last decade or so that principals have been required to be the instructional leaders in their schools as well as the managers of the building. Principals are woefully underprepared for supporting changes in teaching practice. I felt comfortable with the pedagogy but how to lead a group towards change, that was another thing altogether. My colleagues felt the same and many chose to concentrate on the management of the building and leave instructional leadership on the back burner. My reflections on having to learn something new— throw pots—helped me to see that I had been going about it all wrong. Like my desire to throw a perfect pot, the teachers needed to want to change something. Then, as they were learning to do something new, they had to have the freedom to muck about, adjusting their craft as they reflected and learned more. Maybe the end vision wasn't clear and that had to be okay. I would be Louis, offering support as needed but recognizing that it would be a long process, not a quick fix.

Jim's team of intermediate teachers was meeting to discuss how to teach differently so that the students were doing more of the work and the teachers were doing less lecturing. The Thursday after Thanksgiving was our second meeting. The intermediate grade teachers gathered in the seminar room. The table was strewn with papers and teaching books and curriculum guidelines. Jim was there, as were Mac, Mike, Harriet, and Leanne. Tara, blond, fashionable, and smart, was clearly the leader. She had already approached me about supporting her application to be vice-principal. Mac was disheveled and friendly. He was always looking for his glasses and his papers were the ones strewn about the table. While he was disorganized, the kids loved him. He, like Jim, tended to lecture a lot in a booming but captivating voice. Harriet had arrived without any papers. Leanne was a diminutive young mother. This was her first year at school after two back-to-back maternity leaves. She was soft-spoken and hadn't said very much during our last meeting. After that meeting she had come to my office apologetically.

"So much is new after being off for six years," she lamented. "I feel like I have a lot to catch up on, particularly with all the technology." In our district teachers can elect to take up to five years for each maternity leave (four of them with no pay), and maintain their position at the same school.

"I think that recognizing it is a big first step. No one expects you to be up to speed right away. I've heard great things about you." Leanne listened a lot. Her classroom was a bit traditional, but she had solid classroom management. I wasn't worried.

Lindsay, the learning consultant from the board who was attached to our school, was also joining us. Lindsay was an experienced intermediate teacher and had respect among the teachers. She'd worked at this school last year but had confided to me that the teachers weren't very interested in her ideas and liked to do things the same way they had for years. That wasn't unusual in schools. Change is hard and once teachers have found a rhythm and routine that works for them, they don't tend to go looking to upset the applecart. Some, like Harriet, don't realize that what they are doing is not working. Tara was already trying a number of new teaching ideas. Mike, too, was trying some new things but was not yet ready to share too much. Jim, Mac, and Leanne were less innovative, but maybe willing to try something new if I could incite their passion for teaching.

"Good morning, all. We have two and a half hours to work together. I will try to stay, barring any emergencies in the office," I began. "Last time we met, you had identified that you wanted your students to do more of the thinking and talking and you wanted to find ways to talk less. Shall we start by sharing how that is going?"

"I tried putting my students in groups but they talk too much so I went back to rows," stated Mac.

"I've got them in groups," said Jim, "but the student talk is not really on topic."

"My students are doing book clubs. I'm using this book to guide me," Tara said, showing a copy of the *Reader's Notebook*. I had lent it to her the week before. Tara went on to explain the ideas behind having different groups of students read different books. She'd chosen books all on the theme of "what makes a hero," so that her lessons could tie all the titles together. I had given her permission to buy some new titles as well. Mac, Mike, Leanne, and Jim all had questions about this method of teaching. Lindsay and I threw in our comments. Harriet was quiet. The talk went around in circles, but I wanted to see what the teachers came up with. They were intrigued but also wary of trying a new way of teaching literature.

"When are the kids going to have time to read the novels? Tara, you said you were doing the whole unit in three weeks. My kids won't read at home," Jim said, worried.

"I usually give them a good chunk of time in class to read," Tara responded. I could see that Jim was still not convinced and I knew the issue was that he wasn't going to have enough time to do his lecturing and let them read.

"So, how long are most of your lessons?" I asked innocently, already knowing the answer. "These days we talk about mini-lessons of just one main teaching point. Do you guys use the mini-lesson format?" Nods around the table indicated this was familiar language. "So how long are your mini-lessons?"

"About thirty to forty minutes," answered Mac, and Jim nodded in agreement.

Leanne said, "Sometimes mine are about twenty-five minutes but then I feel rushed."

Harriet said nothing.

I must have made a face because Jim asked, "How long do you think they should be?"

I didn't really think there was a magic number, but I said, "About seven minutes. The research shows that you shouldn't talk for more than seven minutes without letting the kids do some talking or work." Honestly, I made the number up. I wanted to force a bit of a shock. I vaguely remembered some research that said a kid's attention span was about as long as their age. So in grade 7 and 8 it would actually be 12–13 minutes. But 7 was the number that came out so we went with that. I was curious to see the reaction. Surprised faces are what I got from everyone but Harriet, who remained smiling and passive.

"Seven minutes! That's not long."

"That would mean I would really have to adjust how I do things." As I listened to them grapple with this suggestion, I decided to leave 7 minutes as the guideline. I knew that 7 minutes was not very much time and that the teachers would go over. But I decided that going over to 15 minutes was fine. If I changed my number to 15 they would go over to 30 and that wouldn't solve the problem.

They spent the next hour coming up with a structure to have

7-minute mini-lessons and book clubs. There was a buzz in the room. I slipped out to check on the office and Lindsay followed me.

"They are really excited about all this," she offered, "but I think they might be overwhelmed, Leanne in particular. There are so many new ideas being thrown about. Maybe I should rein them in a bit."

"I'm okay with messy," I said. "The ideas have to be ones they want to try, even if you or I don't think some of them will work." Lindsay looked at me dubiously, but I knew from experience that *giving* teachers the ideas didn't work. I was willing to try something different and hoped Lindsay would support me. I don't think she truly did, but sometimes there are advantages to being the principal and one of them is that rarely will you be disagreed with publicly. Eventually the staff would get to the point where they would feel safe enough to disagree, but we weren't there yet.

When I came back to the seminar room, the teachers had come up with a new structure. They wanted funds to buy novels and a copy of the *Reader's Notebook* for each of them. They had a plan. What did I think?

"Looks good. Try something new; no one will die," I told them. There was nervous laughter. I had used that phrase for the first time a few years before. When I had left that school to come to this one, Karen, one of the teachers, had made me a wooden sign for my office that had the phrase painted in beautiful calligraphy. I asked her why it had resonated so powerfully with them, and her response was eye-opening.

"You gave us permission to look at our own practices, see what wasn't working for us, and try new ideas," she told me. "I never felt like it had to be perfect or that you'd be coming in to make sure it was working. It was freeing after years of being told what and how to implement changes even when I disagreed with them."

So I would see if this new staff would be as receptive to the phrase. For now I think they thought I was crazy. In my early years of being a principal I had wanted everything to be my way—I was the expert, the boss, the one to lead. That hadn't worked so well. Teachers did what I asked but nothing really changed. Trusting the teachers and letting them try things (even when I knew they wouldn't work as well as they hoped) was harder for me, but it had resulted in more change. It couldn't be a free-for-all, though. They knew that I understood pedagogy and they trusted my opinions and advice. But the relationships I had with teachers had evolved into a professional dialogue instead of prescribed solutions. Could I develop the same types of relationships with this new staff? I wondered. Had the synergy I had eventually felt with that last staff been just a fluke or could this approach be part of a leadership strategy that worked? I wasn't sure. As the teachers energetically packed up their materials, eager to put their new ideas in motion, Leanne lingered behind, taking a long time to gather her books.

"So, Leanne, how are you feeling about the book clubs?"

"It seems like a good idea," she began nervously, "but it is so different than what I would normally do. Usually about now we would be starting a unit on *The Outsiders*."

*The Outsiders* again!

"It's a great book. Is it the right reading level for all your students?"

"Well, for most of them, but I read some of it out loud or have the kids read out loud." This was a typical teaching approach when teachers had multiple reading levels in a single class (and all do), but listening to literature, while important, was not reading.

"If you are reading most of it out loud then you can't really assess their ability to read and understand, though." She looked at me, puzzled. "It would be a listening comprehension mark, not a reading mark." It is amazing how much classroom time is taken up with teachers reading aloud. Faced with a class of diverse reading abilities, teachers often default to this strategy all the way through high school, believing they are teaching reading because the students discuss or write about the text. Read-alouds do have an important place in the English class. But the goal is that students read independently and reading aloud isn't going to teach that. Leanne's class was by no means an exception.

"Really? I hadn't thought of it like that before. Still, *The Outsiders* unit always works so well."

"It is a good book," I reiterated. I could see that Leanne was very nervous about trying a new approach. I had to find a middle ground for her. "I wonder if you could adopt some of the book club principles to *The Outsiders*? Perhaps you could have groups of students talk about the book or write about it instead of some of the activities you have done in the past. Maybe you could identify those students who couldn't cope with that level of text and they could listen to an audio version while the others read it, which would save you having to read out loud to everyone? I know that Lindsay would be happy to work with you on this or we could sit down and come up with some ideas."

She agreed to talk to Lindsay, and added, "I did like the meeting this morning. It was so much freer than other professional development sessions we have had where at the end I had no idea what we had spent the time on. And it was good you stayed the whole time. I've never had a principal do that before."

Leanne went back to class and I headed to my office. Lindsay was already sitting at my table.

"Wow. I've never seen that group so engaged before. I still think they might be a bit overwhelmed and I don't think they really know where they are going, except maybe Tara. Did you see Leanne's body language? I don't know that she is fully on board."

"I thought the session went quite well. I'm not too worried yet. It is early days, and it's fine for it not to be perfect." Then I asked her to casually check in with Mac and Jim in a few days. I went on to fill her in on the conversation I'd had with Leanne. Lindsay thought she could help her adopt a few new ideas while letting her stick with her tried-and-true unit. In past years, I might have insisted Leanne try the book clubs, but I was trying something new, too. I hoped that as we all continued to work together, Leanne would adopt book clubs on her own. And when she did, she would own the idea.

"And Harriet?" she asked. Clearly, I wasn't the only one with concerns about her involvement, but Lindsay was a teacher and I couldn't share my thoughts with her without crossing union lines. I just smiled and said I would follow up with her.

Right before Thanksgiving weekend, another parent had called to complain that his son, Jonathan, was bored silly in Harriet's class and wasn't learning anything. I'd gone through the same conversation I'd had with Mrs. MacDonald—and yes, the parent had called and left messages that hadn't been returned. On Tuesday, the first day back from the holiday, Harriet and I had had a similar conversation to the first one. I checked and she had a prep period last thing today. It was time for yet another chat.

Generally, I tried to have difficult conversations with teachers in their classrooms, not my office. It was less formal than being summoned to my office and it meant that I controlled when the conversation was over since I could leave. I wandered down to her classroom around 3 p.m. The door was shut so I knocked before entering. She was slouched at her desk, laptop open. I glanced about the room. There was still nothing on the bulletin boards and the boxes were still piled in a corner, unpacked.

"Do you have a few minutes?" I asked, although my tone suggested that the answer should be yes.

"Sure. I was just about to look at my email, but I guess that can wait."

"Did you have a chance to call Jonathan's dad back? I saw that he called me again this morning while we were meeting and I wanted to check in with you before I returned his phone call."

"Oh, yeah. I was going to do that this evening from home," Harriet replied calmly. I took a deep breath. She did not seem disturbed at all.

"I would appreciate it if you could call him right after we finish," I directed. "We spoke about this on Tuesday morning and it is important at this school that we have strong ties with the parents."

"Okay. I will do that."

"I will wait then until four o'clock to return his call to me." Hopefully that would add some pressure. "Do let me know after you talk to him if there is anything I need to be aware of." I decided to switch the conversation to this morning's PD session.

"You were pretty quiet this morning. What were your thoughts about book clubs?"

"Oh, you know, Kristin, I've been teaching a long time. I tried book clubs a couple years ago at my last school." I was dubious about this, but I let it go.

"Did you find it was a good way to engage students? Did they like them?"

"Well, it was a bit unmanageable to keep track of it all, to tell the truth. I think there are better ways," Harriet answered confidently.

"What kinds of things are you thinking?"

She ignored that question and responded, "I'm still finishing up the read-alouds." I groaned inwardly.

"It has been six weeks now. I am concerned that you will not have enough assessment to write the progress report cards due to the office in two weeks," I reminded her.

"Well, we are nearly done. Then we will go on to something else."

"What have you got planned?" I queried.

"I'm still finalizing the plans. Maybe I could show you later."

"Given that we are doing your TPA this year, why don't we meet next week. You can show me your plans for the rest of the semester and we can look at how you organize your assessment data. Can you make an appointment with Joan, please?" Perhaps that would galvanize her into action.

"Maybe two weeks would give me more time to get it all organized?"

I would have to hold a tougher line here. "Make the appointment for Thursday or Friday next week. After all, you said you were almost done with the read-alouds, so you will have to have the next unit planned."

"Yeah, of course, I'll do that."

"Great. We will chat next week. And you will let me know if I need to know anything before I call Jonathan's dad back at four, right?" I reminded her.

"Yeah, I'm sure I have his number somewhere."

"Call Joan if you need it. She will look it up." And I left. I worried as I headed down the hall. I had read her file. These were not new problems, but they had gone unaddressed. This was not the fun part of the job. I would have to be supportive through the appraisal process, but I wasn't going to let it go. The students in her classes deserved a good education. The research was clear. A poor teacher holds back student learning.

The students were filing out into the halls. I passed Rafi and glanced at his hat, which he removed sheepishly. Angelina ran up and gave me a hug. I saw Myles and smiled, but he didn't show any recognition—like we didn't spend almost every morning together. He looked sad but Sondra caught my eye and shook her head. I let it be. Carlton Byun passed and I stopped and asked how bedtime was going. He assured me that he and Aimee were going to bed when asked.

"Really?" I probed.

"Yup. Really, Mrs. Phillips. We're good now," he exclaimed with pride.

"Good to hear it!" We high-fived and I made my way to my office. Sarah was first in line. She plopped down in the chair by my desk. Sarah liked to talk pedagogy and teaching but rarely showed up with student concerns, since she handled them expertly. So I was surprised when she sighed and brought up Sawyer.

"He's still not very engaged in learning. Sometimes he will do the independent work if he knows how to do it but he won't do anything in groups and I do a lot of group work. I just don't seem to be connecting with him."

"Have you called his parents?" I asked. Sawyer's dad and I had spoken about the bus difficulties and he had seemed quite supportive and concerned.

"I called during my prep today because Sawyer's been pushing in line and at the coatracks. Dad thinks he is being bullied. He said he himself was bullied throughout his school years and is sure that is why Sawyer is pushing."

"What do you think? Is he being bullied?"

"The other kids don't really like him, but they don't pay that much attention to him except when he pushes them. He has never complained to me that they are bullying him. I've certainly never noticed anything or I would have intervened." I believed her. Sarah wasn't one to back away from a situation that needed her attention.

"What do you want to do?" I asked.

"I was wondering if you could bring it up next time you played backgammon. For now I've made him line captain so that he is always in front of the line."

I laughed. "Line captain? I didn't know you had line captains."

"I don't. I just needed something that the rest of the kids would buy into to let him be at the front of the line. Hopefully no one else will want to be line captain." I appreciated Sarah's creative problem solving. Other teachers might have wanted consequences, but Sarah's solution was clever and innovative. We had already had missed recesses for Sawyer's pushing and it wasn't working.

"Okay, I will explore the bullying and you let me know if being line captain works."

I interacted with a few more teachers. Jim popped in to say thanks for the PD that morning and that he was really excited to try book clubs. Joan stuck her head in while we were chatting to hand me a phone message. Joan had a good sense of when it was fine to interrupt. She handed me the slip. Jonathan's dad had called again.

"He didn't seem very happy and wants you to return his call ASAP."

I glanced at my watch. It was 4:05. Jim intuited that I needed to take care of this and left. I peeked into the office to see if Harriet was waiting. She wasn't. I asked Joan if any teachers had been waiting and she said no. This was not good.

"Hi. This is Kristin Phillips, principal at Jonathan's school," I began.

"Thanks for getting back to me. I just got off the phone with Harriet Davis, Jonathan's English teacher. I have concerns." There was an angry edge to the dad's voice.

"What are those concerns?" I asked calmly.

"Well, first it took her forever to return my call after I left many messages, as I relayed to you last Friday. I asked why all she did was read aloud and she said it was to teach the kids how to analyze a book, that she was showing them how. I said that Jonathan was bored of just sitting and listening every day. She responded that Jonathan needed a better work ethic." I took a deep breath. "Now, Jonathan has always loved school and been an A student. I also asked Mrs. Davis how she was evaluating whether Jonathan was learning how to analyze a book since Jonathan says he hasn't handed in anything yet and it is already the middle of the term! She said she was observing how often Jonathan answered questions in class. Honestly, I don't think this teacher knows what she is doing!"

I could hear the frustration in his voice. Most parents want to support the school system, but it was obvious that Jonathan's dad was at his wits' end. I was getting there, too.

One of the hardest things as a principal is to navigate the space between teachers and parents. It wasn't as if I could just agree with Jonathan's dad and fire Harriet (even though I did agree with his assessment of the situation). Even if I could manage to get through the unsatisfactory appraisal process without union grievances, it would take at least a year. In the meantime, it wouldn't do for the school community to know that I knew I had an ineffective teacher on staff because they would think I was doing nothing. The appraisal process was not shared with parents or other staff.

"I hear you that Jonathan is bored. Just today Mrs. Davis and some other intermediate teachers worked together to look at some different teaching strategies to engage students." This was true; I was just omitting that Harriet hadn't been interested. "I will definitely follow up with Mrs. Davis about starting a new unit. She is new to this grade and sometimes it takes a while to settle in." The former principal had moved Harriet from teaching grade 4 thinking that she'd do better with older students. I didn't like making excuses for bad teaching and was grasping at straws. "Jonathan seems like a great kid"—I had pulled up his file on my computer as we were talking. "Is he enjoying his other classes?"

"He is. He speaks positively about Mrs. Westman for science and he likes Mr. Finley in gym. But every night he is complaining about English. I don't want him to be unprepared for high school next year."

"I see he has done well in English every year, so I think he will be fine in grade nine." I tried to reassure him without specifically stating that this year was going to be a wash. "Could you give it two weeks or so for Mrs. Davis to implement a new unit? But do not hesitate to contact me again if Jonathan continues to be bored," I added. "And do always feel free to contact Mrs. Davis directly. I have ensured that she knows how to retrieve her voicemail messages." I hoped Jonathan's dad could read between the lines here.

"Well. All right. I guess I have no choice," he responded, somewhat calmer. "Have a good evening and thanks for listening. I really don't want to be one of those parents that complain all the time." I assured him he was not and that I was always available to listen to concerns.

I wrote "HARRIET" on a sticky and stuck it on my computer screen. I would have to talk to her first thing in the morning about how to talk to parents without antagonizing them. I gathered my bags and headed out the door, exhausted.

# EIGHT

# Bullying

"MR. TAYLOR? THIS IS KRISTIN PHILLIPS CALLING, principal at school. I'd like to talk to you about Zachary."

Dead silence on the other end.

"Zachary was in my office after recess today. He was threatening to beat up another boy on the bus after school. He was pushing him as well."

Still silence.

I barged ahead, my heart racing. "As we have discussed before, I do believe this is bullying behaviour. The other boy was not provoking Zachary in any way and this is not the first instance. Last time Zachary had some recess detentions but this time I am going to suspend him for tomorrow."

No response.

"I can keep him in the office for the remainder of the day or you can come and pick him up now."

I waited a good ten seconds. Nothing but dead air.

"The suspension letter will be in his backpack and he is welcome back at school the day after tomorrow." I waited again. "Well, thank you for your support." I hung up the phone. My palms were sweaty. I took some deep breaths and tried to calm myself down.

Zachary was a good-looking boy in grade 4. He had a charismatic smile and his sandy hair swept across his handsome face. Brand-name clothes attested to his family's wealth. I couldn't really figure Zachary out. Despite above-average intelligence and everything in his favour, he had few friends at school. I gathered that Zachary was also a gifted athlete. Outside of school, he played rep soccer and during school games he played very competitively and I had spoken to him before about losing graciously. Warren, another student, was his sidekick, and they were alternately friends and enemies. While Warren got into trouble because of his impulsivity, Zachary was mean. He always confessed to his crimes but also always had an excuse to justify his behaviour. But Zachary was also a sad boy, the youngest child in a family of four. I'd asked the teachers about the family and learned that the other three kids had been little trouble at school.

For whatever reasons, Zachary was a bully. So was his dad. The first time I had called home his mother had answered and been very apologetic. Since then, however, either Dad had always answered or it went to voicemail. No one returned those messages. The first time I had spoken with Dad he had responded, but this silence was his more recent response—his own bullying intimidation tactic. And it worked. I hated making the phone calls and was always shaken afterwards. Did I sometimes not call? For sure. It was scary. It didn't matter what I said or how I phrased it, silence was the response. His bullying tactic worked on me.

Bullying is a problem in schools. Research shows that teachers are only ever aware of about 7 percent of all bullying incidents. Schools require mandatory consequences for all instances of bullying and I had been to countless workshops on the subject. In the past, bullying had been brushed under the carpet—"kids will be kids." But our understanding of the harm it can cause has grown.

The National Centre Against Bullying defines bullying as "an ongoing and deliberate misuse of power in relationships through repeated verbal, physical, and/or social behaviour that intends to cause physical, social, and/or psychological harm. It can involve an individual or a group misusing their power, or perceived power, over one or more persons who feel unable to stop it from happening" (ncab.org.au). The imbalance and misuse of power is a key point. Zachary wasn't angry when he was intimidating the other student. He wanted the other student to be afraid of him. His dad wanted me to be afraid—and he succeeded. The fact that it is repetitive is also important. Mr. Taylor used the same silent treatment on me time and again. Zachary targeted the same students over and over.

We had other students who bullied, but in more subtle ways. Michael, in grade 6, lorded over the coatrack outside his classroom and decided who used which hooks. Lauryn used her social power among the grade 7 girls to determine who was cool and who was not, and other girls brought her makeup and clothing in order to gain favour. As these instances were reported they were dealt with swiftly and it was always a difficult parent conversation. No one wants to hear that their child is bullying others.

The school pulled from two socially and economically distinct neighbourhoods and there were far more bullying incidents among the students from the more affluent area. There were more incidents of fighting among the students from the less affluent neighbourhood, but it was rarely bullying. Sadly, I think that the poorer students already saw themselves at the bottom of the social heap. They didn't always have problem-solving skills and used fighting and aggression to remedy conflict. Students from the affluent neighbourhood, however, rarely engaged in fighting but bullying was more frequent. CEOs in the making? I was surprised at the discrepancy.

But the vast majority of the behaviour problems at schools were not bullying. Bullying has received so much press in recent years, as it should—but the result is that students and parents alike tend to ascribe bullying to any altercation. At least once a month I would have this conversation with a student:

STUDENT: I'm being bullied.

ME: Oh, dear. What happened?

STUDENT: So-and-so kicked me.

ME: What were you doing when this happened?

STUDENT: Playing soccer.

ME: Oh, yeah. Did you have the ball when this happened?

STUDENT: Yes! And so-and-so kicked my leg.

ME: Do you think that maybe so-and-so was trying to get the ball from you when this happened?

STUDENT: Maybe.

Bullying is often the go-to reaction whenever students are hurt emotionally or physically. While bullying is a serious problem that needs to be dealt with, I wonder if we are not using the moniker to relieve students from responsibility and the ups and downs of growing up. I remember Julie's mom calling me to complain that the other girls in Julie's grade 3 class were bullying her. I knew Julie because she would always find me on recess duty, her shoes untied and sweater buttoned up skewed. She wanted to be able to jump rope but couldn't figure out how to get in. I would turn the rope and yell "now," but she'd trip up every time. She was best friends with Charlie, who liked digging in the mud for worms.

"Mrs. Phillips, I really don't know what to do here. Julie came home in tears yesterday. The other girls in the class are being mean to her. Now she doesn't want to go to school anymore."

"Do you have any idea how the other girls are being mean?" I asked, reaching for my notebook in which I recorded all interactions with parents and students. I'd learned from experience to document everything.

"Jessica—you know her, she's in Julie's class—is having a birthday party on Saturday and did not invite Julie. She invited all the other girls and not Julie." Jessica was a popular girl and was always the centre of the grade 3 girls. But she wasn't mean. In fact, the other day I'd noticed her colouring with Julie during indoor recess. "This is clearly a case of bullying behaviour and I want you to stop it."

I get it. Parents love their kids and don't want to see them hurt. I felt the same way about my own kids when they would come home upset about something. I also thought it was funny that parents thought I could just call up Jessica's mother and insist that she invite Julie to the birthday party. I honestly didn't have that kind of power, nor did I want to.

"I can understand that Julie must be disappointed and sad that she wasn't invited to the party," I began before I was interrupted.

"Sad? She's devastated. She cried all night. You really can't allow this kind of behaviour to go on in your school. Kids should not be allowed to bully each other."

"It is certainly a challenging situation," I agreed. How was I going to turn the tide of this conversation? "I am a mom, too, and it is so hard to watch our kids be hurt, isn't it?"

"It is. I hate to see her so unhappy."

"Are she and Jessica good friends?"

"They live the next street over. In junior kindergarten they loved to play together but now not so much. Jessica's got this whole group of new friends now and ignores Julie."

"Who would you say are Julie's friends?" I asked.

"Charlie is always over here. I think they are best friends. I hardly ever see her playing with anyone else."

"Yes. I've seen them playing at school as well. They like to collect worms," I said, laughing. Julie's mom laughed, too. I continued: "I know that Julie is disappointed. It is hard to feel left out. Personally, I hate that feeling, too." I wanted Julie's mom to see that these were normal feelings. "Social bullying is really when someone is excluding another person over and over again to be mean and gain social power. I'm not sure this is happening here unless Julie is complaining that Jessica is always leaving her out of things." I let this sit for a moment.

"No . . . She doesn't really talk about Jessica that much. She was so unhappy not to be invited to the party, though."

"With my own kids, I often used these situations to help them see that sometimes we get disappointed in life but that it will be okay. You and I, as grown-ups, know that this isn't the last time she is going to have to deal with being left out." I could feel Julie's mom on the other end of the phone calming down. "Maybe you could arrange a worm search at the park with Charlie on Saturday?" Julie's mom laughed again and thanked me for my time. Julie's mom would help her daughter navigate the social world; Zachary's dad would not.

I had no sooner hung up the phone with Zachary's dad than Joan stopped in my office door saying Sawyer's dad, John, was on the phone.

"Hi, John, Kristin Phillips here. How are you today?"

"I'm fine, thanks. I wanted to talk to you about Sawyer. He keeps getting in trouble for pushing but I think he is being bullied and that's why he is pushing." I turned the page in my notebook.

"Why do you think so?" I asked, pen poised.

"You know, I was bullied all through school. None of the kids were ever nice to me and I was being pushed around all the time. I've told Sawyer that he doesn't have to put up with that kind of shit. I wish I hadn't."

"Sounds like your school days were not that great," I sympathized. "Sawyer sometimes has a hard time as well. Can you tell me how you think he is being bullied?"

"He says the other kids call him names all the time and grab his backpack." This was the first I had heard of this.

"Is this an everyday occurrence or just once?" I asked.

"He tells me stories about the other kids every day. I know what it is like. I went through it myself. I'm not going to let him have the same experience. You need to do something. You can't let bullying happen in that school." John's voice was elevated now. "If you don't do something about it, I will call the board."

Upset parents frequently threaten to "call the board" or the superintendent. It used to bother me a lot because I felt like I had failed to resolve the conflict, but I had learned over the years that parents rarely followed through. I'd also learned to call my superintendent's secretary with a heads-up and my side of the facts ASAP. Sawyer had problems with the other kids and John was assuming the issue was bullying, based on his own past experiences. Parents love their kids and I had to remember not to get defensive and to reassure John that I was taking things seriously.

"I will certainly look into it. I want Sawyer to be successful at school, too. Do you know who is bothering him?" I was reluctant to use the bullying word until we were sure that was the case.

"No. I can't remember. But it's all the time. You know he had problems at his other school, too. That's why I moved him. This has to stop." I hadn't realized that was why Sawyer had moved from the other school. I jotted a note to call them.

"I'm going to chat with Sawyer about it, and I will call you back later today, okay?" John was appeased for now. It was going to be one of those days. Goodbye, instructional leadership, hello, managing student behaviour. I left my office to go check if Adam knew whether Sawyer had complained of bullying, but he hadn't had any interactions with him. The recess bell rang and I stood up and grabbed my jacket. I needed some fresh air and maybe a game of foursquare.

Coming in from recess I grabbed my now-cold coffee and warmed it up in the microwave. There was a muffin left over from the breakfast club as well. We fed more than forty kids a day for breakfast. The muffins were a donation from the local coffee shop. I grabbed a muffin for Joan, too. The phone had been ringing off the hook and the October enrolment report was due this week. I knew that she, too, was having quite the day.

"There were two muffins left. Care for a stale snack?" I asked, setting it down on her desk.

"Sure. Stale is fine." Joan nodded towards the office chairs. A student I didn't know was sitting there fuming. He looked to be about eleven, grade 6? Short, stocky, buzz cut, wearing a sports shirt and baggy jeans. He was breathing heavily, fists clutched.

"Hi. I'm Mrs. Phillips. Want to come and chat a bit in my office?" I offered. The boy got up, brushed past me, and stomped into my office. I entered and he was standing in the middle of the room. "Why don't you have a seat at the table?" He sat down and slouched immediately.

"What's your name?"

"TJ."

"Who's your teacher?"

"Mr. Crewson." Grade 5. I was close.

"What can I do for you?"

He took a breath. "You know Avery?" I nodded yes. She was also in grade 5. She'd recently been diagnosed with Tourette's. Avery's mom had called me in late August, distraught. Seemingly out of nowhere Avery had begun to exhibit odd tics and vocalizations over the summer. Worried that kids would make fun of her, Avery's parents were afraid to send her to school. I had suggested that we have a chat with her class and explain the diagnosis and the symptoms. It was better to acknowledge the elephant in the room than to pretend it wasn't there. Avery had been fine with the plan and even stayed in the room while I discussed it with the class.

"I do know Avery. Are you guys friends?" Experience had taught me that no matter what the altercation between kids, it was useful to know if they were friends or not. Friends fought between themselves but usually made up easily. When two kids really didn't have a relationship and there was an altercation, it was a different matter altogether.

"We were. Until recess."

"Hmm. What happened?" I grabbed my notebook again and flipped the page.

"We were just hanging out by the trees and then she called me the N-word."

This was serious. I needed more details. "Can you tell me more about what you were doing while hanging out?"

"Well. A bunch of us were there. We were throwing sticks, seeing how far they could go. Avery threw one right at me. Hit my back and it hurt. So I threw one at her. Then she just calls me the N-word. Three times! That's racist. That's bullying. She can't do that. She should be suspended."

I knew Avery. She was clumsy. I'd be surprised if she could throw a stick and hit someone on purpose. I also knew that involuntary swearing and racial slurs were associated with some forms of Tourette's. So far, I had only noticed facial tics and grunting.

"You are right. That is a hateful word. It is not okay for people to say that word. Has she done it before or called you names?"

"Nah."

"Okay. Stay here for a bit and I am going to go talk to Avery. There's some Lego there in the bucket if you want to build something while you wait." I walked down to Avery's classroom. The students were busy making paper airplanes, working with gears as part of their science unit. I motioned Mr. Crewson over.

"How's Avery?"

"She came in from recess distressed and quiet. I've just given her some space right now," he said, and motioned to the corner where Avery was sitting with her head down.

"What's TJ like? I have him down at the office. He and Avery had problems at recess."

Mr. Crewson laughed. "Those two. On-again, off-again friends. TJ is quick to react but generally a good kid. What happened?"

"He says they were throwing sticks and then Avery called him the N-word."

Mr. Crewson frowned. "Doesn't sound like Avery. I've never heard her say cruel things."

"I'm going to grab her for a chat." I went over to the corner and knelt down so my voice could be low.

"Avery, can you come chat with me a bit?" At first she didn't move but then she reluctantly rose and followed me out of the room. I didn't want to take her down to my office so we found a quiet corner in the special education room.

"Can you tell me what happened with TJ at recess?" Avery kept her gaze on the table. Her neck was jerking to the left repeatedly.

"He th-threw a st-stick at me. Then I called him the N-word. It just came out. Then I ran away."

"Were you angry or was it a vocalization of the Tourette's?"

"I don't know." She sobbed quietly. This was all new to her. My heart ached for her.

"You know that is a bad word, right?"

"Yeah. It just cc-came out." She put her head back down.

"Okay. I'm going to chat some more with TJ and call your mom."

"Don't call my mom. She'll be so angry."

"I have to call your mom, Avery. Why don't you stay here and calm down a bit?" I left, notebook in hand; made arrangements with Maria, the special education teacher, to have Avery sit in her room; and made my way back to my office. I mulled over what to do. I wanted to find out if Avery had swearing vocalizations at home. How would TJ's parents react to this situation? In other circumstances I would have zero tolerance for racial slurs. Was this a racial slur or a symptom of the Tourette's? There are times as principal when you wish someone else would make the decisions. TJ was building with Legos when I returned and seemed calmer.

"Hey, TJ. Cool car," I said, acknowledging his creation. "I chatted with Avery and she agrees that is what happened. She said the word slipped out. Remember when I talked to the class about her Tourette's?" TJ nodded. "Sometimes people with Tourette's say bad words. Kind of like the way her head jerks. She doesn't mean to jerk her head and she doesn't mean the bad words."

"Nope. She's racist. She can't call me that. I'm telling my parents."

"I agree it is a racist word. Let me look into things a bit more. I will call your parents, too. Are you okay to go back to class? Avery isn't there right now."

"She should be expelled," TJ insisted. I understood his anger.

"It is a hateful word. I get why you are angry. We'll talk later this afternoon, all right?" TJ was not appeased but headed back to class. I gave Mr. Crewson a quick call to explain where Avery was and that TJ was headed back. I looked up Avery's mom's phone number. Her work number was at an insurance company. I wasn't sure if she'd want to be interrupted at work with this situation, but it needed to be handled immediately.

"Hi. It's Kristin Phillips calling."

"Is everything all right with Avery? What's happened?" She was worried. I would worry, too. I knew what it was like to have a kid with problems others didn't understand, problems I didn't really understand myself.

"She's okay but there has been a bit of a recess issue. She called another boy the N-word. The boy is Black."

She gasped. "Oh, no! Why would she do that?"

"Have you ever heard her make swearing or name-calling vocalizations with Tourette's before at home?"

She paused. "Lately the F-word has been coming out a lot. Usually when she is frustrated but sometimes just because. She repeats it over and over."

"I spoke with Avery and she says this word just came out. I don't think she meant it. Usually they are friends. But the boy is very upset."

"She's a good kid. I don't think she would do that. We don't allow that at home. I think it must have been a vocalization. Is she going to be suspended?" This was the rub. There were clear guidelines that she should be suspended unless there were mitigating circumstances. There were indeed clear mitigating circumstances, but would TJ's parents agree?

"She's pretty upset about things. Could you possibly pick her up and take her home for the rest of the day?" This would give Avery a bit of respite from school and it might look like she'd been suspended to the rest of the class. I wasn't sure it would appease TJ's parents. Avery's mom agreed to come and get her right away. I called Avery down to the office and explained the situation. I reiterated that although it was a very bad word I didn't think she'd meant it.

"Can I tell TJ I'm s-sorry?"

"How about you and TJ and I talk together tomorrow? I think it would be good to say sorry. I know you guys are friends." Avery left with her mom. She shot me a look of gratitude and sadness. I knew what it was like to have your life go topsy-turvy with little warning—looking back, I wish I could have better communicated all that. I found TJ's phone number and called home. His father answered. I explained the situation. He was furious.

"What do you mean she said it by mistake? That isn't a mistake. That is racial bullying. You'd better do something about this. I'm not going to have my son bullied like that. This is racism. There is zero tolerance for this at the school board." We had had numerous workshops on racism and the systemic issues of discrimination. White and upper middle class, I could never truly understand his reality, but I could listen and support him. Had any other child made a racial slur against TJ, I would have suspended him without a second thought. I tried again to explain about Tourette's. Under other circumstances I believed that TJ's dad would be more understanding but not in this case. It was too personal. My palms were sweaty. How could I navigate this?

"I do understand how hurtful this is to TJ and your family. I do not condone racial slurs. Avery has gone home for the day. She has already expressed a desire to apologize to TJ. I will meet with both of them tomorrow. I truly do not believe that this was bullying or racism but rather an unfortunate result of a difficult disorder. Avery's mother is also upset this has happened."

"I am very angry about this. TJ should be able to go to school safely. I will be calling the board office about this." I gave him the phone number to reach Max, my superintendent, and ended the conversation. I quickly called Max's secretary and gave her the details and a heads-up. My experience was that parents only followed through about 20 percent of the time, but I didn't want Max to be blindsided. I was hopeful that after some time TJ's dad would calm down. His reaction was understandable and maybe he didn't believe me about the Tourette's. Perhaps it seemed like I was making excuses or trying to avoid the situation. And I was questioning my response as well—had I made the right call here?

I was not having a good day. Kids mess up and make mistakes. They can be mean to each other. They have issues and, sometimes, complex disorders. At times I felt that parents thought I had some sort of magical power that could just make all kids behave, could stop them from acting out, swearing, and engaging in name-calling.

On top of that, kids didn't always make reliable witnesses. The investigation of a behaviour issue could take hours. In the end, for every situation, I had to call both sets of parents and needed to be fair in my assessment of the situation. I knew as a parent that it was difficult to believe your own child had behaved poorly.

The afternoon break had come and gone. It was Tuesday and Sawyer would be showing up for backgammon soon. I looked forward to our visits but today I would have to explore the bullying that his dad was concerned about. Sawyer appeared at my door right on time, sticky note in hand. His hair was messy as usual and he sported his black hoodie, hood up. I smiled and he came in and set up the board. No small talk for Sawyer.

"Maybe today will be 'Let the Principal Win Day,'" I joked. He smiled and made his first move. We played in silence for a while. I wasn't sure how to bring up the subject, as I didn't want to disrupt the peaceful silence of our backgammon game. I knew this was a highlight in Sawyer's week. After a few moves I asked how his day was going.

"Okay." I had two of my pieces sitting on the bar and Sawyer was well on his way to having his pieces on his home board. Winning backgammon often comes down to luck in the roll of the dice but strategy was a key piece as well. It was a bit embarrassing to be beaten by a ten-year-old week after week. I didn't try very hard, but I wasn't purposely losing anymore.

"Are you making any friends at school now?"

"I don't know."

"Who do you play with at recess?"

"I don't know." I wasn't getting very far with the indirect approach.

"Your dad called me today." Sawyer looked up from the board. "He's a bit worried about you." I paused to see if he'd bite. Nope. "Do you know what about?" Silence. We played two more moves each. It was clear it was not going to be "Let the Principal Win Day."

"Your dad says other kids are bullying you, bothering you all the time."

"Yeah. They don't let me play with them. And they tell me to get lost all the time."

"Hmm. That doesn't sound fun. When does this happen?"

"I don't know." I sighed inwardly. Was he reluctant to say or was it nonspecific or did he really not know?

"Who bothers you? Which boys?"

"A lot of them," and he named about eight boys.

"What do you want to play?"

"Mini-sticks. I want to play but they never ask me."

"Do they know that you want to play?"

"I don't know."

"Do you ever ask if you can play?"

"Nope. I just start playing and then they tell me to get lost."

"Oh. Maybe they have their teams already organized," I suggested. It sounded like Sawyer just didn't know how to interact with the other boys. I would ask Stephanie, our Child and Youth Worker, if she could add him to her recess group. This group had been formed to help lost kids figure out how to negotiate the social world of play. I began to wonder if all the pushing was an indicator that Sawyer just wanted to interact with the other boys and didn't know how. Was the other boys' reaction bullying? I wasn't convinced. I think they were annoyed. But to Sawyer's dad it would appear like bullying and be reminiscent of his own schooling years. Sawyer and I confirmed our date for next Tuesday. I wrote the sticky note for him and then made a note to talk to Stephanie and Sarah, Sawyer's teacher.

The end-of-day bell rang and the line of teachers formed outside my office. I was pleased that more of the conversations today were to share stories about teaching rather than make complaints about kids and resources. Jim and Mac were excited about their book clubs. Maggie popped in to give me an update on Ana, who had put her hand up to answer a question today. Kate plopped down to discuss her smiley-face system. She didn't think it was having the desired effects. Again, I suggested some routines and structures from the book I'd given her and she left promising to read it that night.

Joan stuck her head in the door. "Tough day?"

"Yeah, it was nonstop. Is it a full moon?" She laughed. It was an ongoing joke. There must be some explanation for the crazy days. She handed me a handful of messages and said goodbye. One was from Joey. I glanced at my cell phone: three texts. Pizza? Did the child never tire of pizza? Avery's mom had called, as had Sawyer's dad. I called Avery's mom first. She was apologetic again and devastated. They had made an appointment at the doctor's for Avery for tomorrow and she wouldn't be at school. That was good for me; it would appear to the other kids that she was suspended. I hung up and called John. I repeated the conversation Sawyer and I had had. I suggested that support from Stephanie might be helpful. Although he was amenable, he was still convinced there was bullying occurring. I said that I would monitor the situation and urged him to let me know of any further instances, no matter how small.

As I packed up my bag, debating the gym on the way to the car, I mentally reviewed the day. Zachary's dad had never picked him up and he had done his work in the office all day. The suspension would be for tomorrow. Zachary was a bully, but he was a sad boy hiding behind a lot of bravado. I wondered how much his dad bullied him. I wasn't sure the suspension was going to make a difference to his behaviour, but I didn't know what else to do. Some days I just didn't feel equipped to deal with all the complex issues of student behaviour. Maybe Joey's wish would come true tonight. I'd go to the gym and pick up a pizza on my way home. There were snowflakes on my windshield. Winter had arrived in southern Ontario. Hopefully it wouldn't stay, as I really didn't want to deal with snowball issues all day tomorrow.

# Winter

NINE

# Bouncy Boundaries

TWO DAYS AFTER THE FIRST SNOW, I awoke to my cell phone ringing at 5:45 a.m. Groggily, I answered it—school buses were cancelled but schools were open. Great. That meant a messy drive, a half-empty school, slushy hallways, and snowball fights. I peered into the dark and it had snowed heavily overnight. There must have been at least fifteen centimeters of wet snow blanketing the roads and the driveway. I pulled on my sweats and went to rouse the kids—we'd have to shovel the driveway and leave before the plow arrived to block us back in. While our divorce was amicable, I hated my ex-husband every time it snowed.

"Kids, get up! We have to shovel!" I yelled, banging on bedroom doors. I bet principals in California were happy. November in southern Ontario is just the beginning of winter; it will not loosen its hold until the end of April. I tramped into the garage, grabbed a shovel, and started. I saw that Fred the neighbor next door had his snowblower out. *I should get one of those,* I mused. I used to think he would offer to do our driveway, but he never did. He actually stopped exactly at the property line on the sidewalk.

"Mom, watch out!" A snowball landed on my shoulder. I looked up and Joey was grinning. He grabbed another shovel and started racing up and down the driveway. For him, clearing the snow is a challenge. He loves it. He might not be the most dedicated student but I can count on him for hard work. Lily, bundled to her nose, dragged herself into the fray, halfheartedly shoveling a few random snowflakes. After we had cleared half the driveway, I asked if anyone had heard Frankie get up. I was met with looks of disbelief and eye-rolling. It wasn't the battle to fight, I decided.

Driveway and sidewalk cleared (what made us buy a corner lot?), we retreated to the warmth of the house to begin the mad scramble to get the four of us out the door in forty-five minutes. I quickly glanced at my emails to see if I had any teachers absent that day and if I had supply teachers to cover them. Five teachers away and three supply teachers. Par for the course. Snow days, Fridays, and Mondays all saw an increase in teacher absences and the lack of supply teachers was a province-wide problem. I'd be able to collapse a class or two with buses cancelled and have one teacher cover two classes. I could cancel Special Education and have Maria take a class, or Adam or I could cover a class. I texted him some thoughts in case he got there first. *This is a VP job,* I thought wryly. We all managed to get into the car almost on time, even Frankie, albeit not pleasantly, and just as I began to back out of the driveway the snowplow appeared.

"Lily—jump out and stand in the road and stop that plow!" I yelled. Was this putting my daughter in harm's way? I didn't care. Giving me a look that could kill, she complied and halted the plow while I backed out. Joey laughed and found some obnoxiously loud music to blare as we made our way down the street. I dropped them off at the high school door, none of them dressed for the winter weather. Certainly I had purchased snow boots for all three. How could they be wearing shoes? Was

Lily wearing ballet flats? Didn't any of them own mittens or hats? Was I a terrible mother? As I slowly drove to school on slushy and unplowed roads, I resolved to be understanding of the students who would arrive at school underdressed for the weather.

Pulling into the school parking lot, I laughed at the group of roly-poly primary students bundled in snowsuits building snowmen and snow forts, thrilled at the first major storm of the year. Huddled in a corner of the schoolyard was a sullen group of grade 7 and 8 students who didn't ride the bus. I could imagine their disdain for their parents who made them come to school despite the fact that many of their friends who rode the bus had the day off. Sure enough, none of them wore boots or mittens or hats. The girls typically had short bomber jackets atop skintight jeans, sockless, with ballet flats. The boys wore hoodies and jeans and running shoes. They did not have bad parents. As I made my way to the front door, a parent was dropping her children off and rolled down her window to talk to me.

"Good morning, Mrs. Phillips. I don't understand why you cancelled the buses. The roads aren't that bad and we all have to go to work." I sympathized with her frustrations.

"Sorry," I replied. "The decision to cancel buses is made at the board office, not by me. The weather forecast is calling for the snow to continue today and it is important to keep the kids safe. Thanks for bringing your kids to school." Actually, I had no idea how they decided when to cancel buses or school, but I was glad the decision wasn't mine! I got enough flack calling an indoor recess. Years later, when I worked more closely with the superintendents, I learned that it was the most reviled job in the board. You rarely got it right. I entered the front hall and met Vince, mop in hand. He would spend all day mopping floors, trying to stay on top of the slush.

"I put a coffee on your desk, but it might be cold by now," he said with a smile. Thank God for Vince. He was a gem.

"I owe you one. I will nuke it. It will be a wet day. Thanks for getting the walks shoveled already." He nodded and moved on. The office was busy. The phone was ringing and I grabbed it as I walked in.

"Good morning. Yes. The school is open today." Joan, phone to her ear, rolled her eyes and said the same thing into her receiver as another line rang. Adam walked by, purposefully, notepad in hand.

"I think I've got all the classes covered. You don't have to cover any except maybe last period. I'll let you know." He scurried out.

"Kristin." Mac had come into the office. "There are already kids throwing snowballs in the yard. You'd better make an announcement." Another parent wandered into the office, holding her daughter's hand. I didn't recognize them.

"Can I help you?" I said. "I'm Mrs. Phillips, the principal."

"Oh, yeah, great. My daughter here has a cold so she will need to stay in for recess today." This was a tricky one. I had to ensure that all students were supervised during recess and could not ask teachers to do extra supervision duty, due to contract obligations. Teachers had to do 80 minutes of lunch, recess, or bus duty per week. Not 83 and not 75. Eighty. The schedule was created and adhered to. I could not ask Joan to supervise students during recess. While Adam or I could do it, we were often busy and I didn't want to set a precedent. From a parent's point of view, I understood. Your kid is sniffly and wants to stay home. You think they can go to school and you can get to work. It seems like a good compromise to tell the child they can stay in at recess. But from a school organizational standpoint it was not easy.

"I'm so sorry your daughter isn't feeling well. Unfortunately, I don't have any supervision for sick children at recess time. If she is too ill to go outside then she should probably stay home." My fingers were crossed that the mom would accept this answer.

"That's ridiculous!" Nope, she wouldn't. "I can't take Emma home. I am already late for work today and I have no one to look after her." She stood there glaring at me. It is important to have rules. It is also important to know when to let them bend. Plus, I was now beginning to get that scratchy, sweaty feeling as I was still bundled in my outdoor coat despite having been in the building for fifteen minutes.

"I'll tell you what I will do today since we have a reduced school population." That actually had nothing to do with it, but it provided me with an excuse to break my rules. "Emma can stay in today at the office and read but if she is still feeling ill tomorrow you will have to keep her home. If she feels worse throughout the day, we will give you a call to come and get her." I wasn't sure the parent was totally appeased but she nodded her agreement. "And don't tell anyone I made an exception to my rule," I joked. She smiled and agreed.

The morning bell rang and the day began. I managed to hang up my coat and remove my boots, which had created a puddle on the office floor before "O Canada" was played. I made my announcement reminding students that snowmen, snow angels, and snow forts were all permissible but snowball throwing was not. I didn't think it would make much difference and knew Adam and I would deal with infractions at recess for sure. Some days I thought I should just allow snowball throwing but if a kid got seriously hurt it would be my ass on the line. It was better to have the rule.

Into my office barreled Myles, the educational assistant trailing behind.

"That didn't take long," I said to Kim, glancing at the wall clock. "Anything in particular this morning?"

Kim sighed. She had a heart of gold. "Not that I could see," she replied. "He had some trouble getting his boots off and then sat in a puddle on the floor. Threw his coat down the hall, screamed his favourite word, and ran down here." Myles did not cope well with the ups and downs of life. He had so few problem-solving skills.

"I've got it now. I'll bring him back when he is settled." I wandered into my office and Myles was sitting in his spaceship muttering to himself. I let him sit while I perused my email. He was comfortable in my office now that we spent so much time together. It wasn't as if I could reason with him. He was five. I provided a safe place to calm down. Other students used Maria's special education room or Stephanie's office for the same thing. After about ten minutes he climbed out of his spaceship and handed me *Mortimer.* I could read this book with my eyes closed by now. On one page was a picture of all of Mortimer's "seventeen brothers and sisters." Last week Myles had asked me what their names were and I'd made up some, but now he expected me to remember them! I was thinking of hiding *Mortimer.* Myles clambered into one of the chairs around my table and pulled his knees up to his chest, feet on the seat. His blue jeans were baggy and his T-shirt had a rip at the neckline. His socks (no shoes) were slouching down and wet on the bottoms. I never saw Myles in any other outfit. He never wore sweatshirts or sweaters. I suspect he generated enough body heat. We read the book and he corrected me when I got the imaginary names of the seventeen brothers and sisters incorrect.

"I hate it when I can't get my boots off," I ventured. "It is so frustrating." Myles slouched farther into the chair and picked his nose. I nudged the tissue box towards him but he ignored it. "Remember that you were going to try and say 'yucky' not 'fuck' when you were frustrated."

The conversation required repeating the word. A five-year-old doesn't necessarily know what "the F-word" is. I was always direct. Plus, he wouldn't be shocked to hear me say it. It was part of his vocabulary already.

"I forgot," he mumbled. "And my socks were bunched. And there was snow all over the floor."

"It was a frustrating time," I agreed. We sat in silence a bit and he looked at me, a puzzled look on his face.

"You know, Mrs. Phillips, you wear different clothes but you are always the same." I was stunned. Such insight for a five-year-old. There wasn't much in his home life that was stable. Tiffany, his mother, tried her best, but she was overwhelmed. Most likely the rules came and went like the wind. Myles liked me because I was the same every day, despite the changes in attire. Maybe I could use this to my advantage. Perhaps some of the morning tantrums were just a need to ensure that I was here.

"I am always the same. I like to see you, but I like seeing you when you are happier, not angry." I let that sit a bit. "Do you think you are good to go back to class? I think your class is on their way to the gym soon."

"Okay." He untangled himself from the chair and took my hand and we went back to class. When we arrived I motioned Sondra to the doorway. She had a skeleton class today, so hopefully Myles would manage without further issues. I relayed the conversation Myles and I had had.

"So I am wondering if maybe we should take control of this situation and have him come to see me every morning *before* he tantrums. Kim could bring him down right away and we could have a little visit. Maybe he needs to know I am there." Sondra looked at me dubiously but nodded.

"We can try. What else have we got to lose? Nothing else is working." Later that day I explained the plan to Kim. We would start tomorrow and see what happened. I knew that there were a handful of teachers in the school who doubted my methods. They wanted rules, and for me to come down with a hard line on student behaviour. Many principals operated this way, with inflexible consequences for each infraction. Parents, too, often wanted this type of punishment system, usually when their child was the victim, not the perpetrator. But I preferred "bouncy boundaries." If an older student swore like Myles did, there would definitely be stronger consequences, but that's because I believed the consequence would help the student to change. Recess detentions or school suspension was not going to stop the swearing. A "zero tolerance" consequence might appear to be a good idea but if it didn't change the undesirable behaviour then it wasn't working.

I remembered back to the first school in which I was vice-principal.

The principal I worked for was very much in favour of strict consequences and since it was my first position, I didn't know what to do. In those days a school's suspension numbers were circulated internally and he seemed proud that our school suspended a lot of students. I guess he thought it made him seem tough and able to manage a school in a rough neighbourhood.

One student was trouble. I met him the first week of school and dealt with him every week thereafter. Dawson, the youngest of four brothers, would get into fights, mouth off at teachers, swear, vandalize, and steal—though he looked like an angel with long, flowing blond curls and a slight build. Following the principal's direction, I suspended Dawson for one to five days for each infraction. By the end of the year, he had been suspended seventy-four days! Nothing ever changed. No sooner would he return to school than I'd be suspending him again. His parents accepted the suspensions without comment and the teachers didn't miss him. Dawson had no one at school who liked him. He had no positive relationships with staff or students.

That same year there was another student, Brody. Also in grade 7, also a street-savvy kid, Brody either showed up late or skipped school. As vice-principal I was in charge of attendance and lates and had implemented a system of consequences for them. There were very clear boundaries that everyone knew. The lineup for late slips in the mornings no longer snaked out the office and down the hall. But Brody was still late every day despite the consequences. So I tried something different with Brody. I told my secretary to welcome him when he showed up, say we were glad to see him, and send him to class, no consequences. I told Brody that this was special, just for him, because he was one of my favourite students.

"I am?" he asked, puzzled.

"You are," I stated firmly. "One of my favourites." Often we would spend a few minutes chatting when he arrived. Brody needed a grown-up to care. One day in the spring he showed up in the morning complaining that his fingers were sprained. Unofficial nurse, I looked at them and saw no swelling.

"Can you move them?" He wiggled them without hesitation.

"But it really hurts."

"Hmm. How about some ice?" Ice is the school's answer to any injury.

"I think it needs to be bandaged," he said. So I got out the first aid kit and wrapped his fingers with reams of gauze and tape. It looked like he had suffered third-degree burns. Brody beamed. "It feels way better." Shaking my head, I sent him off to class. At the end of the day he returned and gave me back the bandages.

"You can keep them on," I said.

"Nah. It's okay." Brody left but the next morning he was back, late, and I rebandaged his hand. We did this for a week. By the end of the school year, Brody was still late most days but he rarely skipped school. I felt better about the relationship I'd built with Brody than with Dawson. I often wonder if I could have made a difference with Dawson if I had taken the time to bandage his wounds.

I stopped in at Mr. Crewson's class to check on Avery and TJ. Both had walked to school. Mr. Crewson had his students involved in a math game and Avery and TJ were playing together. The previous day the three of us had sat down to discuss the racial slur. I still didn't know if I had handled it correctly or not. TJ had expressed his hurt and Avery had apologized. I had explained again about the vocalizations that happened with Tourette's syndrome. I hadn't heard from my superintendent, Max, so I assumed TJ's dad hadn't called the board office.

Recess came and went. Emma brought a book to the office. I didn't hear a single cough or sneeze. Sure enough, there was a lineup of students in the office sent in for throwing snowballs. Adam and I talked to them and gave them the job of creating "No Throwing Snowballs" posters for the hallways. How reasonable was it to expect Canadian students to not throw snowballs? I wished that the teachers could manage this better as part of their recess supervision duty and the students weren't sent to the office. Maybe we would need to talk about bouncy boundaries at the next staff meeting. I spent a few minutes counting how many more days until the end of April.

The day was nearing the end and Joan interrupted me to say that the vice-principal of my own kids' high school was on the phone. My heart flipped. Frankie?

"Hello?" I said warily.

"Hi, Kristin. Joe Waldon here. Joey's vice-principal." My heart stilled. This was not about Frankie. But what was Joey up to? He didn't usually get into trouble. "Joey has been skipping classes. He usually is missing third or fourth period. He will be suspended from school for three days." What?

"Pardon? Skipping class? Why haven't I been informed about this before you move to suspension?" Three days at home, unsupervised? How was that going to help?

"Kristin, our automated system calls parents for every absence. This is the phone number we have on file." He read out our home phone line. And then I figured it out. Recently we had had a large number of "marketing" phone calls around dinnertime. The phone would ring and Joey would jump to answer it, saying it was a solicitation call. I hadn't thought much of it, being in the business of getting supper on the table. That scammer! He would definitely be grounded for this.

"That is our number but could you please change it to my mobile number?" I gave it to him. "Joe, I'm wondering if you'd consider an in-school suspension? I know you have a full-time CYW [Child and Youth Worker] who manages in-school suspensions. I'd rather Joey not be at home and I can't take three days off work. Plus, as you may know, his dad and I have recently divorced and perhaps he could use some support?" Was I becoming one of those difficult parents?

"Well . . . I suppose I can do that this time, but if the behaviour continues then next time it will have to be out of school."

"Thanks so much, Joe. I really appreciate this and I know it will be better for Joey. I will drop him off at the office tomorrow morning myself." I wondered if Joe had bouncy boundaries or whether he was doing me a favour since I was a colleague. I texted Joey that I'd had the call and he was to go directly home and shovel the driveway. I got a "Sorry" back. Joan came in and asked if everything was all right and I told her the story. She laughed about the marketing phone calls and I had to admit it was rather clever. Joan had three kids of her own and we exchanged stories for a bit, but I didn't share about Frankie. That I never talked about.

Adam came in. "Have a second?" Joan got the hint and left. Adam settled into the chair by my desk and pulled out his notes.

"I just had an angry phone call from a dad. His son was pelted with snowballs on the way home from school by Rafi Nader."

"Grade eight, slouchy jeans, untied shoes, baseball cap?"

"That's the one. I've been dealing with him a fair bit lately. I get a lot of kids complaining about him—he pushes, calls them names. According to this dad, Rafi bothers his son almost every day on the way home."

Students are our responsibility on their way to and from school as well as on school property. We have to ensure they are safe coming and going. In fact, if an issue is part of the school community broadly, it is our problem. There are limits, of course; if there is an issue at a party or the mall, that's not on us. But if there are ramifications that come into the building, then potentially it becomes our problem. It can be a slippery slope.

"You think he might be bullying?"

"I don't know. Whenever I look into an incident it seems like there are problems on both sides. But his name is coming up more and more."

"What kinds of consequences have you had?"

"We've had warnings and recess detentions."

"I've seen him in the hallways quite a bit. I think he gets kicked out of class a lot." Adam nodded in agreement. "Well, investigate tomorrow morning and maybe we need to up the consequences to an in-school suspension."

"I'm at meetings all day tomorrow," Adam said sheepishly and handed me the notes. Some principals had their VPs do almost all the student behaviour but Adam knew that I would share in it. There are no rules or guidelines on how to mentor a vice-principal. I thought back to my first experience when I'd been expected to suspend students even when I wasn't convinced it was the right decision. Adam and I often talked about our philosophies and shared the load. In the end, big decisions were always mine, but I tried to give him a fair amount of leeway. I thought he would be a good principal himself one day.

"All right, I've got a meeting in the afternoon. I will deal with this in the morning." Some principals also tried to ensure that at least one of the administrators, either principal or vice-principal, was in the school at all times. I didn't follow that protocol, either, if it meant that we would miss important meetings. I chose Jim to be in charge and he would call if there was a problem. I also trusted my teachers to deal with school behaviour. Adam and I could not be the only authority figures in the building.

I looked out the window and it was snowing again. Bundling against the cold, Adam and I headed out together. I swept off my car. The snow was wet and heavy. Perfect for snowballs. I looked around. The parking lot was empty except for our two cars. I carefully formed a snowball and threw it at Adam. I have terrible aim and it landed short. He laughed and got in his car. Guess he knew better than to throw snowballs at the principal!

# TEN

# "Bad Egg"

IT WAS 9:01 A.M. AND, RIGHT ON time, a little boy bounced into my office. I heard Kim's voice chastising: "We have to knock first." A soft knock followed and I looked up.

"Good morning, Myles."

"Morning." He shuffled his feet and looked at the ground. Despite having been in my office almost daily, he'd never arrived calmly and officially.

"Would you like to come in for a visit before you go to class?"

He beamed.

"Yeah." He wandered about my office aimlessly. Climbed in and out of his spaceship. Fingered the toys on my table. Looked out the window. And then settled himself in one of the chairs at the table.

"What did you have for breakfast?" I asked. "I had peanut butter toast."

"I had Cheerios," he answered amicably. "And my sister had Rice Krispies. The baby had baby food. I don't like baby food. He's a messy baby. Sometimes I help feed him when my mom is busy."

This was the longest speech I'd ever heard from Myles that wasn't a swearing rant. He went on to tell me about the cartoons he'd watched that morning and that he and his sister had made a snowman after school the previous day.

"I like it when you come to visit me in the mornings, Myles. It helps me start my day happy. Maybe Ms. Zeigler can bring you every day first thing and we can have a little visit."

Myles nodded.

"You heading off to class now? Ms. Zeigler can walk you back."

"Okay."

"See you tomorrow." Touch wood he wouldn't have a tantrum upon entering the class. We would see how this plan worked. I wasn't expecting miracles, but I knew that forming relationships with kids was important. Every year there would be a handful of kids that were "mine." Some years they continued to connect with me and other times they didn't need the relationship as much. Jose, a not-as-tough-as-he-appeared grade 4 boy, and I had played cards and he cheated terribly in order to win. I cheated to lose. Ruby, a feisty grade 1 girl, used to come for "Princess Time" when she'd been having a good day and behaving like a princess. We would wear Dollar Store tiaras and colour pictures of ponies and unicorns and rainbows. Bailey, a sad young man who never wanted to come to school, used to have tea with me whenever he arrived, be it 9 or 10 a.m. or even 1 p.m. All these kids ended up in my office for behavioural problems, and they continued to struggle with peer interactions or dealing with authority. But we had a relationship and they felt guilty when they messed up. Guilt is a useful emotion in trying to change behaviour.

I read over Adam's notes about Rafi Nader and the other young man from the previous day. It was TJ. I wandered down to Mr. Crewson's class to find him. The kids were all reading silently, so, making eye contact with Mr. Crewson, I made my way over to TJ and asked if he could come see me when he came to a stopping spot. I waited in the hall. TJ found his stopping spot quickly.

I asked him about what he was reading and we talked about his book as we made our way to my office.

Grabbing my spiral-bound notebook, I turned to a clean page and asked him about his walk home the night before.

"Avery and I were walking home together and throwing snowballs at each other. It's okay to throw them off school property, you know." I nodded in agreement. "So then this Rafi kid. He lives on my street. He is walking behind us and is yelling that I throw like a girl. He says that we are punks. He was swearing, too." There was a pause. "And then he tackled me and pushed my face into the snow. He's a bully." In his notes Adam wondered if this was bullying as well. I had enough experience with Rafi to suspect this was not the first time he had bothered TJ on the way home.

"Did he bother Avery, too?" I hadn't heard from Avery's parents.

"Yeah. He was bullying both of us. He always does."

"What else has he done?"

"You know. He follows us. Calls us names. Bugs us. He was making fun of the way Avery talks."

"Okay. Let's walk back to class. I'm going to talk to some other kids." I had a quick chat with Avery, who corroborated the story. I headed towards Rafi's class only to find him sitting out in the hall.

"Already?" I questioned. I let his teacher know I was taking him to the office. Rafi shrugged nonchalantly and shuffled down the hall behind me.

"Tell me what happened on the way home from school last night."

"Nothing." He scowled, looking at me like I had two heads.

"Hmm. I heard you were bugging TJ and Avery."

"Who are they?" he retorted. They were in different grades so it wasn't surprising he didn't know their names. I got out my student directory and showed him their pictures.

"Oh, yeah, that kid," he said, pointing to TJ's picture. "He threw a snowball at me."

"Really? Why did he do that?"

"I don't know. He's always bugging people." Bullying instances are never as clear-cut as they are on the made-for-TV movies.

"Was he bugging you last night?" Silence. "I heard you were bugging them. Calling them names. Making fun of Avery. And then you pushed TJ into the snow." I waited.

"He started it. He deserved it."

"I'm going to get TJ." I left my office and went to get TJ from class again. I didn't like disrupting student learning like this, but these incidents took a long time to muddle through. Document, document. The three of us settled around the table in my office. The boys did not acknowledge each other or make eye contact. It was clear they were not friends.

"So this is what I think happened. When I'm done you can tell me if anything I have said is incorrect, okay?" They nodded. "Avery and TJ were walking home together and throwing snowballs happily with each other. They are friends. Rafi was walking behind and calling them names and saying TJ threw snowballs like a girl. This made TJ angry so he threw a snowball at Rafi." I waited but no one disagreed. "Then Rafi was angry so he tackled TJ in the snow." Neither boy said a word.

"Rafi. You do not get to call people names. It makes them angry. I can understand why TJ threw a snowball at you. TJ says this isn't the first time you've been bugging them on the way home. If you keep bugging them then that is bullying behaviour." I purposely used the bullying word and defined it for everyone involved. The word is often bandied about to refer to any altercation. It was clear here that the snowballs TJ and Avery were throwing were friendly but that Rafi's continual intimidation of the two was bullying. All instances of student behaviour are also opportunities to educate. "TJ and Avery get to feel safe walking home." Rafi just looked at the table. "TJ, I know you were mad at Rafi. But if you throw a snowball at someone, chances are they will fight back." We sat in silence for a bit while I tried to think of appropriate consequences. This was the first instance we'd heard of Rafi bullying kids on the way home. TJ hadn't been able to be specific about what else Rafi had done. Some principals would have given consequences to TJ for not walking away but honestly, I hadn't had a lot of success with the line "Couldn't you have just walked away?" when talking to angry boys. Generally the answer is no, they don't just let it slide. I don't condone aggression but one needs to be realistic. "TJ, the very next time Rafi bugs you either after school or at school, I want you to come and tell me. I can't stop bullying if I don't know it's happening. Can you do that?"

"Yeah," he mumbled.

"TJ, you can go back to class. Rafi, you and I are going to spend more time together. It is not okay to bully other kids on the way home or at school." I had a look at the computerized behaviour tracking program Adam and I used. Rafi had had some recess detentions and calls home. "You will serve an in-school suspension this morning and tomorrow morning." I would have made it a full day but I had that meeting this afternoon. It was mandatory for all principals with grades 7 and 8. Some new policy. "Let's walk to your locker and get your lunch and I will get you some work to do."

"Can I go out for recess?" I raised my eyebrows. He scoffed. "Thought I'd try." Rafi had a certain charm when he wasn't scowling. I settled him in Adam's office, where I could keep an eye on him but have the privacy to make the phone calls home. I checked Rafi's family and saw that he lived with his aunt and uncle. Neither parent was listed as having custody or access. His uncle answered the phone. His voice was raspy.

"What's that kid done now? I swear he is always getting into trouble. Just like his dad did and I can see Rafi heading in the same direction. His mom just up and left when he was a baby. Well, you do whatever you gotta do. I'll punish him when he gets home. In-school suspension, you say? Does that mean you are sending him home or keeping him?" It was clear that Rafi's uncle had had many calls home in previous years and was frustrated. I felt for him. Certainly Rafi hadn't had an easy life so far and the uncle probably hadn't signed up for this.

"It means that I am keeping him here in the office this morning and then tomorrow morning as well. He can do his schoolwork in the office but he can't be with his class."

"Oh, yeah, that's fine."

"These seem to be new behaviours for Rafi. I don't see any instances before grade six."

"He turned into a teenager and then who knows what happened. Bad egg, that kid. Like my brother."

"Thanks for your support, Mr. Nader." I wondered what kind of support Rafi got at home if his uncle thought he was a "bad egg." My decision for an in-school suspension was confirmed. Sending a student home for a suspension is risky. Will the kid be supervised? Will the parent react in a productive yet firm manner? Will the kid be overly punished? In this case I would have worried.

I didn't believe in suspensions. It was the worst consequence schools had available except for expulsion. Suspensions were easy to dole out. Principals have broad powers to suspend. For some infractions suspensions were mandatory, including bullying, but for others the decision was arbitrary. Principals could suspend for "actions that are injurious to the moral tone of the school." Really it meant that if all else had failed— the chats, the detentions, the calls home, the behaviour modification— suspension was it. As I had learned with Dawson, it didn't mean that behaviours would stop but it made parents, students, and teachers feel like you were doing something. You were in control of the situation. But again, I tried to avoid them. The research on the effect of suspensions is very clear: they don't work. Students who are suspended frequently are more likely to fail courses, drop out of school, and have repeat offenses. So the only alternative when you've reached the end of the line is an in-school suspension. Personally I find they are more effective. It is really, really boring sitting in my office all day doing your work. I will help them with schoolwork but I don't engage. They don't go for recess or lunch. I walk them to the washroom and to get a drink. But it is work on my part.

I had a feeling that an out-of-school suspension for Rafi would not go well at home. I didn't know if his uncle would just throw up his hands or punish him. Also, I worried about what kind of punishment it would be. It did seem that Rafi was not coping well with the onset of puberty. Really, would anyone choose to be thirteen again? Rafi's early childhood had obviously been a struggle. I quickly looked back at his record and it seemed that the aunt and uncle had custody of Rafi when he entered school in kindergarten. The background story for students is often hidden—we can't assume they all come to school with the same suitcase.

I dialed the number for TJ's dad. I explained the situation, including TJ's role in throwing the snowball at Rafi.

"Damn that kid. He can lose his temper quickly. I've told him to just walk away so many times." I agreed TJ could be impulsive and that walking away was a better but challenging solution. However, Rafi had clearly started it and there would be increasingly more severe consequences if the bullying continued. I suspect TJ's dad wanted an out-of-school suspension but he was accepting.

"Whether this is bullying or not, TJ or you have to let me know if it happens again. A bully will keep going if he or she thinks they will get away with it. I've been very clear with Rafi that this is to stop. If he does something again and nothing happens, then he will continue. You aren't bothering me if you call, and I will check in with TJ regularly." Dad agreed and we ended the call.

Checking in on Rafi, I tried to engage him in conversation about the incident, but he didn't bite. He wasn't very communicative. I looked at the math he was doing and he had a fair handle on the work despite the fact that he spent so much time in the hallway. It was obvious that he could do the academic work but the behaviour was getting in the way. The bell rang for lunch and I sat and ate my yogurt while he ate his food. He told me all about skateboarding but any personal questions were met with reflection back to a nonthreatening subject. As the lunch break ended, I sent him back to class with the expectation that he would return to the office tomorrow morning to serve another half-day suspension. I glanced at the clock. I was going to be late for the mandatory meeting if I didn't scurry.

Principals are called out of their schools for a variety of reasons: policy and procedure changes, system-level committees, professional development, health and safety training, Ministry of Education meetings, regional meetings, meetings with the superintendent, community agency meetings, and the list goes on. After so many years in the role I had figured out which ones I could skip. Adam was still keen and I let him go to most of them. Often the meetings just felt like another version of the movie *Groundhog Day*—same people, same rhetoric, nothing new. At first I had been eager to go, excited to talk to colleagues about what was happening in education and in their schools. But rarely did that happen. Principals work in isolation and only get to know each other through these outside meetings. Because we don't ever really work together, it is hard to build trust for the robust discussion I craved. There was a lot of superficial talk and a fair amount of gossip, but often I felt the information could have been delivered in a memo.

Within two years on the job, I had become disillusioned and had seriously considered returning to the classroom. As a teacher you had community, a group of teachers all working together in the same environment. Being a principal was often lonely. It was much more difficult to be part of the teaching staff and, I found, difficult to find community with the other principals. While most people wouldn't think so upon meeting me, I am socially very shy. Within a work environment I am confident and articulate, but I had not found it easy to make the personal relationships among my colleagues that I desired. Today's meeting was about a policy change. I hadn't read the memo very carefully except for the word "mandatory." I quickly touched base with Jim, said my goodbyes to Joan, and drove to the board office.

Coats piled one on top of the other on the rack. Name tags were strewn on the table and mine stood out as one of only three left unclaimed. Pinning it on my suit jacket, I stood at the back of the room looking for an empty seat. All the back seats, of course, were taken. The advantage of arriving late was that I didn't have to make small talk; the disadvantage was that I would have to sit near the front. It reminded me of university lecture halls—only in grade 1 do the kids clamour to sit in front as close to the teacher as possible! I spied an empty chair towards the front and off to the side. I made eye contact with Marg, the principal sitting next to the vacant chair, and she motioned it was free and I squeezed myself through the cramped room to take a seat. Tables were littered with scraps of lunches and coffee cups. Budget cuts meant that we didn't get food at meetings anymore. I missed the banana bread they used to entice us with. Most principals had their computers open and phones out. Meetings were an opportunity to get caught up with email although some might have been taking notes.

Grace was talking. Grace was the head social worker with the board. I liked her. She was a no-nonsense person but full of compassion. Looking up at the PowerPoint she had just begun, I saw the title was "Self-harm and Suicide Ideation in Teens." My throat thickened and my heart raced. There was a bowling-ball-sized weight in my gut. I consciously tried to slow my breathing. I could do this. Grace's voice droned on and I paid scant attention. Cutting was becoming more common among young teens and the board had created a policy. Teachers and principals were to follow prescribed steps upon the discovery of self-harm or suicidal talk. Had none of Frankie's teachers ever noticed her scars? Her change in behaviour? Her mood swings? Tears were pooling in my eyes and I looked down. I had to get out of there.

I pretended someone was phoning, gathered my things, and pushed my way out of the room, avoiding eye contact with anyone. Damn—it was snowing again. Without brushing off my car I huddled in the safety of it. I turned it on for heat but didn't engage the engine. I let the tears stream down my face.

# ELEVEN

# Frankie

SHORTLY AFTER THAT DAY IN LATE JUNE when we had learned Frankie had been cutting, we found her a therapist. The diagnosis was unclear: anxiety or depression or something else. No one suggested that the rest of the family should enter counseling as well and in hindsight that was a mistake. My husband and I coped very differently with Frankie's mental health issues and it was one of the factors that eventually pulled us apart. Add a teen with mental health issues to an already faltering marriage and it only makes things worse. I read everything I could about teen depression, cutting, and suicide among teens. Surely, if I knew what was going on we could fix it. I couldn't.

The next school year, when she started grade 8, we mostly ignored the issue. None of us knew what to do. The family doctor had recommended a counselor and Frankie went three times before quitting. Over the course of the year, we tried two other counselors but Frankie quit after three sessions each time (I had made a rule that she had to try a new counselor at least three times). I had gathered that the first three sessions were get-to-know-you meetings but once the real work started Frankie would quit. The battle to get her to stick with it at that point wasn't worth it and I would phone yet another therapist. The family doctor had prescribed a number of antidepressants, but Frankie didn't like them and I would find them in the garbage. Throughout grade 8, she spent lots of time in her bedroom and wore the same clothes a lot of the time. But many days were fine and she was the daughter I knew and loved. Maybe this was just a stage. No one at school ever called with concerns.

The following year, Frankie began high school with little fanfare. I had not told the school about Frankie's issues. This was private and we would get through it. Ironically, as a principal I expected parents to inform me of any major issues that might be affecting their child's school life, but as a parent I was ashamed. I didn't tell anyone.

The next November was the first time I took Frankie to the hospital. Frankie had announced she wasn't returning to see the counselor and we were in her bedroom, she screaming and me scrambling to stay calm. I wanted to talk logically but she wanted to rant.

"I hate you. I hate my life. I hate my counselor. I'm not taking these stupid pills anymore. I wish I was dead." She ran into the bathroom and flushed them down the toilet. My heart was breaking. How could I make my baby happy? I tried to gather her into my arms but she pushed away.

"Are you still cutting?" I asked. It was hard to know since she wore long sleeves all the time, and short of grabbing her arm and pushing up the sleeves there was no way to tell. Sobbing, she pushed her sleeves up and her arms were covered in angry red slashes.

I would stay calm. I had read the books. Cutting wasn't necessarily a precursor to suicide. The experts said that the physical pain was preferable to the cutter than emotional pain. But the books also said that teens who were cutting were at a higher risk for suicide and the question to ask was, "Do you have a plan to kill yourself?" I gathered my courage and asked the question. In response she got down on her knees, reached under her bed, and pulled out a shoebox.

"Here!" She threw the box on the bed. Gingerly I opened it. There was a collection of razors and other sharp objects as well as a bottle of pills. The pills must have been mostly Tylenol as we didn't have anything else in the house, but I wasn't sure. I didn't ask. I sat there for a few moments, letting this new information permeate my thoughts. This was serious. It wasn't getting better. Frankie was sobbing uncontrollably, taking huge hiccupping gulps of air, clutching at her arms, fingernails digging in.

"I think we should go to the hospital," I said as calmly as I could. Frankie nodded. I wrapped her coat around her shoulders and walked her downstairs. I told my husband, who was already in bed, what we were doing. I didn't ask his opinion. We didn't discuss it.

We arrived at the emergency room, Frankie still sobbing, me stoic. We told our story to the triage nurse and were escorted to a private waiting room. The room was three by five feet with two chairs and a metal hospital table. The door was left open. We sat in silence. No one came by. We could watch the comings and goings of the ER from our perch, an inside view of paramedics, stretchers, nurses, and doctors scurrying about in scrubs, but no one came to our room. An hour went by and Frankie had calmed down. We sat and, funny as it sounds, began to chat normally about everyday stuff: school, TV shows, Christmas. Another hour went by and still no one. It was midnight now and a school night. Frankie was calm and seemed herself. I clutched the shoebox. Frankie wanted to go home. I wanted to go home. I didn't want to be one of those mothers who had to bring their child to the emergency room. I told the charge nurse and no one tried to dissuade us. We left.

I had already learned that accessing mental health services was not easy. When I had tried to find Frankie yet another new counselor, I had to call random names from the directory. Therapists, I learned, rarely have a secretary who answers the phone and you have to leave a message. You have to tell your problems to a stranger's message service. Most phone back but invariably end up leaving a message, too. Some don't return the call. Apparently hauling your daughter to the hospital with a box of razors she kept hidden under her bed was not an emergency.

For the next year life was up and down. Frankie stopped taking any medication and refused to see a counselor. I tried not to pester her about her feelings or the cutting, as it always ended in a fight. There were good times and grumpy times. She failed grade 9 math but no one at the school phoned to tell me.

I am the eldest of three siblings. My parents were academics. They loved me and I remember a relatively peaceful childhood. I was not particularly close with my brothers growing up, but we didn't fight. My family was not overly demonstrative or affectionate. We didn't discuss feelings. We were logical people—reason reigned. Thrown into the midst of this turmoil, I wanted to reason it out. I did not want to feel. I certainly didn't want the world to know that I was not a good mother. I felt shame. As a principal, I was someone people looked up to. I was an expert on children. I counseled parents with difficult children. I went to meetings about other people's children.

In the spring of grade 10, Frankie's school called me at work. She had disclosed to the guidance counselor that she was cutting and feeling suicidal. I thought back to that morning and it hadn't been any worse than usual. The guidance counselor was taking her to the hospital. I called her father and said I'd meet him there. With a lump in my throat, I mumbled some excuse to Joan about why I had to leave, a sudden migraine maybe, and drove in a haze to the hospital.

Each step to the psych ward is a step in realizing that this is really happening. Scrambling in the bottom of my purse for change for the parking meter. Asking at the front desk which floor to go to. Waiting for the elevator that took forever. Not making eye contact in the elevator as I got off at the ninth floor: Child and Adolescent Psychiatric Ward. The doors to the ward are locked. You have to announce yourself. I am buzzed in and met by a nurse in scrubs. She takes me to a hospital room where Frankie is huddled on a thin hospital bed, knees up, wearing sweats and a hoodie pulled up. Her running shoes have no laces. It takes me a moment but then I realize that it is a suicide prevention measure. I want to take her in my arms but one look at her and I know it is not a good idea.

I sat down on the bed next to her and put my hand on her knee. She flinched but didn't move it away. I can't remember what we said. Small talk and murmurings and crying. After an hour (your emergency is not theirs, I discovered quickly enough) a doctor came by. He said that they were keeping Frankie on a Form 1 (as if I knew what that was). He explained that meant they could keep her for observation for seventy-two hours. They would assess her mental state and look at medication. They would inform the school and there was a teacher on the unit who could help her stay caught up. She would partake in group therapy on the floor. We could visit. He would see us later.

And that was it. My daughter had been admitted to the psych ward. This wasn't our family. This wasn't our life. I felt dead inside but to the outside world I remained calm and in control, determined to keep our family intact.

In the end they kept her for forty-eight hours. I expected that at the end of the ordeal there would be a plan. There was not. Upon discharge the psychiatrist handed us a new prescription and a list of psychiatrists who worked with teens. No one asked how the rest of the family was coping. No one offered to help find a psychiatrist. No one talked about the fact that Frankie would continue to cut. No one had any ideas on how to get her to take the medication. We just went home. I filled the prescription, but she refused to take it. I made ten phone calls to psychiatrists and left messages. A few phoned back and Frankie started seeing someone—for three visits before she quit.

Towards the end of that school year, Frankie was on counselor number 6, and I got a phone call in the middle of a meeting. It was the counselor. She had taken Frankie back to the hospital due to suicide ideation. Again, that morning had been no worse than usual. We had actually been having more good days than bad.

The story repeated itself. They kept her for seventy-two hours this time. A new psychiatrist saw her and changed the medication that she wasn't taking anyway. I got the same list of psychiatrists to phone. I was left to fumble about in the dark without much support.

Getting support for children's mental health isn't straightforward or easy. And I was an educated, articulate parent with private health insurance benefits. Thinking back on the number of times I had, as principal, suggested to parents that they seek mental health support for their children, I wondered how some of them had fared—they were often poor, intimidated by authority, or new Canadians.

Joey had been born prematurely and stayed in the hospital for the first eight weeks of his life. Afterwards people would ask me how I coped during that time. I remember that you just do. You don't think about it, you just do it. It was the same with Frankie. Her mental illness became the norm in our family dynamic. My husband and I didn't share the struggle with friends or even our own parents. We barely talked about it between ourselves as the marriage continued to disintegrate. Everyone was cautious around Frankie—what would her mood be today? Some days she was like a regular teenager: she fell in love, went to the movies, and had a part-time job. Other days were hell: she would tantrum, scream at us, or sulk for hours in her bedroom. I knew the cutting continued but she was so defensive when I brought it up that I rarely spoke of it. Lily in particular took it upon herself to take care of Frankie. I worried that Lily was afraid to express her own growing pains for fear of adding to the family dynamic. Lily was afraid to be a bad kid.

Back in that parking lot, as I was pulling myself together after the mandatory meeting, the car was getting uncomfortably warm. I got out and brushed off the snow and decided to drive home. I took the long way so I wouldn't drive past the hospital. It would be years before I could drive past without tears. I would read the policy on self-harm and suicide ideation another day.

## TWELVE

# Good Teachers Matter

THE ROOM IS CALM. STUDENTS ARE WORKING at their learning centres. Kate is concentrating on teaching reading to a small group. I am sitting at the back of the room, notepad in hand, doing her TPA. A small, lanky boy starts to talk loudly at the listening centre. Kate pauses her lesson and softly says the boy's name, motioning to him to come to her. He scuffles over and they have a quiet conversation.

"Mikey, you are getting loud. Go get a drink and then come back ready to listen quietly," Kate says firmly yet with compassion. I smile and put a star next to the interaction on my paper. As the reading time comes to a close, Kate grabs a small rain stick from beside her chair and shakes it. With the sound all her students stop and wave their fingers in the air, turning to face her. "Thank you for listening," she says. "It is time to tidy up and get ready for recess." Kate dismisses her small group, tidies her materials, and moves to the classroom door. On the way she picks up a book of poetry. As a small group begins to assemble by the door to line up, she begins to read poems. This entices the rest of the students to join the line quickly so they can hear the poems. Maggie did that, too. Had Kate reached out? I make another star on my paper.

"So, how do you think the lesson went?" I ask Kate. I am now seated across from her at a little table, both of us awkwardly sitting in student-sized chairs. With the students out for recess we are debriefing this formal observation.

"Good?" she says tentatively.

"I agree," I say with a smile. "What do you think went well?"

"Well, I think I managed to get the kids at the reading table to understand the role of the silent *e*." I nod. "And I felt like the rest of the kids were on task at their learning centres. The girls with the big book on the carpet were a bit chatty but still on task. I don't know what to do with Mikey. His attention span is so short."

"I think you handled it very well. You took control of the situation before it got out of hand and gave him a bit of a movement break." Kate beams. "You've obviously made some changes with classroom management. It was very calm and productive today. I liked how you got the kids to line up."

"Yeah, Maggie gave me some suggestions about transitioning activities, and I did read the book you gave me, finally." We continue to talk about the lesson. I make a few pedagogical suggestions but am pleased with what I saw.

"Based on my observations from September, and the last three formal observations this month, your first TPA will be satisfactory," I state, smiling. Kate is visibly relieved. While I had been worried at the beginning of the year, she has made a strong effort to find strategies that work for her. Kate is one of those teachers who will be just fine. She is reflective and changes her practices when they aren't working. And she has obviously sought out support from a colleague, Maggie—always a good sign.

What makes a good teacher? I'd spent a lifetime trying to figure that out. Certainly classroom management, as Kate had discovered, was key.

No learning could really take place without a calm learning environment. But that wasn't all. Bryce had a calm classroom, but I didn't think there was a lot of rigorous learning going on. Harriet had a calm classroom, but it was because the kids were half-asleep. Conversely, Debra's science classroom was often noisy, but that's because the kids were engaged and talking.

Structure and routines are the first step, but they don't complete the picture. Teacher-student relationships are key in creating a strong learning environment, and recent research suggests that positive relationships are the most consistent predictor of student achievement. While most students are captivated by teachers who are friendly and chatty—like Bryce—the relationships that are the most effective are those based in the learning: teachers who take the time to know their students as learners, who know their strengths and weaknesses, and who show a belief in their students' abilities to succeed.

When I was twenty-four, I taught grade 10 math in summer school for the first time. Anthony was seventeen and taking it for the third time. I had a ponytail; Anthony had a beard. He was a good half foot taller than me. Truth be told, I found him a bit scary. He was a tough kid. I think if we had met on the sidewalk at night, I would have clutched my bag closer and crossed the street.

Summer school was held in an old, three-story redbrick building that had been built in the early twentieth century. My classroom was on the third floor, with big windows, wooden floors, rickety desks, and no air-conditioning. On a good day there was a bit of a breeze. We packed thirty-five students into the classroom—every desk was full and some students perched on the windowsills. Classes were two and a half hours long, every morning for three weeks. It was a grueling pace with a group of students who did not see themselves as successful mathematicians. Grade 10 math was compulsory and this was a chance to get the credit without repeating the course next year. Most said they failed during the school year because the teacher didn't like them. I usually replied, somewhat sarcastically, that their plan hadn't worked so well since their teacher was sitting on the beach right now and they were here with me in a stuffy un-air-conditioned classroom.

Anthony showed up late almost every day. He rarely completed his homework and slouched in a seat in the back. Even when he showed up late, he always got a seat; someone would move. I was determined to reach him, however. I greeted him pleasantly when he showed up with the pink late slip. I helped him during class time. I praised him when he got the answers right and didn't nag him when the homework was incomplete. Despite coming late, he showed up every day. He passed every test—barely. On the last day of the course the students could drop in and get their marks. I was packing up my things as the day was over and who should show up but Anthony. He shuffled in, head down, and asked his mark. Fifty-three. He mumbled "okay" and headed out the door. Then he stopped, turned, and said, "Thanks, miss." And he was gone. I hadn't given up on him and he knew it. Forming the relationship with Anthony had been worth it.

Kate was beginning to form a relationship with Mikey. Sarah was forming that relationship with Sawyer. Sondra was forming a relationship with Myles. All those children were a challenge and it would be easy to give up on them. So often in education, blame is laid on the student or the parent and yet the teacher has the power to change the conditions. A germ of an idea was forming as I wandered the halls during lunch. How could we as a staff believe in the kids who needed us the most? And, in this school, this idea would go hand in hand with the teachers believing in the families as well. I needed to continue to work on that family connection that had been so damaged in the past years. Teaching is hard. Making a real difference is harder. The PA signal went and I was being paged to the office. I would think about this later.

The school-based team was meeting again that afternoon. This meeting of special education teachers and consultants along with some teachers was our monthly opportunity to support students who were a mystery to us—why weren't they succeeding? An update on Olivia revealed that little progress had been made. Stephanie was meeting with her in the mornings to work on personal hygiene but having limited success. Olivia was still tantruming and doing little in class. We decided to have a meeting with her parents and the special education consultant from the board office. Perhaps we needed to look at a treatment setting for Olivia.

Sarah arrived to talk about Sawyer. "He doesn't engage with the other students but seems to understand the concepts being taught. He likes to read but won't write a word."

"Is there a psychological assessment in his file?" Mary, the special education consultant, asked. Maria riffled through his student record and shook her head. I related what I had learned about Sawyer from our backgammon playing and conversations with his dad. Stephanie reported that he attended her recess group but struggled to figure out how to play with the other boys. She had noticed he did better with smaller groups than if the group decided to play soccer.

"He certainly seems to be struggling with some academics and with social relationships," I summarize. "Is he a candidate for a psychological assessment?" Our school was granted two psychological assessments from the board per year. We had six hundred students. If a parent paid for one privately it would cost about $2,500. Some of our families could afford that and had benefits that would cover it. But many did not. Every year we chose from among ten candidates. A psychological assessment would identify things such as learning disabilities, intellectual challenges, autism, and behavioural problems. Knowing what the issues were sometimes helped to point us towards effective strategies but not always. Olivia had had two psychological assessments and we didn't have a clue what to do with her. The discussion went back and forth and we finally agreed that Sawyer was a big enough mystery to warrant an assessment. I said I would call the dad and suggest it. Not all parents agreed to having an assessment done, funnily enough.

Recognizing and admitting that your child was having difficulties was hard. I knew that firsthand. No mother ever holds her newborn baby and looks down and coos, "I hope you grow up to have a learning disability." No, we all believe our children will grow up to be perfect. And when that doesn't happen it is devastating.

May was a precocious grade 2 girl I'd met a few years back when her teacher had called me one September morning. "Can you pop in? One of my students just put up her hand and asked in front of the whole class if I could help wipe her bum because she had to go poo!" Stifling a laugh, I said I'd be right there. I walked into Nancy's classroom and she indicated May, wearing a purple flowered dress with puffy sleeves and a wide skirt. The waist was adorned with a wide sash tied in a bow. It was in contrast to the other girls, who were in leggings and T-shirts. Her dark hair was in curled pigtails tied with pink ribbons. As we walked down to my office on the pretense of a get-to-know-the-new-students visit, May spoke animatedly and constantly in a rather clipped tone. Her vocabulary was advanced for a seven-year-old and she was obviously comfortable with adults.

"I love your dress," I said when I could get a word in. "Your teacher says you want some help going to the bathroom."

May giggled. "No. I know how to go to the bathroom. I do need you to wipe, though, please." She was not embarrassed.

"You are a big girl; don't you do that yourself?" I asked.

"Nope. My mummy does that part. I don't like doing that." May wasn't concerned and chatted happily down the hall. Entering my room, she did a tour talking about the pictures on the wall and the toys on the table. She was delightful but definitely not your typical seven-year-old. I called her mom to explain the situation; she was embarrassed and arrived shortly to help with the toileting. Although we had EAs who could have helped, that was usually with kindergarten students. We had a quick chat and she promised to work on the toileting at home. May's family had lived overseas and she had attended an international school prior to arriving in grade 2. She was their only child. Mom seemed to be in her early forties, well dressed, and professional. In fact, she told me, she was on her way to work.

Something niggled at me about May and when I spoke to Nancy, she also had concerns. May was obviously bright, writing and reading much above grade level. She was articulate and fastidious. But already Nancy had noticed she had difficulties engaging with the other students and could become agitated easily when things didn't go her way. We called in the school psychiatrist to have a quick peek and she was also concerned. Increasingly, May would become easily frustrated in social situations or when things did not go as planned. She had difficulties with games when she didn't win or when other students didn't follow the rules. May was most definitely a black-and-white thinker—there were no shades of gray. She was charming with adults, most of the time, but struggled to make friends. We all suspected May fell on the autism spectrum and the psychologist was recommending a full assessment. However, when I broached the assessment idea with May's parents, careful not to mention the word "autism," but rather stating that we wanted to understand her better, they initially refused. As older parents, all their friends' children were much older than their daughter—May was the only seven-year-old they knew. To them she was delightful and they had never seen her interacting with her peers.

I gently probed about her early toddler years. Had there been lots of tantrums? Did May like things to be a certain way? Her parents were unsure. It took most of the year, with May experiencing increasing social difficulties, before the parents agreed to the assessment. When the diagnosis came back that May did indeed fall on the spectrum, it was another few months supporting the parents as they came to terms with it. Over the next few years May's parents became strong advocates for their daughter in the school system; they understood her needs well. The early school years were bumpy but with support May was able to flourish at school.

However, it was a lesson for me to tread cautiously with parents when suggesting that the love of their life may have significant issues. Often the school is the first to notice. I would proceed cautiously with Sawyer's parents as well. Although we were giving one of our coveted psychological assessments to their child, the parents might not see it the same way.

The last thing for me today was another TPA visit, this time to Bryce's classroom. I had been in to observe informally a number of times already. His students were always quiet and working. He had a very relaxed manner with the kids and I knew they all loved Mr. B. Frequently he would play basketball with the students at recess, or talk music videos. He formed relationships with his students. However, the schoolwork was rote and mostly worksheets. He didn't push his students to achieve at high levels. He continued to adhere to the binders he'd been given and only paid lip service to collaborating with the other teachers in the junior division. While his teaching partner, Mike, had fully embraced our school initiative to engage students in critical thinking, I wasn't sure that Bryce really understood what that meant. He saw himself as the person who delivered the information to the students, while Mike was beginning to see himself as the facilitator of student thinking.

Bryce was giving a writing lesson as I entered his room. I sat quietly at the back and began to document the visit. Formal TPA visits were always documented; informal drop-ins were not. I wrote down everything that happened—what he said and how the students responded. He had told me the lesson would be about descriptive writing.

"Today, class, we are going to write descriptive paragraphs. You need to have lots of adjectives in your paragraph. Who can tell me what an adjective is?" No one raised their hand. "Well, an adjective is like a describing word. What words would you use to describe me?"

"Tall."

"Fun."

"Athletic."

"Right on!" Bryce responded enthusiastically. "Those are adjectives. Now, everyone take out a piece of paper and write a descriptive paragraph about a person or a pet you know. Try to put in as many adjectives as you can." Most of the students obediently found some paper and started to write. Some, I noticed, took a long time to get going, but they weren't disruptive. Bryce wandered around the classroom, peering over students' shoulders. I heard a phone ping and he wandered past his desk to glance at it. The phone again—I made a note. When the period was over, the students handed in their paragraphs. Three students handed in nothing. He didn't notice. While Bryce was dismissing the students for home time, I gathered my thoughts.

It was not a brilliant lesson. Bryce was not a hardworking, creative teacher. He managed the class and assigned tasks. Unlike Kate, he wasn't reflective and he didn't hear the suggestions I gave, although at least today he wasn't chewing gum! If I gave him an unsatisfactory, he would be devastated, but I wasn't sure it would entice him to change. I could give him a satisfactory but with a number of suggestions for improvement embedded. As a new contract teacher, he would be appraised again in the spring, and if things hadn't improved, I could go down the road of unsatisfactory then if I wanted.

"So, how did you think that lesson went?" I asked.

"Pretty good, Kristin. Yeah, the kids got it. They all finished the paragraph. I will mark them tonight."

"I noticed that a few students didn't hand anything in."

Bryce looked puzzled. "Oh? Well, maybe they weren't finished. You know some of the IEP kids have trouble getting work done." I tried hard to say "kids with IEPs" to indicate students who had special education needs, but I guessed Bryce hadn't picked up on that yet. I didn't want teachers to see the IEP as defining the student.

"Do you modify the work for them per the IEP? Was this task appropriate for them?"

"Ummm. You know, that's a great point, Kristin. I will check with

Maria about that. Maybe she can take them." That was not the answer I'd hoped for.

"I'd like you to know what is on their IEP and how to modify lessons for them. That is the point of the IEP—to support the students in the classroom with the appropriate level of work."

"Oh, yeah, of course, of course, Kristin. Definitely. You're right. I will look them over tonight."

I made a few more suggestions about how the lesson might have been more robust and Bryce nodded vigorously while sitting back in his chair. He was relaxed. He took no notes. Then I had to address the final concern.

"I noticed your cell phone was pinging during class. We have a school policy that students can't have their cell phones out, so I think that should pertain to teachers, too. Good modeling and all."

"Oh, my God, yes, Kristin. I totally forgot to put it on silent." He wasn't getting the point.

"I think during class it needs to be in your bag or desk drawer, not on your desk." Bryce said nothing. I am quite sure he thought me an old fuddy-duddy, out of touch with reality. I wasn't sure either how to navigate cell phones and teaching and classrooms, but the staff was quite clear they didn't want student cell phones in the classrooms and if we were going to have that rule then it couldn't be different for staff.

"I am going to write this first TPA, Bryce. It will be satisfactory," I began. He looked smug. "However, I do have a number of concerns that we have talked about that I will also list. You will need to work on those things over the course of the year for the second TPA to also be satisfactory."

"Oh, for sure, Kristin. I definitely will. Thanks so much for doing this." With that he stood up, effectively ending the conversation. I walked back to the main office, walked into Adam's office, shut the door, and began to rant. Bryce irked me. He didn't hear. He was everything in a teacher that made the system mediocre. Adam laughed.

"You aren't going to win them all, you know." He was right, but I wanted to win them all. I wanted every teacher in the building to be great. I just didn't quite know how to do that.

"Joey called." Adam smiled. "Is it a pizza night?"

Maybe.

# THIRTEEN

# Mom to the Whole School

I PULLED INTO THE SCHOOL PARKING LOT, tires sinking into puddles as I searched for a spot. A cloudy gray sky heralded a risk of another indoor recess. I was already in a grumpy mood as I arrived from a meeting at the board office.

In principal groups we had discussed our school improvement plans. I had initially been excited to share my ideas to move teachers away from traditional forms of teaching and into twenty-first-century skills (What Doesn't Siri Know?), but the conversation had quickly lapsed into complaints about the shortage of supply teachers and the lack of resources for special education teachers. I felt those constraints as well but still believed we could make a difference in our schools. Certainly there had to be more to leading a school than management concerns—otherwise nothing would ever change.

Putting my frustrations aside, I hurried into the building since I had received a text that Myles was on the warpath. Our plan to meet in the mornings had reduced the number of behaviour incidents, but this had been the first morning I hadn't been in my office when he came to visit. I hadn't thought through that contingency.

Joan offered a sympathetic look as I entered my office. The four visitor chairs around my table were knocked over. The children's storybooks I kept on a shelf were scattered helter-skelter on the floor. The box of Legos was overturned. Myles was huddled in his rocket ship. Kim sat slumped in my office chair. She came to the door to chat.

"Sorry. We got here and Joan said you were at a meeting. I tried to explain to Myles that we'd come back later to see you but he just lost it. It all happened so fast. Stephanie came down as well but we just decided to let him at it. Adam tried to calm him, too, but no luck." She sounded defeated.

"You did the right thing. It's just stuff. Don't worry about it. I guess I didn't think through what would happen if I wasn't here in the mornings. We know better than to expect him to cope with changes like that." Kim offered to help tidy up but I sent her to the staff room for a coffee and a break. Taking off my coat, I busied myself in my office, not saying anything at first. Myles looked up but immediately lowered his gaze and sank deeper into the box. His mouth was set in a grimace but his eyes were full of fear, and they followed me as I righted the chairs around the table and sat down at one.

"I guess you were pretty disappointed when you came for your visit this morning and I wasn't here." I waited. His shoes were quietly kicking the inside of the box. "I am so sorry about that. I had an important meeting this morning so I was late getting to school. I forgot to tell Ms. Zeigler." We sat in silence for a few moments. Giving Myles a quick smile, I got up and started to pick up the books and put them back on the shelf. There are some adults who would say that the mess was his to clean up. I didn't think he needed a punishment at this point. Kids don't get out of control on purpose; his feelings overwhelmed him. I sat down on the floor and started on the Lego pieces. "Do you want to help?"

Slowly Myles clambered out of the spaceship and sat on the floor next to me and we returned the pieces to the bin in silence.

Throughout the early 2000s, suspensions for students grew in response to zero tolerance. Although more recently school boards across North America have been reevaluating suspensions, especially for young children, with some districts banning suspensions altogether for them, thousands of kindergartners are suspended each year, usually for verbal or physical outbursts. A suspension as a consequence suggests that the student could have chosen to act differently. I do not think that Myles could have chosen differently in this situation. His feelings had been hurt, his expectations dashed. We already knew that he didn't manage his emotions well. More than anything Myles needed reassurance that I was still here—and I needed a plan to deal with the mornings I wouldn't be in my office.

With the office tidied, we read *Mortimer*, and I walked him back to class hand in hand. At his classroom door he looked up at me and mumbled, "Bye. Sorry." My throat caught.

"Have a great day, Myles." I knew I had another meeting tomorrow, first thing in the morning. There was a meeting with Family and Children's Services about a new foster child coming into the school after Christmas. We did not need a repeat of today, but I wasn't sure how to handle this. I couldn't be at school every morning. Although I could transfer Myles to someone else on staff, I didn't want to. For one thing, I liked the relationships I formed with kids. I wanted to be involved. I remembered principals I had worked for as a teacher who seemed so removed from the students and teaching. I didn't want to be that kind of principal. Plus, I got into this business to work with kids. Just because I had this role, I wasn't giving up the fun part of the job. And Myles needed me to be there—always the same but in different clothes.

The halls were decorated with holiday wreaths and snowmen and red and green paper chains. I looked for evidence of other cultural celebrations, to no avail. In a school of thirty different languages and many new

Canadians we needed to be sensitive to the fact that not all our families would celebrate Christmas. How would we meld the Judeo-Christian traditions that were entrenched in the school system with a changing school community? It was on the agenda for the staff meeting this afternoon. There were strong feelings among some staff that we should put up the Christmas tree and sing carols in the mornings. Despite our school population being racially diverse, the teaching staff was not. All the teachers were white. Most of them were female. Only the fact that we had grades 7 and 8 meant that the staff had a greater male representation. Some smaller primary schools often had no male teachers at all.

Arriving back at my office, I found Rafi Nader sprawled at my table, eating his lunch, running shoes untied, baseball cap on. I nodded at the hat. He smirked but removed it.

"Do you have a detention?" I asked. I couldn't remember giving him one. In fact, I hadn't seen him since the snowball in-school suspension. Maybe Adam had dealt with it and needed my office space.

"Nah." I raised my eyebrows and tilted my head. "Can I eat my lunch here?" he asked. I was puzzled. Thirteen-year-old boys like Rafi didn't tend to choose to eat their lunch with the principal.

"Sure. How come?"

"Ya know." I didn't but left it at that. I settled down across from him with my yogurt and fruit. He hadn't been kicked out of class. He hadn't been in trouble. There wasn't a problem with anyone. We, or rather he, talked skateboarding.

"What will your family do for the holidays?" I ventured. I didn't have a handle on Rafi, couldn't figure out what made him tick.

"Nothin' probably."

"You live with your uncle, right?" He nodded affirmatively. "Do you ever see your mom or dad?"

"Not my mom. Not since I was a baby. My dad comes 'round sometimes," he said.

"Do you get along with your dad?"

"Yeah, I guess. Sorta. He fights with my uncle a lot."

"Have you always lived with your aunt and uncle?" I asked.

"Yeah. I guess." He didn't sound very enthusiastic about family life, but I didn't know if that was just normal teenage hesitancy or something else. I let it be. The bell rang and he shuffled off without a word.

In the coming weeks, this would become a regular pattern. I'd look up from my computer and he would just be sitting at the table in my office. Rafi began having lunch in my office most days. He wasn't in trouble and didn't want to talk about much except skateboarding. I couldn't engage him in conversations about friends, his family, or schoolwork. Then, just before the holiday break, I asked him why he always came for lunch. I wondered if we had built up enough of a relationship for him to open up. He mumbled that the kids weren't nice to him in class. *He was lonely.* But it probably looked to the other kids like he was always in trouble, eating lunch in my office. It gave him an out from the social scene while maintaining his tough-guy exterior.

Standing at my office door as the bell rang for class to begin, Joan caught my eye and motioned towards the hallway. Mr. Byun was lurking, hat in hand. "He's been pacing out there for half an hour but won't come in."

"Mr. Byun, how nice to see you," I began. "Did you want to come in and chat with me?"

"Ah, no, I'm okay." I waited. "Well, maybe for a minute if you have some time." We settled in at the table. Mr. Byun perched on the edge of his seat, nervously playing with his wool cap.

"How is bedtime going?" I asked. I had been checking in with Carlton and Aimee when I saw them in the halls and they assured me they were getting to bed on time.

"Good. Good. They listen now." He paused. "You know, Mrs. Phillips, they only want me to pack junk food in their lunches. At dinner I try to make good food but they say it is no good and always want me to buy McDonald's, or pizza." I smiled, thinking of Joey.

"My son, Joey, wishes we could have pizza every night, too," I shared. "But we parents have to be firm and have treats only for special times."

"They don't listen to me. They listen to you. Can you tell them they have to eat what I say?" Mr. Byun pleaded. What had I done? Were Mr. Byun and I going to coparent Carlton and Aimee all year? On the other hand, it took courage to come and ask for my help. I called their classrooms and asked for them to come to the office. They looked sheepish as they spied their dad sitting there.

"We are going to bed on time," Carlton stated emphatically as he sat down.

"Yeah. We do," reiterated Aimee defensively.

"Great," I replied. "Your dad says so, too." The two children visibly relaxed. "But your dad is worried you aren't eating healthy meals." Guilt replaced relief. I guided Mr. Byun and his children through a discussion on how many treats would be reasonable in a given week, which healthy foods they liked for lunches, and why their brains needed good nutrition. After the kids returned to class, I mentioned that parenting support groups were available in the community, since many, many parents had these kinds of problems with their kids.

"No, I just have this one little problem and you helped me with it. Thank you."

"You are most welcome, Mr. Byun. I'm glad you came." I knew that asking for help was hard. I certainly didn't want to air my troubles with Frankie in a room full of strangers. Coparenting with Mr. Byun might be outside the formal duties of my role, but I wanted him to feel part of the school community. I had helped Myles through a tantrum, had lunch with a lonely teenage boy, and provided parenting support to Mr. Byun. Some days it felt more like I was "mom" to the whole school rather than the principal.

Peeking at the time, I saw that I only had an hour before the staff meeting and I needed to prepare. I told Adam and Joan I was closing my door and to interrupt only if there was a catastrophe.

# FOURTEEN

# School Culture

MOST JURISDICTIONS ACROSS NORTH AMERICA HAVE NEGOTIATED limits on staff meetings. In our district the union had successfully bargained for one seventy-five-minute meeting per month. It was the only meeting outside the school day that I could insist teachers attend. Although most teachers were happy to meet voluntarily at other times during the month, this one was mandatory and I controlled the agenda. I was thankful that in our district we had maintained the right to set the agenda, since many other boards had relinquished that right through contract negotiations and principals were not allowed to use staff meeting times for professional development (PD). Nevertheless, the unions frequently admonished teachers that professional development was at their own discretion, that as professionals they could decide what type of professional development they required.

Teachers were often caught in the middle of the push and pull between their contractual obligations and the union rhetoric. I remembered a few years earlier I had a committed grade 6 teacher who did not show up to a staff meeting. The union was in full swing of contract negotiations. When I questioned him the next day, he replied that the union said he didn't have to go to PD that he thought was not useful to him.

I tried to be understanding. I could see why he thought it wouldn't be useful—we were talking about math, which he wasn't teaching that year, but he could be the following year. And while the union says teachers can choose the PD they attend, that doesn't apply to staff meetings; they have to attend those. I was ready for a confrontation, but the teacher acquiesced.

"I just wish the board and the union could get their messages straight," he said. I could see his confusion. With such a powerful union, teachers often forgot that they worked for the board, not the union.

"They aren't really friends," I joked, but I don't know that he understood that the union and the board were often on opposite sides.

As a principal I tried to use every minute possible of my staff meetings to improve the teaching in the building. When I first began as principal, I would have the administrative items first and then we would move on to PD. Except we never moved on to PD, as the administrative items and the ensuing discussion could easily take over the seventy-five minutes. A few years back, I changed to having the PD first, with the administrative items at the end of the meeting. I found that we got through the administrative items much quicker the closer it got to home time! In our board all elementary schools had their staff meetings on the same night and I had already received a few texts from my old school's staff: "We miss your meetings! This is sooooo boring. We aren't learning anything!" Although my nonadministrative staff meetings were usually met with resistance when I first started at a school, because they were different, soon teachers found that a seventy-five-minute meeting of learning was far more engaging than a thirty-item agenda of information points.

Debra had just finished a quick presentation about how she was creating an inquiry-based model in her science classes by following a makerspace workshop, creative spaces in which students could demonstrate scientific concepts by building with a wide variety of materials. After our first meeting about how to get the kids more engaged in learning, I had passed on an article about makerspaces to Debra. Her presentation promised a change from earlier in the year, when all the students built the same gadget from a set of instructions. In education we tended to stifle creativity by having all kids do the same thing. I had been thrilled when Debra came to me bubbling over with new ideas. Although it was still in the infancy stage, I wanted her to share her enthusiasm with the staff.

The grade groups were now discussing what they had tried in their classrooms since the last month. Adam had distributed the commitments they had made the month previous. I sat down with the intermediate team. Tara was energetically talking about her book clubs.

"I can't believe how excited the kids are to read and talk about the books they are reading. They have all read a whole novel in a month! I shudder to think that last year we only read one novel all year." I noticed Leanne paying attention. I knew that she hadn't quite bought in yet, but having the other teachers excited about what they were doing was making her rethink her ten-week unit on *The Outsiders*.

"I've got my kids all reading during class and talking about their books, too," ventured Mac. "But I am having trouble getting around to all the groups to hear what they are doing." Tara and Jim jumped in and offered ideas. I suggested that having some kids write and some kids talk might help. Leanne asked some practical questions about how she could get started after the holidays. Harriet said nothing.

The discussion was lively for 4:30 p.m. after a day of teaching. I was pleased that the conversation flowed naturally even when I added my two cents. I felt like one of the gang—not the principal. I was just another teacher at the table. Looking around the room, I could see that other groups were just as engaged. I noticed Adam, elbows on the table, leaning in with the primary teachers. This was so much better than the dull and monotonous staff meetings I remembered as a teacher. But we had to address the Christmas issues, and we were running out of time. I stood up and had them bring their discussions to a close, asking each staff member to record what new thing they were going to try before the staff meeting in February, recognizing that with a two-week break, and report cards due at the end of January, they wouldn't have time before then to dig their teeth into a new idea.

Navigating contentious issues around school culture is tricky. All schools have ways they have done things forever: Halloween parades or Orange and Black Day, Christmas concerts or lunches, Valentine's Day traditions, Easter egg hunts, Mother's Day cards and presents. Twenty years ago, no one thought twice about such celebrations. As a teacher it was just part of the rhythm of my year. Now, though, we need to be more culturally responsive to our communities. There are traditions that belong to the community and the school that are sacred. In some neighbourhoods, parents went to the same school their children now go to, and in those instances the parents are often the ones reluctant to examine current practices. A colleague of mine spent an entire year working with staff and parents to replace the culturally biased school logo of a warrior. The debate made the local papers! My school had been around for twenty years, but the community composition had changed over the last five years. Our school registration practices do not collect religious or racial information, but I knew that over 40 percent of the school students had been born in a country other than Canada and that thirty different languages were listed as our students' first language at home. However, my teaching staff was unchanged. Most of the teachers had been working at the school for at least ten years.

"I want to show you some statistics about our student population," I began. I presented the slide with the demographic information. I had had some requests to decorate the main foyer with a Christmas tree and had noticed some holiday decorations already in the hallways. "I don't know what the right answer is here, but I think it behooves us to think about how we respond to the holidays, school traditions, and to the many students and families in our school community who may not celebrate Christmas." I paused. The atmosphere had gone from excited buzz to tension in under thirty seconds. "On the paper at your table I am going to give you two minutes to list all the school traditions we typically do at this time of year. Please think of both classroom and school-wide activities."

We created a staff list: holiday worksheets, holiday arts and crafts, making Christmas presents for parents, holiday songs on the announcements, carol-singing assemblies, Christmas tree in the foyer, staff Christmas party, and treats; some classes had parties on the day before the holidays, decorating classroom doors contests, Secret Santa, charity gift cards for needy families, cookie exchanges, Red and Green Day. It was an extensive list but not unusual in my experience. Schools knew how to do celebrations and capitalized on the students' excitement. Christmas was a big event. Once we had the list up, I could tell there was a bit of discomfort. Like many excesses, you often don't recognize it until it is laid out in front you.

I split the room in two. One half of the table groups was assigned to list all the reasons why we should keep most or all of the traditions we had around the Christmas holiday. The other group was to list all the reasons why we should change what we do. It didn't matter what your personal beliefs were at this point, I said. We just wanted all our thinking on the table. At the end of five minutes the groups put up their lists. At that point anyone from the room could add to either list. This method ensured that those with the loudest opinions didn't dominate the discussion. I mixed up the table groups next so that we had voices across grades at every table, and asked each group to come up with their best thinking. I would collect all the thoughts and share them back. I told them I would do the same activity that evening with the parent council. If traditions were going to change, we needed everyone's input.

I suggested that the teachers might also want to do a similar activity with their classes so that students could have a say as well. Any student groups were welcome to bring me their thinking. At exactly 5:00 p.m., seventy-five minutes after we began, the meeting ended. I never went over time. It is always best to play in the union sandbox.

Adam and I went out for dinner between the staff meeting and the parent council meeting. It was a long day and we didn't usually plan for the meetings to go back-to-back. He approved of how the discussion was organized and said, "I think I would have just opened up the floor for discussion."

"That's one way to have staff discussions," I said, "but I am always wary that it can go off the rails quickly when it's a free-for-all. You know me, I like to have some structure."

Adam continued: "I noticed that Julia, who has been here since the school opened, was on the side that had to list all the reasons to change."

"Uh-huh. I had her in mind when I made the decision about which side would do which task. It's always good when people have to think outside their comfort zone."

Adam then echoed my earlier thoughts, that discussions like this can often be hijacked by whoever talks the loudest, so it was good we avoided any grandstanding or tempers. Then we looked over the notes to see where the common threads were. We wanted to take the ideas that best matched with current thinking around culturally appropriate celebrations and come up with a plan. I wasn't sure where we'd land exactly, but it was a start and, importantly, the staff had had a say in the decision. We pored over the responses and were pleased that most groups were suggesting both cutting back on Christmas activities and being sensitive to those students who celebrated differently. There were suggestions about how to be aware of other holidays and celebrations that we usually ignored or passed over. A few groups suggested a staff committee.

"So," Adam said, "do you mind if I run the activity at the parent council meeting? I'd like to try my hand at it." Of course, I agreed. It had been my plan all along. I would jump in if need be, but I felt Adam would do fine and he did. The parents came up with almost the same list as the teachers. There were a few more discussions about what a shame it would be to forgo all the things they remembered as students. The previous month, Cathy had brought up the lack of diversity on the parent council, and there was a lot of brainstorming. One of the ideas was that each member would try to invite a parent who didn't usually attend the meetings. I saw a few new faces in the audience this evening—one Black father, two Muslim mothers—but the vast majority were white. We needed to do more.

By 9:00 p.m. I was sitting at my desk, shoes off, feet aching. It had been a long day. Adam and I had agreed to look at the parents' suggestions the next day. Packing up my desk, I remembered Myles and the fact that I had a morning meeting again. He needed to know I was still there when I wasn't. I grabbed a piece of school letterhead and penned the following:

*Dear Myles,*

*This is Mrs. Phillips writing. I have an important meeting this morning. That is why I am not in my office. When I get back to school, I will telephone you in your classroom. The next day I will be here and we can have a visit and read* Mortimer. *I hope you have a wonderful day!*

*Mrs. Phillips*

I put the letter in an envelope and wrote his name on the front. I propped it up on my keyboard, where it was easily visible. I sent a quick email to Adam, Sondra, Kim, and Joan to let them know what I had done and to wish them good luck.

The following morning, as soon as my meeting was done, I called Adam to check in. I hadn't received any harried texts. Adam assured me all had gone smoothly. Myles had beamed at getting mail, as I thought he might. When I arrived at school, I called his classroom. Sondra answered and said the morning was going well.

"Myles, you have a phone call." All kids love to talk on the phone.

"Hello," whispered a shy voice.

"Hello, Myles. This is Mrs. Phillips calling. I am back at school now. Did you get my letter?"

"Yeah," he whispered.

"Are you having a good day?"

"Yeah." Pause. "Bye." I heard the click of the receiver. Disaster diverted. From then on, I tried to remember to leave a letter for Myles on the mornings I was out. A few weeks later I forgot again but there was no meltdown. Kim confided that she kept one of the letters and that if I forgot, she put it on my keyboard herself in the morning. Teamwork.

# FIFTEEN

# Best-Teacher-Ever Feeling

THE HOLIDAY BREAK HAD PROVIDED A MUCH-NEEDED respite for everyone. Lazy mornings with time to finish a cup of coffee in one sitting, cross-country skiing and snowshoeing with my kids, trashy novels. Even Frankie had been more relaxed away from school and friends up north at my parents' cabin. Perhaps she kept it together better since her grandparents were around. Perhaps it was the release of stress from school and social issues. Whatever it was, the change had been welcome.

Although the beginning of January isn't the same as the first day of school, it is a fresh start. Teachers, like me, have had a break, and contrary to popular opinion, the students are excited to be back and see their friends. Out in the schoolyard, kids clambered up and down the mountainous piles of snow left by the plows. I noticed orange cones encircling patches of ice. I wondered who had put them out. The playground was littered with small snowmen, and snow forts abounded. Red-cheeked primary students decked out in puffy snowsuits lined up at the bell, and a few last snowballs hurled through the air. I would make an announcement this morning now that winter was here to stay. I wondered what principals in California announce—earthquake threats?

Hallways were abuzz with chatter. Many were parading their new outfits and the younger children had snuck new toys into their backpacks to show their friends. Sarah was standing in the hall as her students disrobed and piled snowsuits, hats, mitts, and boots onto hooks that are suitable for light summer jackets.

"Good holiday?" I asked.

"Wonderful. I so needed the break. But glad to be back." We watched Sawyer trudge slowly down the hall, dragging his backpack behind him through the slush.

"I spoke with his parents right before the break," I said. "They were reluctant at first but have agreed to the psychological assessment. I will call the psychologist today to let her know."

"That's great news. I thought about him a lot over the break." Of course she did. "I am going to try some new strategies to help him get some of the work done. I am just going to assume he has some processing issues and see what happens." I nodded. Good teachers didn't throw up their hands or wait for the expert to tell them what to do. Good teachers kept trying new things until something worked.

"I wonder if chunking his writing assignments and giving shorter instructions would help?" Often students with processing deficits had troubles with longer tasks.

"I was thinking that," Sarah said. "And I want him to be able to share his thinking in groups instead of avoiding them altogether. Got any ideas about that?"

"You know, he is a bright kid. What if you paired him with someone else, equally bright but maybe stronger on the written side? Maybe just one other student would be easier for him than a group of four? Chat with Stephanie."

"I'll try that today and let you know." Sawyer had slowly disengaged himself from his coat but left his snow pants and boots on. The usual black hoodie was pulled up over his head.

"Good morning, Sawyer," I chimed. "Ready for backgammon tomorrow?" He nodded but didn't make eye contact. "See you tomorrow." I was heading to my office when I ran into Myles tearing down the hall with Kim in pursuit.

"He's going somewhere fast," I said, falling into step next to Kim.

"Has been in a state since he walked in," she replied, slightly out of breath. "I mentioned your office as usual and he was off." Most kids relish the holidays but for some it is added stress. Their routines are thrown off, they aren't confident things will be the same when they return, and family dynamics can be stressful. I was sure that Tiffany had found the two weeks long, stuck in a small apartment with three kids under the age of five and no other support. She had mentioned once that she wasn't connected to her family. I remembered the days when I had three young kids and even with all my supports, two weeks at home in the winter had at times been tiring. When I entered my office, Myles was already in the rocket ship. He had pulled the box of Legos in with him. I told Kim she could go and let him play a bit as I changed out of my boots and coat, flicked on my computer to deal with the barrage of Monday emails, and made the morning announcement, welcoming students and staff back and reviewing the no-snowball-throwing rules. As I sat at my computer a small piece of Lego flew through the air and pinged the table. Another landed by my feet.

"Myles," I said as I turned in my chair. "How are you today?"

"Mad," he affirmed. I could tell, but I was pleased he could say it without swearing.

"I can see that. Can you talk about it instead of throwing Lego pieces? What made you mad today?"

"The boys making snow forts. They won't let me in." This was good. He wanted to play with the other kids.

"Snow forts are fun. How do you know they won't let you in?"

"They said go away."

"Hmm. That would hurt your feelings. Why do you think they said that?"

"I accidentally kicked the fort. They said I wrecked it. I was just walking by." I doubted that. I suspected he kicked the fort wanting their attention and not knowing what else to do. Mentally I counted the days to spring.

"Maybe you could make a fort with one of the boys from your class at recess. What about Jalal?" I knew he and Jalal played together sometimes.

"I don't know how to make a fort. Those boys had a good fort."

"I bet you and Jalal could make a great fort." He thought for a bit and began to build some Legos. We talked about what he was building and I asked how the holiday had been at home.

"Boring. Mom yelled a lot. The baby cried a lot. We never even got to go outside and play." I grabbed a sticky note and wrote, "Tiffany—social worker." Maybe Tiffany would be amenable to some family support. Asking her about it right after the holiday, which sounded like it had been stressful, might be a good time. It took longer than usual for Myles to be ready to return to class but eventually I was able to walk him back. I stopped by Stephanie's office to ask if she could check in on him at recess and see how he was doing with the snow forts. I hated snow forts. The students defended their forts like medieval fortresses.

I decided to pop into Harriet's class. I would be starting the formal process of her performance appraisal in the next two weeks. She had assured me before the break that she had a new plan for teaching English. I opened the door. The desks were in rows and she was at the front of the class. By now the other teachers had all their desks in groups in order to facilitate student discussion. I sat down at her desk at the back. The boxes were still unpacked.

"Throwing snowballs is just not okay. I heard a story of a young boy who was permanently blinded by a rogue snowball. You know, often a piece of ice can get stuck . . ." I glanced about the room. The class was quiet but bored—heads down, arms crossed. What was she talking about? It was twenty minutes into the period and she was lecturing on snowball throwing? "So . . . um . . . today you are going to write about why we shouldn't throw snowballs at school. You have the rest of the period." This was a grade 8 class. Surely this was not an engaging topic for them. What teaching had preceded this? What were they learning? For the full ten years these students had been in school, they'd known about this rule. What was the point? I could feel myself getting frustrated and needed to watch that my face wasn't betraying my feelings in front of the students. I decided to leave and talk to Harriet later. Her daybook was open on her desk. There was nothing written down for today's lessons, but she had a prep period next. I'd come back.

While I was waiting, I wandered into Mac's class. His grade 8 students were seated in groups of five. All the kids were talking animatedly in their groups. I didn't see Mac at first, but he was sitting with a group at the back. I pulled up a chair next to another table. They barely acknowledged me before returning to their discussion.

Each student had a copy of a newspaper article that had been highlighted. On the front board was the question, "Would Tamir Rice have been shot if he had been white?" Before the break, a Black twelve-year-old boy in Ohio had been shot and killed by police for carrying a toy gun. I skimmed the article quickly. Mac didn't shy away from difficult discussions. From my vantage point I also listened in to the discussion he was having with his group. He was ensuring that the students understood some key words from the article. I recognized that some of the students were having challenges with reading, yet he had not given them easier text. Instead, he was ensuring they could access the same article as their peers. The students in my group were referring to comments from the article to prove their points. The conversation was high-level and I smiled inwardly. As I got up to leave, Mac waylaid me at the door.

"Look at these kids argue!" he exclaimed proudly. "They are so engaged."

"I was impressed that the kids at my table were using the text to defend their thinking. Very impressive."

"I gotta say, Kristin, I wouldn't have ever thought it. I am really trying to keep my own talking to a minimum." I smiled and he continued. "Yeah, I know. Hard for me—I do like to talk. But I learn so much more about what they are thinking when I do this."

"How will you finish this up? Is there a follow-up activity?" I asked.

"They are going to individually answer the question on the board. Tara did this article with her group before the break and said that the kids did a great job on their writing after they had had a chance to discuss it."

"Oh, the whole intermediate team is planning this?"

"Yeah, we got together in early December and found some articles that we thought would highlight some issues around equity. Right after that staff meeting about the holidays."

"Great. Love to hear more about it when your team meets next week." I could see Mac had that "best-teacher-ever feeling." When I had first begun as principal, I thought that teachers would change their practice if they had data to show their students weren't doing well. Nope, they didn't. I thought that if they learned how new pedagogies made more sense they would change. Still not. What *did* work was when they tried something new and saw their students being successful. Teachers change their practice when their students are successful— every time. I was thrilled that Mac was seeing that. He would take off now as he sought the best-teacher-ever feeling more often. As I made my way back to Harriet's room, I was even more frustrated. There were great things going on with her colleagues and she was lecturing about snowballs!

"Hope you had a restful holiday, Harriet," I said, although I really didn't want to make small talk. She told me about her family trip to

Manitoba and I nodded in the appropriate places. "Tell me about your lesson today."

"I just thought I would capitalize on your announcement this morning. Give the kids something to think about and reinforce your message."

"Do you think there is a problem with snowball throwing in that class?"

"Uh, I guess there always is room to think about appropriate behaviour." I truly believed that you have to start where teachers are when trying to support changes in practice. I honestly couldn't figure out where she was.

"I guess I think that by grade eight they are pretty familiar with the snowball rules. When I was here, you'd been talking for longer than the seven-minute rule"—I meant this to be a joke but she didn't react. So I plowed ahead. "You assigned the same writing task to all of them. What type of writing are you hoping to see? What was the goal of the lesson?" She said nothing.

"Harriet, I think we need to work together to have your lessons more planned and purposeful. I noticed that your teacher plan was not filled out for today or this week. It sort of seemed like this was an off-the-cuff lesson because you were unprepared." This time I just waited in uncomfortable silence. I could hear the classroom clock ticking. She didn't respond and after an uncomfortably long time I gave up.

"As we have talked before, I have concerns about the lack of planning in your classes. Parents have complained. This month I will begin your performance appraisal. The other teachers on your team are planning together but you do not seem to want to join in. Would you rather sit down and you and I plan together? I can release you for a half day. I want your performance appraisal to be positive, but I am worried. What can we do before we get to that stage?" I didn't really believe she could turn this around, but I had to offer.

First, if the TPA was unsatisfactory we were in for the long haul and

I needed to have a positive relationship with her. There was no way she would make any effort at all if she thought I was hounding her. Second, I would have to document that I had offered support. Teachers' unions, even when they know the teacher is bad, will target the administration for being unsupportive and nitpicking. The ministry guide for performance appraisals lists numerous criteria for successful teaching, which are valid but broadly worded, such as "The teacher is dedicated in his or her efforts to teach and support pupil learning and achievement." And every time I write an appraisal I have to read these lists and try to figure out what each item really means. Teaching is a complex process: part technique, part knowledge, part art, part psychology. Pinpointing where a teacher is going wrong is not always easy. In Harriet's case, however, we would start with simple lesson planning.

She reluctantly agreed to spend a half day later in the week planning a week of lessons together. I sent her some planning templates to look over and asked her to gather some resources and ideas for our meeting. She'd been in the profession a long time. This couldn't be a completely new process to her.

The end-of-day bell had rung and I could hear the buzz of teachers outside my door. I looked forward to these moments, like a proud parent at the end of the school day. Mac was there to talk more about his diversity unit and to show me some of the writing his students had done. Early in the year Mac had been a teacher who left at the bell—not anymore. Leanne trailed in behind him, both listening to his excitement and telling me about her own attempt to try the unit. Her confidence was increasing and she was feeling supported by her peers. She had Rafi in her class and said that even he had been engaged in discussing the article. Sarah waited until the crowd had thinned and plopped down in the chair next to my desk.

"Well, I paired Sawyer with Paul today for math. They are both kind of geeky kids but bright. I also gave them only one part of the problem at a time." I nodded approval. "At first they just worked side by side but when I came to check they had different answers. I pointed this out and then walked away. I wanted to see what they would do."

I was pleased. Most teachers help their students way too much. Many would have been tempted at this point to sit down and explain what had gone wrong, but Sarah showed her students she trusted them to figure things out by walking away. I wasn't sure how this strategy would work with two kids who were reluctant to engage with each other, though. Would a blowup be the end result?

"And the next time I looked over they were arguing with each other about how to do the problem!" Sarah glowed triumphantly. She also had that best-teacher-ever feeling.

## SIXTEEN

# Starfish

MS. O'GRADY WAS FRANKIE'S LIFELINE AT SCHOOL. I had met her only once, at parent-teacher night when Frankie was in grade 9. She taught Frankie art. But she had made a connection with Frankie that had endured throughout the years. Ms. O'Grady never contacted me, but Frankie, when she was talking to me, mentioned her. They talked music and art; Frankie would go to the art office and have lunch with her. I was so grateful for this teacher.

Over the holidays I had been mulling over how to change our perception about challenging students. I had seen some evidence of teachers empathizing with students but there was an undercurrent of blame. Conversations in the staff room were derogatory at times, complaining that kids didn't try or that parents didn't care. I got that. I'd done that as a teacher, too. The staff room was a safe place to rant against the frustrations of the job. But now I cringed, imagining what teachers said about Frankie and her mother in the staff room. I had a plan for the staff meeting but I needed to tug at heartstrings, not reason. Stories were the best way to do that. Should I risk telling some of Frankie's story? My therapist would say yes. And I would tell another principal to go ahead and be vulnerable. I wasn't sure I would do it myself, though. As an escape, I wandered down to grade 1 to read with kids.

There is an old story about a young girl walking on the beach among washed-up starfish. She begins throwing them back into the ocean when a man comes walking by.

"What are you doing?" he asks.

"Throwing the starfish back into the sea," she replies matter-of-factly.

"Why bother? You will never save them all," he responds with derision.

She throws another into the sea. "I saved that one."

I began the staff meeting by playing a YouTube animation of the story. "Sometimes," I began, "I think teaching feels like saving starfish. In everyone's class there are so many needs that it feels impossible some days." I could see the nods of agreement. It was January and we knew who our needs were. Any student who had been hiding in the fall had come out of the woodwork. The weather was dreary and first-term report cards loomed.

"My daughter Frankie is Ms. O'Grady's starfish." Breathe. Don't cry. "High school hasn't been a good experience for Frankie and she has struggled with mental health issues." I could feel the attention of my audience, sense them leaning in. "In grade seven she began cutting. She skips school and failed grade nine math. We have been getting her counseling support, but I will admit that the road has been bumpy for sure." I paused. Swallowed. Gathered my strength. Pushed back the tears. "Sometimes I wonder what the teachers at her school must say about her, and me the unfit mother. It's hard." Pause. Tears were welling, I knew. "But I am grateful for Ms. O'Grady. She was Frankie's art teacher in grade nine but she still connects with Frankie. Some days I think she is Frankie's lifeline at school. Frankie is Ms. O'Grady's starfish." I paused to collect myself and looked around. The room was quiet. Their faces were empathetic, and perhaps a bit shocked. I didn't ever share these types of feelings.

Things needed to get a bit lighter. "And then there is Joey." I often told funny stories about Joey. While I also worried about my son, there was a joy to him, and his antics were typical teenage boy stuff. "I am fairly certain Joey doesn't even know he goes to school." Laughter. "He could be the poster boy for disengaged boys in high school. But Mr. Jackson, the phys ed teacher, keeps his eye on him. Mr. Jackson calls me every once in a while. I am grateful for him, too.

"We need to make sure that we are saving starfish—one kid at a time. We need to remember that all those kids who drive you nuts, the ones who seem disengaged or act out or don't do their work, are someone's kid. And those parents love their kids. A lot. We can't give up. Maybe we can't save them all, but we can all save one. I am going to give everyone a paper starfish. I want you to think of a kid in your class this year that you can throw back into the sea. Who will you pay extra attention to? Write their name on the back of the starfish. You can talk about who you are choosing or not." I gave everyone a few minutes to chat and do the task. I made a point of giving one to Adam and one to myself. I wrote down Sawyer's name.

"Stand up. Walk back to your classroom and pin the starfish to your bulletin board by your desk or paste it on the cover of your daybook or tape it to your desk. Somewhere you will see it every day. Make sure the student's name is facing down and not visible." I waited and there was little movement. "No. Go now and do it and then come back." I was afraid that if we didn't all do it now, the starfish would get lost in the shuffle of papers on their desks at the end of the day. I left as well and put one on my office door, a paper starfish with Sawyer's name hidden on the back. Adam caught up with me in the hallway.

"Kristin, I didn't know. It must be rough."

"Thanks. It is. You know me—not something I like to talk about."

"Yeah. I know. You like to look perfect. But I think it resonated with them. A lot. I was watching their faces."

"Think so?" I took a breath. "Let's head back. You are leading the section on report card expectations, right?" Back to business as usual, where I was much more comfortable.

The following few days, as I was making the rounds of classroom visits, every teacher had a starfish displayed somewhere near their desk, even Harriet. I made a point of not asking whom they had chosen but many volunteered the information as we stood side by side in the hallways or walked recess duty together. Sarah had also chosen Sawyer—surely together we could get him back in the ocean. There have been many research studies that demonstrate that teachers who concentrate on the learning of one or two students actually end up affecting far more. Often the research refers to "marker students." That seemed rather impersonal to me. I thought starfish had a better chance of making a lasting impression on teachers. When I first began as a principal, I passed out research studies like free grocery store samples, except no one wanted to taste. Most teachers don't like to read the research because it feels so far removed from their daily lives. And, often, although it shouldn't be, teachers think that research is a criticism of how they are doing their job. So I left out the research studies and was going to capitalize on the certainty that most teachers cared about the kids they taught. We would see what happened. I repeated to myself—try something new; no one will die.

I was surprised that many of the teachers shared with me their own stories about their own children's challenges and sympathized about Frankie. People were understanding, not critical. But shame is often like that. You imagine the worst and then, of course, it isn't so bad. I felt lighter. It wasn't a big, big secret anymore. I wasn't going to share all the details, but I could share enough.

Harriet and I met at the end of the week. *Maybe she is my starfish teacher,* I thought ruefully. We met in a small seminar room with no windows, lined with shelves of forgotten books and teaching materials. I brought copies of the curriculum, the planning templates I had shared with her, and some books on teaching English. She arrived with nothing.

"Good morning, Harriet. How are you today?"

"I'm fine, thanks."

"We were going to spend the morning planning your next English unit. Did you have a chance to look over the templates and come up with some ideas?"

"Yeah, well, I gave them a quick look over."

"And . . . ?" I was wondering how I was going to save this morning. Obviously, she was totally unprepared. She didn't reply.

"Do you have any ideas about where you'd like to go next? Which curriculum expectations do you need to address with your class?"

"Well . . . umm . . . I think maybe another novel. My friend has this unit on the book *Holes* that she said I could have." Was my face expressing the grimaces I felt inside?

"I don't think we have class sets of that book," I said as steadily as I could.

"Oh. Well, I could read it aloud to them." Did she not remember all the kerfuffle with the last fourteen weeks of read-aloud? She continued: "Then she has all these great worksheets that get into the main idea and vocabulary and stuff."

It's not unusual for teachers to share materials like this, and when they are good lesson plans, I'm all for it. But generally, I believe teachers should be involved in their own curriculum design and assessment. Clearly this was not going to happen with Harriet. Maybe I could get her working with the team and she would learn from her colleagues, who were generating original ideas. I'd tried to nudge her towards this before—time now for a push.

"I think we need to go in a different direction. You know, the other intermediate teachers have put together some readings about equity. Mac was saying just the other day how well it was going."

"Yeah, I think they were talking about that the last time we met."

"Sometimes it is easier to work with others when you are trying new things. And they have done a lot of the heavy lifting already with finding the articles and determining the sequence of activities. They have also created the assessments. The other classes have been very engaged with the unit so far, I believe." Short of trying to order Harriet to work with Mac, there wasn't anything more I could say.

The rest of the morning was like paddling a canoe upriver against a headwind. Harriet was agreeable to everything I said but contributed nothing on her own. I asked if she wanted to change anything. No. I asked if she had some articles of her own to contribute. No. I asked if she had ever had her students work in groups before. No. Clearly the expectation was that she needed to be able to plan on her own. Clearly she couldn't. So we would try this approach of support with the understanding that she would come up with the next unit on her own. I was explicit on that last point. I offered to team-teach the next unit, but she declined. By the end of the two hours she had the templates filled out—mostly by me—and the next week planned out for grade 8. Her grade 7 class was not planned, but perhaps she would use some of these ideas for them.

"Harriet," I said as the morning drew to a close, "you need to be able to plan like this and follow through with your students in order to receive a satisfactory on your TPA." I could not have been more blunt.

"Of course. Thanks for your help. I think this will work." She wasn't worried or reflective like Kate. She wasn't even cocky and confident like Bryce. She was bland.

"I enjoyed the morning planning," I said because it was the right thing to say. "I will be popping by to see how things are going next week. You'd better get going. The bell for your next class is about to ring."

Rafi fell into step beside me as I walked back to my office. I didn't really get our relationship. Sometimes he showed up when he'd been kicked out of class, but often I would just find him sitting at my office table at lunch or even during class time. The teachers had started to refer to him as my shadow. Even so, he didn't ever really want to talk about what was bugging him and he would shut down as soon as I asked too many questions.

"Hey, Rafi. What's up?"

"Nothin'."

"Where are you headed? What class do you have?"

"Math," he grumbled.

"Want to have lunch today?" I asked.

"I don't know," he mumbled under his breath, but I saw the glimpse of a smile.

"Well, I will be there if you want." We parted ways. Sure enough, he showed up at the lunch bell. Rafi was a conundrum. He was often unruly in class but at other times he was compliant. He could do the work and I didn't think there were any learning difficulties. Past teachers remembered him as being a pleasant kid in his younger years, no behaviour issues. These days teenage attitude seeped from his pores. And although his attitude, clothing, and language were all appropriate for the teenage social scene, Rafi didn't quite fit in with some of our more popular teens. The bell rang and Rafi shuffled out, but he came back and picked up his garbage at my throat clearing. Then he headed to class. I reached for a leftover paper starfish, wrote his name on the back, and stuck it on my office door.

# SEVENTEEN

# Connecting Dots

THE END OF JANUARY IS A STRESSFUL time. The snow is never-ending yet no snowstorm appears to warrant a snow day respite. The renewed energy of the holiday break has succumbed to the stress of report card writing.

Vanessa, who taught grade 2, plopped herself down in the chair next to my desk. She was an excellent and conscientious teacher, and as principal I never worried about her. But she was in a quandary this cold winter day. She needed to report on four of the five math strands and one she had chosen was measurement. A major unit in measurement is telling time to the quarter hour, a grade 2 curriculum expectation.

"So," she sighed. "I taught my time unit for the required two weeks and all my kids can tell time to the half hour. But almost none of them can tell time to the quarter hour. What do I do? Do I give every kid a C?"

I was frequently called upon to provide all sorts of advice and guidance to my teachers. I positioned myself as a fellow teacher in the school, avoiding the hierarchical power my job held whenever possible. But here Vanessa wanted an answer that was fair and, more importantly, that I would support with parents who might complain. I understood her dilemma. The Ontario math curriculum, like many in the Western world, is crammed full of expectations. The broad scope of the curriculum means that a cursory brush is applied to many concepts. Most topics are taught in blocks of two to six weeks and then not returned to until the following year. It is not uncommon for teachers to believe that the previous year's teacher didn't teach a particular concept at all, given how little students often remember. It is kind of like remembering how to operate an appliance you rarely use, or how to change the clock in your car in the olden days before it all happened for you. When we learn something, we need to use it, or we lose it.

"Well," I responded, trying to give myself some think time, "do you think that if you kept working on telling time to the quarter hour your students would get it?"

"Most definitely," she replied without skipping a beat. "Can I do that?"

We looked at each other and lightbulbs went on. We were so stuck with the board-recommended timelines for units of study that we had forgotten that all curriculum expectations were for the end of the year. There was nothing that said students had to master any curriculum expectation in January. We agreed that Vanessa could give the majority of her students a B in measurement on the January report card since they had mastered telling time to the half hour. She would make time to keep working on the quarter hour over the course of the rest of the year and see if the kids had mastered it by June.

In the world of mathematical proficiency and comprehension, telling time to the quarter hour is small potatoes. But that interchange led me to begin thinking about our mathematics instruction differently. Why were we stuck to this rigid system of breaking up the math concepts into units of discrete learning? As a classroom teacher I was always concerned that my students often had to relearn the previous year's understanding of fractions or multiplication because it had been a year since they'd had to use it. I began to wonder if the way we were teaching mathematics was actually hindering the students' retention of concepts.

Earlier that year my junior teachers and I had been participating in lesson study in mathematics at another school. Lesson study, which originated in Japan, involves groups of teachers working on a lesson plan together, observing the lesson as taught by one teacher, and then debriefing and tweaking the lesson afterwards. It is a powerful method of professional development that has been shown to develop teacher skills further than a traditional workshop approach. The classroom for the lesson was in a neighbouring school; a teacher named Melissa would be running the lesson for her grade 4 classroom. As we were planning it, I had a puzzling conversation with Melissa.

"What do you think your students' biggest challenge with the lesson we've planned is going to be?" I asked as we walked to her classroom. We'd worked for an hour to plan a mathematical provocation that would get the students to subtract large numbers.

Without missing a beat, Melissa responded, "Oh, I know already. They will all add." I had been so puzzled by her answer that I didn't say anything at all. I couldn't imagine why she thought they'd all add to solve the problem. Certainly a few might be confused, but all of them? Melissa set up the provocation problem and got the students into pairs to solve it, just as we'd planned. The rest of us wandered around to observe how the students approached the problem. Sure enough, every single pair of students immediately started to add the two numbers. I leaned over one pair and, pointing to their work, asked them to explain their thinking.

"Oh, we are adding the numbers," one of the students responded confidently.

"Why did you decide to add?" I asked.

"We've been doing addition problems for two weeks. It's adding," the student again responded confidently. His partner nodded affirmatively. It is tempting to blame the students for not reading and thinking critically at this point, but perhaps the fault was in how we approached the curriculum. Almost all problems we have in education, we have created ourselves, usually inadvertently and with the best of intentions. Perhaps, in order to not overwhelm students, we taught math one concept at a time. But clearly this was not always beneficial. What if this parsing of the math curriculum meant that students did less critical thinking?

I remembered trying to help Joey with his math homework earlier that year. He had been given a series of simple-interest problems to do. I was trying to explain each one to him, but he had already figured out that you could just apply all the numbers to the formula given. He had no idea what simple interest or a percent was. Nor was he interested in me explaining it to him. Joey's goal was to complete the questions as quickly as possible. Avoiding a confrontation, I had let it be. But it was part and parcel of the same issue—we often teach, and particularly in math, so that students don't have to think very much at all; they simply follow a given procedure for a unit of study. Joey was following the formula for simple-interest problems; Melissa's class saw two numbers and added them.

That January afternoon, Chloe popped by as well with a report card writing question. Chloe had a grade 5 class, mostly boys. The year had been challenging with so much energy in her classroom.

"I've got myself into a bit of a pickle with my math report card marks," she stated matter-of-factly as she leaned against my office door. Chloe was a no-nonsense kind of teacher—strict but fair and the kids respected her. She was petite and always dressed to the nines, today sporting heeled boots with a green knit dress and blazer. I felt frumpy in comparison and couldn't imagine how she taught all day in heels. I raised my eyebrows in response.

"My kids this year are so squirrelly that when they were getting frustrated with long division after a few lessons I just gave up in despair and went on to something else. I probably shouldn't have but I couldn't keep them focused. They are so busy!" The exasperation in her voice was evidence of the challenges of this particular class. "But I didn't drop long division altogether, if you are worried about that. I just came back to it, and then stopped when they got frustrated and picked it up again. I guess over the term we tackled long division about four times, in short bursts." She gauged my reaction for a second and then continued when I said nothing. Maybe she was on to something here. "So now they can all do long division! Even those kids who were really struggling at the beginning have got it now. Really, I've never had a class all get it before." Chloe stopped for a breath.

"Sounds like a great way to teach it. What's the pickle?"

"Well, one, I think that my class average is going up because of this and I didn't want you to think I was inflating marks. But second, they really bombed some of the quizzes they did in the fall on long division. It seems like those quizzes shouldn't count."

I agreed. If they could do the long division now, that's what counted on the report card. "It's like taking your driver's license test," I said. "No one counts all the miserable attempts you made while learning to parallel park. You only have to be able to do it on the day of the test. If you are like me, you never parallel park again! But your kids can do long division now. Don't worry about what they did in October even if you'd planned to do the whole unit then. And don't feel you have to use those test results."

With that settled, I returned to the potential larger question.

"Before you go, I'm wondering if you might like to get together with a few other teachers and do some brainstorming about how we teach math." I relayed the conversation I'd had with Vanessa earlier that day. "We came to the realization that really we don't have to master any of the math concepts before the end of June. Vanessa is going to continue to teach telling time to the quarter hour for the rest of the year and it sounds like you did the same thing with long division. You just kept coming back to it. We won't meet before the report cards are due," I reassured her.

"Sure. That sounds interesting. Invite Sarah. She's all into math. I've got to get to class before the next period."

My brain was spinning. Part of my job as principal was to observe and connect the dots. I had two strong teachers doing some interesting things. Teaching is often very isolating. Each teacher's classroom is a small kingdom and mostly what goes on is private. In many schools today, and certainly in the past, the principal rarely visits. The business of the school day and the limits that unions put on the ability to call meetings outside of school hours mean that teachers have few formal times to share their teaching practices. Deep sharing of practices requires trust, and trust requires time. It was a vicious circle. But I had access to what everyone was doing in their classrooms and here I saw an opportunity to bring some teachers together to talk about how we taught math. Could we come up with a system that might avoid some of the issues that Vanessa and Chloe had noticed, and some of the issues I'd been thinking about?

Days like this reminded me why I love education. It was all about the what-ifs. I drove to the gym with energy pulsing through my veins. I texted Joey that we weren't ordering pizza but I'd make something yummy for supper when I got home.

"Homemade pizza?" he asked. I laughed. Good days give you hope.

# EIGHTEEN

# Report Cards

**THE VERY WORST PART OF BEING A** teacher, bar none, is writing report cards. Gathering all your assessment data of the term, you have to come up with a single grade that you believe—and can defend to parents—accurately reflects the student's learning. You write comments for every subject and although you can cut and paste, there is an expectation that the comments will be somewhat personalized. A class set of report cards from start to finish can take upwards of twenty hours to do, often more. Invariably teachers find they want a bit more assessment information and kids are bombarded with tests and last-minute assignments leading up to the end of January. There is a time-consuming series of events: writing and proofing comments, building report cards, proofreading again, submitting them to the principal, making corrections, signing the final copy, and stuffing them into envelopes. Everyone hates it except the brand-new teachers, and they learn to hate it after the first round. I was old enough to remember doing the whole process by hand and thought the cut-and-paste options were actually more time consuming, but I kept those thoughts to myself.

The very worst part of being a principal, bar none, is reading report cards. I would choose any day to write a class set over reading them. Adam and I would split them, but it still meant just over three hundred for each of us. They tended to be formulaic—not an interesting read. Some teachers would hand them in riddled with spelling and punctuation errors. The worst was when, in the cutting and pasting, a teacher would have the wrong name in the report card. In my early years in the principal's chair, I took the report cards very seriously, reading each one carefully and trying to enforce my own stylistic preferences. Just like everything else in the principalship, you naively assume that all teachers will take the same care that you did as a teacher. I wanted perfection.

When I was a first-year principal, Daniel was a seasoned French teacher. French teachers write the French comment on the report card of every student they teach, often close to 250. I'd read Daniel's report card comments, red pen in hand, with an editor's scrutiny and returned them to his mailbox full of red squiggles. He came storming into my office like a tornado ripping across the prairies.

"What the fuck is this?" he said angrily, brandishing the offending page in my face. "I have been teaching for fifteen years and never, NEVER, has any principal ever, EVER, made comments like this!" He slammed the page down on my desk and left. The door had been open the whole time. I walked into the main office to dead silence. Everyone quickly looked down, refusing to make eye contact. Returning to my office and closing the door, I sat down and cried. I was the principal. How dare he question my authority? The report card comments were not up to snuff. But as I settled down, I began to see it from his point of view. I would have been mortified as a teacher if my principal had made even one correction, let alone massacred the page in red. An hour later, tail between my legs, I apologized, and, luckily, Daniel was gracious.

"You're good as principal, Kristin. But you can't do stuff like that. Not to report cards." After that I calmed down with my expectations. I went from taking two hours to read a class set of report cards to being able to do it in thirty to forty minutes. I switched to purple pen—a less alarming colour—and if I read the first five and there were a lot of errors, I just returned them with a note suggesting that perhaps the teacher had been too busy to proofread. As a parent I reflected that I rarely even read the comments on the report cards, which tended to be full of educational jargon (which as a teacher I actually understood). Like most parents, I looked at the mark and gave the rest a cursory read.

Over the years, I discovered that I shouldn't focus on report cards at all. When I worked with teachers to change how they taught, invariably they'd show up at my office door wanting to talk about how to write their report cards better to reflect what they now understood about their students. When these conversations happened, I knew that the teachers were thinking deeply about how their teaching and assessment were connected. Usually I just listened and agreed that their new comments would be just fine. It was a sign of professionalism that teachers wanted the report cards to be meaningful and not an exercise in compliance.

This would be my first set of report cards at this new school. I knew that I wouldn't love how they were written but I also was willing to let it go (except for the misuse of the semicolon, which drove me nuts). I knew that as we focused on our teaching practices, conversations about report cards would invariably follow. Reading all the report cards can provide valuable information about instructional practices in the school. As I began this Herculean task, I would scan for teachers who gave too many high or low marks, teachers who seemed to know their students well, and students who were doing poorly that I didn't know about. I was looking for patterns.

A few years back I had noticed that Karen, an experienced teacher but new to grade 2, had given most of her class a "Needs Improvement" when it came to independent work. I questioned her about it and she said that almost none of her students could sit quietly at their desks and complete their work. When I asked how long she expected them to work quietly, she replied with exasperation, "Well, they can't even manage thirty minutes." A conversation ensued about reasonable expectations of seven-year-olds. She was used to grade 5 students, for whom thirty minutes would be normal. She adjusted both her expectations and the report cards before they went home.

Another time I noticed that Joanne, a grade 8 English teacher, had given an extraordinary number of Ds, mostly to boys. When I questioned this, she replied, also in frustration, that they were simply not completing any of their writing assignments. I'd been by her classroom a number of times, and although it was lively, it had seemed that she had control of the class and the students were engaged. But in our conversation I got the distinct feeling that if the students chose not to work during class time, she didn't worry about it. Joanne didn't see it as her responsibility to ensure that the students were completing the work. This is fairly common as students get older and teachers abdicate responsibility to the kid. While a teacher cannot absolutely force a child to get the work done, just like a parent can't force a child to sleep, there are numerous strategies that teachers can use to ensure students are working. But your average teen is pretty savvy and if they can figure out how to not do something, they won't.

Teachers and parents often believe that a poor mark will motivate a student to do better. The research is very clear that it does not. Joanne's attitude was that she would "show them," as opposed to working to engage her students and find out why they weren't getting the work done. Study after study shows that while grades may work as a positive reinforcement (students who get good grades are motivated to keep it up), they do not work as an effective "punishment." The problem is, of course, that individual parents and teachers will say that a poor grade did make them work harder. However, they are usually people who received only one poor grade in a sea of good marks. They knew that it was possible to do better and would not make the same mistake again. But students who struggle simply assume they will get poor grades. In Joanne's class the students who received the poor grades didn't have a good relationship with the teacher and just blamed her, much like the students who took my summer school math course who attributed their failing math grades to poor teachers.

Report card grades carry a lot of power in school systems. Parents scrutinize them, teachers agonize over them, and students rip open report card envelopes before they get home even though we admonish them not to. The grade is meant to be an accurate measurement of how well a student is doing, in the context of prescribed expectations. The problem is that report card grades are highly subjective and may or may not be an accurate portrayal of how the students are doing.

In the second week of school that year, Mrs. Chen had called me about her daughter Amelia's grade 2 mark in geometry. It was a B, not an A like all the other math marks. The teacher who had given the mark last June was now on maternity leave, so I couldn't pass off the phone call. Although I tried to convince her that this B in geometry in grade 2 was not the end of the world, she was very concerned. I knew that there were a million reasons why Amelia might have received a B and not an A and that most of them had nothing to do with whether Amelia deserved it. It could have been that the teacher had done very little work in geometry and didn't have a lot of data. It could have been that the teacher hadn't known how to assess the different levels of thinking. It could have been that Amelia really didn't understand geometry as well as patterning. Report cards are supposed to be an objective reflection of a student's achievement. They are not always that. Arriving at a grade was complex and there were no rules for teachers to follow. Assessment is the hardest thing teachers do. I was tempted just to make the B an A to appease Mrs. Chen but I did not. She hung up dissatisfied.

I had carefully read the math marks in grade 6, as Bryce was not as strong in math as he was in English. His math marks were considerably higher than those of Mike's class. Unless Bryce was a much more gifted math teacher, which I doubted, his marks were likely not a true representation of his students' abilities.

I also paid particular attention to Harriet's report cards. The majority of her students had gotten an A or a B in English. Yet when I'd looked at her assessment book in December, she had had no grades listed! I knew for a fact that she had read aloud to her students and they had done no actual reading on their own. One of the issues I'd raised with her was whether she'd have enough assessment data about her students to generate a defendable mark. Harriet's comments were, not surprisingly, vague. After reading them I decided to hand-deliver them back to her classroom.

"Here are your report cards back. There are a few spelling corrections required before you submit them for the final printing."

Harriet looked up from her desk. "Oh, okay. Thanks a lot."

"I was wondering which assignments you used for your marks," I commented naively. "If you have a minute, could you run me through it?"

"Sure. Let me see. Where is my assessment binder?" She shuffled through the piles on her desk. "Here it is." I pulled up a chair next to her desk and she handed the blue binder to me. A divider marked each class and I turned to grade 7. There was a class list but no marks. No marks at all. I flipped to the next page. Same class list and two students had a mark next to their name. Harriet seemed unperturbed. Grade 8 was the same story.

"Maybe I am missing something, Harriet? I don't really see any grades here."

"Oh, yeah. Ummm . . ." I thought she'd lie and say it was at home and she'd bring it tomorrow, but she didn't.

"How did you arrive at the report card marks?"

"Well, you know, as an experienced teacher you just have a gut instinct for these kinds of things."

"Actually, Harriet, as an experienced teacher I don't really have a gut instinct for what grade a student deserves. You are required to have data. It can be test or assignment marks. It can be anecdotal remarks, but you have to have something."

"I guess I should have more in there. Being a new grade and all, it was a bit of a slower start to the year. You know, I was waiting on that plan from my friend. And then we did that planning together. I probably wasn't as organized as I should have been." I didn't think I could continue the conversation and be polite. I had wanted to ask how her new unit was going but I needed to leave.

"Please determine how you will assess your students from now until March break and give me a copy by the end of the week. I will use it as part of your performance appraisal."

"Oh, okay. That's a good idea." As I left her room I was puzzled by her passivity. Never in my entire career had I heard of a teacher who had no assessment data. What would I do if a parent called? I didn't even want to contemplate the mess that would be.

One of the things I did after reading and signing all the report cards was run a report that gave me all the grades given in the school. Each student received eight marks. Out of 600 students, we had only given out 50 marks of a D—only 8 percent. Seventy-five percent of our grades were an A or a B. This is a trend that is seen in K–8 education across the country, so I was not surprised. I believe in mastery education: teachers teach in a way that all students master the material, and therefore getting an A or a B would be the norm. But I knew that wasn't the case. Our standardized test scores at both the school and board levels had a large group of students sitting below the standard, or the equivalent of a B grade. At our school, in mathematics the spread between the number of students on our report card grades receiving an A or a B and the equivalent grade on the standardized test was 37 points. While standardized testing won't always match report cards since they measure learning differently, there should be a closer correlation. Report cards are subjective.

Plus, it is uncomfortable for teachers to give students, particularly younger ones, a D. So they just don't do it. When I taught grade 1 I hated having to give students a D. They were six years old and doing the best they could. I was worried that parents would get angry at their six-year-old when I knew that the issues were developmental—most kids in grade 1 learn to read but they don't learn to read all at the same time. I would have a session with my little students explaining that a D just meant that the work was tricky for now and they would learn it later. It made me feel better to tell them that, but I was never sure what happened when they got home, even though I provided the same analogy to their parents. However, to listen to the teachers talk in the staff room and at our special education meetings, I knew that we should have identified more students struggling by giving them a D, as yucky as that feels.

I was ready for February's staff meeting in the library. Page after page of rows and columns of pink As, green Bs, yellow Cs, and purple Ds. Student names and teacher names were blacked out and the visual showed an overwhelming spread of pink and green with some yellow and the very occasional purple. (The Ds were often clustered with one or two students.) I also had charts comparing our report cards to our standardized testing scores, the number of students receiving a D who were recent immigrants, special education students, male and female, and who were racialized. The computer program was able to pull out all the identifying factors except race—I did that by hand. Not until recently have school boards asked for student registration information about race. Historically, educators have not wanted to believe that race was a factor. But it is. Later in my career I worked at the board office and had a chance to visit many schools. Walk into any lower-level grade 11 math class and it is often 80 percent Black boys. Walk into an academic stream grade 11 math class and it is 95 percent white or Asian, usually with more girls than boys. Our data showed that the students who were struggling were overwhelmingly special education students, racialized students, and boys. The trend started early in a student's schooling.

"Happy February staff meeting. I see you already found the donuts on the back table." I had left all my coloured charts on the tables and already people were starting to rifle through them as they downed a donut before the meeting began. "I thought we could start today with a look at our collective report card data. I know that you all spent hours and hours working on the report cards and I appreciate your hard work and dedication. Report card writing is not your favourite, I know." Laughter. "And assessment is the hardest thing you do." It is important to remind and commiserate with teachers about this. Assessment is hard to figure out and I often tell new teachers that although it will get easier, you will never master it. So many factors contribute to determining a grade: which curriculum expectations were covered and in how much depth, which types of tests or assignments were given and whether they were marked fairly, which tests and assignments actually counted towards the mark. It would be simplistic to think that teachers can automatically design tests and assignments that are completely fair and unbiased. Many times in my teaching career I gave a test only to think afterwards that I didn't really get the information I was looking for.

"Today I'd like us to look at the grades we gave and see what sorts of patterns and trends you might notice. Although standardized testing scores are not everything, I would think there would be some correlation between the marks we give and the marks students get on the standardized tests." Scanning the room, I could see some frowns and eye rolling; I knew this was a loaded comment. Teachers' unions are anti–standardized testing and the rhetoric is that they are not that important. I disagreed. Teachers wait anxiously for the test scores and they want their students to do well. No one likes to be judged but standardized test scores, especially when they are low, feel like a judgement. At the school level I don't really believe that we need to agonize over every percentage point—our sample size is too small. In our school, each student was worth about 2–3 percentage points and in smaller schools it could be as much as 5 percent. So, in any given year a few students with academic challenges could skew the scores. On the other hand, when we compared our standardized testing scores against the report card marks we were assigning, there was a 30 percent discrepancy year after year. Looking at patterns and trends might reveal why.

"On your tables you have some information. I'd like you to have a look and at each table group, write down anything you notice. I suggest you don't try to explain anything yet—although it will be tempting— just, what are your observations?" The amount of assessment data your average principal can generate is extensive. I had selected only a few key pieces so that it would be manageable. As a teacher I had been subjected to staff meetings where we looked at so much data our heads would spin and at the end we had no clear direction at all. Adam and I sat down with table groups. There was a keen interest in looking at the data. No one was off task. We put the charts of their observations around the library and I was pleased to see common themes:

> We don't give very many Ds but our standardized testing has lots of students below standard.
>
> Most of the kids who get Ds are boys.
>
> Lots of the kids who get Ds are racialized.
>
> Lots of the kids who get Cs are special education students.
>
> Lots of the kids who get Cs are English Language Learners.
>
> The number of As and Bs sometimes differs a lot between classes and grades.

We had a discussion about how giving a D felt wrong, but were we doing students and their families a disservice by avoiding it? If we were giving so many As and Bs but our standardized testing scores showed some real areas of concern, perhaps we weren't assessing the right things. In other words, were we making school too easy for kids? These are difficult questions but they were ones we needed to discuss.

Looking at school data is complex. It is difficult to know what is most important and it is challenging to come up with a plan to address what the data tells you. But now, as we were examining our assessment practices, it was time to look deeply at those students who should be able to do better. Data needs to be action-oriented, to lead you to looking at individual students you can help.

My Joey was disengaged at school by grade 9 and had been diagnosed with a mild learning disability. His IQ was slightly above average and he did not have attention issues. But he was slow to learn to read and still didn't like it, although he loved to be read to. He also liked to discuss ideas and write, albeit without any punctuation. But school made him *feel* stupid, so he had got to the point where he didn't often try hard. I'm sure he was seen to have an attitude. His profile would show marks that ranged all over the place. If a teacher could capture his interest, he did well, but if a teacher didn't try to teach to his learning style or do more to help him succeed, he disengaged. I wish his elementary school had asked, "Why isn't this kid succeeding all the time?"

In a class of twenty to thirty kids it is very difficult to teach to each student's strengths; it is much easier to teach to the middle and hope for the best. As such, teachers don't always move beyond a student's behaviour to see what they are capable of academically. For example, school is not designed for young boys. In fact, if you were going to design a school for boys it would be divided into twenty-minute blocks that rotated between eating, playing, and schoolwork. But we expect young children, boys and girls, to sit quietly and listen for up to forty-five minutes at a time!

Data is important, but it is only useful if we do something with it. I wanted our teachers to recognize that maybe they had some unconscious biases towards boys who were antsy in the classroom, or racialized students, or students with learning disabilities who were smart but found some academic tasks difficult.

Teachers love kids and want to do a good job. It's never easy to examine our own practices, but it's necessary.

As the staff meeting was ending, Bryce approached me. "Hey, Kristin. Good meeting. I think maybe my math marks were a bit high. I know there weren't names, but I could tell which class was mine. Do you think I should mark harder?" It wasn't the solution I was looking for, but I was pleased with the self-reflection.

"I don't think it is about marking harder. I think it is about having a really good sense of what you want students to be able to know and do and ensuring that your math program is rigourous. Perhaps we could meet during your prep tomorrow to do some planning together?" Behind my back I crossed my fingers. Bryce's face revealed that he'd hoped for a quick answer to his query.

"Uh, sure, Kristin. Maybe not the whole prep but let's chat for a few minutes tomorrow."

Small win.

The next day Chloe was waiting outside my office as I arrived. Before I could get my coat off, she followed me into the office, obviously excited about something.

"Great staff meeting yesterday, Kristin. I was up all night thinking about my squirrelly grade fives," she began.

"Glad you liked it. Sorry you didn't get any sleep."

Chloe laughed but continued without pause.

"More than half my class are boys this year and they have been driving me crazy, you know." I did know. Chloe and I had had many discussions about the energy level in her class. She had already begun to have them run around the school when everyone became too squirrelly. "I think I need to embrace their energy, not fight against it."

"What are you thinking?"

"I'd like to replace all my chairs with exercise balls." I stopped and looked up. Novel idea.

"How . . . much money do you need?" School budgets are small. There is rarely much left over, although our fundraising dollars were strong.

"I don't know yet, but I thought I'd make it into a research project for the kids. They could research if it is a good idea, the cost, the problems, and such. Then we will invite you to hear their presentation. I think they will be more committed that way."

I liked Chloe. I liked her enthusiasm and she was a thinker. "Great idea. I like involving the kids. Let me know when you are ready."

Two weeks later Chloe's class sent me an invitation to hear their proposal. The kids had researched the benefits of sitting on exercise balls, how it could help with concentration, how much they cost, and even how they would keep them from rolling around the room when the custodian came in to clean! I was impressed. I found the money and Chloe purchased the balls. For the remainder of the year, whenever I passed her room the kids were all bouncing quietly, but their work was getting done and Chloe wasn't coming to vent about her rambunctious class quite so much.

# NINETEEN

# Mental Health

"WE NEED TO DO SOMETHING ABOUT OLIVIA." Stephanie and Peter were in my office. Olivia's latest tantrum in her room at the end of the day had thrown everyone. Despite all our best efforts, Olivia wasn't improving at school. She was unkempt and isolated from her peers. She completed almost no schoolwork.

"I meet with her every morning but I can't say I have formed a relationship with her," Stephanie reported. "Some days she likes coming with me but other days she refuses, and sometimes she becomes very agitated, throwing things at me and swearing." Stephanie was despondent. She almost always formed solid relationships with our most challenging students.

"I really struggled to give her any grades on her report card," Peter added. "She does no work. And I think the other kids are afraid of her. They give her a wide berth. And you know, my kids are pretty forgiving." He was obviously discouraged. "I can't say I've got much of a relationship with her, either."

"What about her parents?" I asked.

"I talk to them almost every day," Peter said. "They are really struggling, too. She tantrums at home probably more than here." It wasn't unusual for students to be better behaved at school than at home. Home is where everyone can let go, kids included. I knew that Frankie held it together at school most of the time but home was a different story. Frankie was also able to hold down a part-time job at McDonald's— she'd just been promoted to shift manager. Sometimes it made me feel like it must be us at home that was the problem because she was coping well in other areas of her life. Olivia wasn't coping in any area of hers.

Mental health issues flood schools that are ill-equipped to handle them. Schools do best teaching kids who learn easily. Dealing with students with learning challenges or even some behavioural issues is possible but taxes resources. Plus, not all teachers have training in dealing with special education needs and most students with special needs are placed in regular classrooms. School personnel are not equipped at all to deal effectively with mental health issues. Yet accessing support for mental health is cumbersome at best and impossible at other times.

I've always dreamed of a day when all services for children— education, health, childcare, legal services, foster care, disabilities support, even recreation—would be housed together. Wouldn't it be wonderful if within a single institution and ministry, everything to do with children was centralized? Pie-in-the-sky dreams, I know. As it was, parents seeking support for a child in need had to navigate an uncoordinated system, make phone calls to answering machines, get placed on wait lists that were months or even years long, and wait. I had met and dealt with numerous caring and dedicated professionals throughout my career, but I also knew only too well that Olivia's parents would not have an easy time getting the support their daughter required.

I remember a hot July day, early in summer vacation. Joey and Lily were at summer camp for the month. The week before, Frankie had had another weeklong stay in the hospital and had been sulking ever since. Camped out in front of the TV as I was getting ready to go out, she was definitely not having a good day. I offered to skip the gym, but she said no. At the gym I finished my workout and as I was getting into my car I looked at my cell phone. There was a voicemail message from an unknown number. I played it.

"This is the police. We are looking for Kristin Phillips. It's about your daughter Frankie. Would you please call us at the following number?" Fingers shaking, I redial the number and get an answering machine. Panic. I call my husband—he's heard nothing. I ask him to start calling the hospitals to see if she's been admitted anywhere. I call the police again. The same message. I check in with my husband. He is in shock and hasn't called the hospital. Desperation. I call the police switchboard and get transferred to someone. Frankie has been taken to the hospital via ambulance. There is no more information than that. I tell my husband to meet me there. There are no words.

When I arrived, Frankie was in the emergency department wearing a hospital gown, her face and teeth stained black. They had given her a charcoal milk shake to empty her stomach. She had taken an entire bottle of Tylenol, but then called a friend, who had called 911. Police and paramedics had arrived at our house to find her on the floor of the upstairs bathroom. Yet a new psychiatrist came by and said they were keeping her on a Form 3—up to two weeks. Perhaps this time we would get the support we needed. She stayed ten days. At the discharge meeting we were given yet another prescription and the same list of psychiatrists. This time I cried.

"I need help. You can't just send us off like this. It isn't getting any better. You have to do more." Crying, I learned, is the one way to get help. In a system with limited resources, crying gets you to the top of the list. In fact, after that day, when working with parents, I often advised, "Call on your worst day and cry." An appointment was made with a hospital social worker who would see the whole family. I went home, filled the prescription (that she didn't take for long), and started calling the list of psychiatrists. Leaving phone messages. Hating every moment of this. But at least we had an appointment for September with someone who might be able to help us find our way.

We saw the social worker for nine months, until our allotted time ran out. The hospital program gave only a specified number of sessions with the social worker. It was helpful and we got through another year. My husband and I decided to separate and the trauma of that over-shadowed Frankie's issues for a while. Of course, now I realize that the divorce added to her issues. I told no one what was going on at home—not the divorce, not Frankie's mental health issues, not Joey's skipping class and experimenting with marijuana and alcohol. I began privately seeing a professional to try to make sense of the mess my life had turned into: failed parenting and failed marriage. I didn't feel like the successful person the outside world saw.

I was an educated, articulate person who understood how the system worked and I had found it extremely difficult to get support for my own daughter and our family.

Schools frequently suggest that parents seek outside support for mental health issues. "Your child would benefit from counseling," we say, expecting that parents can just make that happen. We don't often recognize the minefield that simple sentence can expose: parents' own feelings of inadequacy, the emotional challenge of admitting your child needs help, the guilt, and then the next-to-impossible task of actually getting services.

I invited Olivia's parents to another meeting—this was not a telephone conversation. Peter, Stephanie, Mary, our special education consultant, and our school psychologist would also join us.

"We really like Olivia and when she is in a good mood she is delightful and has a witty sense of humour," I began. You have to let parents know you like their kid. I went on to outline the difficulties we were having and then asked how things were at home.

"You know Olivia," her mom, Caroline, started. "She has her moments, but it isn't too bad." I noticed Lucas, Olivia's dad, looking at his wife in disbelief, but he said nothing. "Olivia has always struggled with things, but we love her."

"Have you noticed anything different this year? Have things become more challenging?" Mary asked.

"Well, I don't really know," said Caroline. Tears were welling in her eyes. "You know there are good and bad days." I felt for Caroline. Who wants to admit to a group of professionals that their child has problems? That they are on the edge of coping?

"Lucas, what's your impression?" I asked.

"Frankly, it is not good. We are having lots more bad days than good days," he stated matter-of-factly.

"Can you elaborate a bit?" asked the school psychologist gently.

"Every day is a battle. She is becoming more physical with her brother and sister. Bedtimes and meals are always a fight. We can't take her out to the store anymore without a scene." Lucas sounded tired.

"Is she aggressive with you and Caroline?" the psychologist asked, her voice even softer. Caroline reached for a tissue. Lucas and Caroline shared a look of defeat.

"A few times." Lucas choked. "We don't know what to do."

Clearly this was a child and family in need of more support than we could provide. Unfortunately, the school program that the district ran in conjunction with the local mental health agency was full. There might be a spot in September. There were no other local options. Olivia was already in a small class and Peter was an excellent and empathetic teacher. We didn't have any other solutions. It is hard for the school system to tell parents they can't really support their child in the ways the child needs. Schools could invoke a piece of legislation that allows them to exclude students from school who can't cope. I didn't like doing that. Olivia's parents both needed to work. They couldn't cope with her at home any better than we could at school.

"Let's put Olivia on the list for the mental health class locally. It could be, a place will open up before September. Also, ask your family doctor for a referral to Dr. Samson, a child psychiatrist I have worked with before. He can see Olivia and maybe adjust her medications. He could also make a referral to CPRI, the regional children's mental health institute." The school personnel were exchanging glances. Everyone knew that the chances of Olivia getting in to see Dr. Samson before next December were slim. "Here's his number," I said, sliding a piece of paper towards Caroline. "I'm going to be honest, it is going to be hard to get an appointment. This is what you need to do. You're going to be triaged, so first, call on a bad day. As parents our instinct is to minimize the concerns. If you call on a bad day you are less likely to do that. Also, cry if you can. Trust me on this one. It will help. You have to sound more desperate than all the other parents who are calling that day. Second, when you are given an appointment for next December, ask to be put on the cancellation list. Tell them that you will take any appointment that comes up. Lastly, you need to call that office every week and ask if there have been any cancellations. With any luck the secretary will get so annoyed that you will get a faster appointment."

The table was chuckling by now at my theatrics, but I was serious. You had to be persistent. It wasn't that psychiatrists didn't want to help. There were simply inadequate resources.

"One last thing you can do. If at any point you feel that Olivia is a danger to yourself or others, you can call the crisis line or take her to the emergency department. This is hard to do as a parent." I knew that first-hand but didn't share. "But if you do, and you are very truthful about the extent of the difficulties, it is sometimes a way into the system."

"Oh, I don't know that Olivia is that bad," Caroline said, jumping in quickly.

"No, of course not. But if it got to that point, don't hesitate to get her the help she needs. And remember, you love her the best. You know her the best. You are the ones who are going to fight for her the best."

Caroline and Lucas also needed support in helping their daughter. Naturally we don't want to impose, we don't want to admit how bad things might be, we don't want this to be happening at all. "Olivia is a good kid. You are good parents. This is a tough time. Call anytime. You are never bothering me." The meeting wrapped up and Caroline and Lucas left. The rest of us just sat in silence. It was disheartening not to be able to do more. I addressed the elephant in the room.

"I know that we could exclude Olivia from school until she gets psychiatric help, but I don't want to do that." I knew that Peter didn't want that, either—he wanted to help. But I also knew he was at the end of his rope. And it was a long rope. He had given everything to this. "Her parents can't afford to have her at home. There is no way even if they could afford it that they could find a babysitter for her all day. Let's brainstorm how we can keep her in school without too many outbursts."

We spent the next half hour coming up with both ridiculous and good solutions. In the end Stephanie agreed to take her one-on-one more often, and Peter and I agreed that academics would be minimized if it kept peace—Olivia would be provided with academic work but not forced to complete it. Peter suggested more frequent reading breaks since that was all she liked to do, and I agreed that if she wanted to talk to someone about her books, she could come and chat with me. I was not currently working with her much besides manning the door during tantrums and might be a novel face. After all, reading was learning. Mary said she'd make a referral to the district behaviour team and maybe they could send out an extra Child and Youth Worker once or twice a week. We had a plan. It wasn't a great one and it was transitional at best, but we would see how it went.

A few days later Caroline called me. She'd called Dr. Samson's office.

"I called on a bad day like you suggested." She laughed nervously. "That morning had been such a struggle getting everyone out the door and on the bus. I had oatmeal on my blouse from the bowl Olivia had thrown and I didn't change it before I called."

"Yuck, but good," I said supportively. "Did you get an appointment?"

"December fourth, just like you predicted. That's so far away," she lamented. I could tell she was close to tears.

"Remember that you are going to call every week and ask about cancellations. Appointments get moved about all the time." I tried to reassure her. With any luck she could get in before the summer. "I know how hard this is, Caroline. We have some plans here at school to try to support her the best we can. Just yesterday Peter sent her down to tell me about the book she was reading about Helen Keller. She is a smart cookie, your Olivia. We just need some help figuring her out."

"Okay. Thanks for all your help with this. Lucas and I know that everyone there is trying and we just feel so bad you have to put up with Olivia." It broke my heart that Caroline was apologizing for her daughter but I got it. It feels a bit like airing your dirty laundry and I knew Caroline was feeling ashamed.

"Don't worry about it," I said consolingly. "We love kids here. That's why we are in this business. Let's just concentrate on getting her the help she needs. We will all work together." I wanted Caroline to know she had our support. I wanted someone to be supporting me with Frankie. I could give Caroline this. "Keep me posted on how getting an appointment is going and call anytime. You are never bothering me."

"You always say that."

"It's always true. Have a good day, Caroline. We'll get this figured out." I hoped we would.

# TWENTY

# Terrible, Horrible, No Good, Very Bad Day

I COULD HEAR HIM BEFORE I COULD see him. "Fuck! I hate this fucking school!"

"Myles, you can't go in. Mrs. Phillips is in a meeting." I could hear Joan's voice pleading outside my closed office door. My superintendent, Max—professional, dressed in the proverbial blue suit and striped tie—was sitting at my table and stopped what he was saying midsentence.

Myles burst through the door anyway, standing with his feet apart, tiny freckled, chubby arms crossed. Max's eyebrows raised and he suppressed a smile. I had forgotten about Myles. All of a sudden it hit me—Sondra and Kim were both absent today. In my rush to get prepared for my biannual meeting with Max, I'd forgotten to let the supply teacher know to bring Myles to my office first thing in the morning. Obviously, that had been a mistake. I mouthed a "sorry" to Max.

"Myles, I see you are angry. You have a new teacher this morning because Mrs. Smith is sick today. So is Ms. Zeigler. So you didn't get to come and see me first thing. I am sorry. That made you disappointed."

Myles responded with a pout, eyebrows gathered, nose wrinkled. I explained to Max, "Myles starts his day by coming to say hello to me. It is a good way to start the day. Myles, this is Mr. Thompson. He is visiting me this morning. When our meeting is over, you could come back to my office and we could read *Mortimer*. How does that sound?" Myles relaxed his face but kept his arms crossed, shifting on the balls of his feet. "Here. I will write a note to the teacher that says you can come to my office after recess." Grudgingly he palmed the note in his little hand, scrunching it into a ball. I called his teacher to say he was coming back to class. It was less of a tantrum than we would have had earlier in the year; I'll take progress where I can get it.

After explaining about Myles to Max, I returned to our agenda. Superintendents supervised the principals of about twenty schools. They also held numerous portfolios at the board level and dealt with parent complaints for all of their schools. While they were also supposed to be intimately involved in the process of school improvement planning for each of their schools, the reality was they usually had very little time for that. Twice a year my superintendent would visit the school. We'd discuss facility and staffing issues, go for a tour, and spend some time discussing how our school improvement plan was progressing. I was excited to talk about the changes our teachers were making in involving students in their own learning, the ideas the math teachers had about returning to key ideas many times over the course of the year—we'd decided to call it spiraling—and how successful identifying starfish had been in getting the teachers to focus on specific student issues. But the more pressing issue for today was Harriet.

"You know that we have Harriet Davis here at this school." Max nodded, frowning slightly. "I am doing her teacher performance appraisal and it is going to be unsatisfactory." Max's frown deepened. An unsatisfactory TPA is almost unheard-of. Most principals try not to travel that road, given the amount of paperwork, the pushback from the union, and the fact that you are rarely successful in making a change.

Unlike in other professions, it is extremely difficult to fire an incompetent teacher. "I have been in her classroom multiple times and had many discussions with her on what needs to change. We even planned a unit together, but she isn't following it. She is frequently off topic, she can't plan and meet curriculum expectations, and I get parent complaints almost weekly. But the worst of it is that she wrote her report cards with absolutely no assessment data. Nothing. And she didn't even try to lie about it! She showed me an empty mark book." Max's jaw dropped. This was a shocking breach of accountability that even Max had not come across before.

"I assume you have everything documented?"

I placed a thick file on the table.

"She's been teaching for eighteen years and this is her fourth school, as you know." Sometimes teachers do move around and that in itself is not alarming. It was the next bit that I wanted to draw his attention to. "The problem, of course, is in her three satisfactory performance appraisals. If you read between the lines, there have always been problems, but the union isn't going to do that, they are just going to say she's been satisfactory up until now, so what gives?" I needed Max's support if I was going down this road. "Honestly, Max, I've tried all sorts of approaches with her and although she is polite and seems to agree with suggestions and plans, nothing ever changes. She just shows up every day and talks to the kids about whatever pops into her head. No plans. No assessment. The kids don't misbehave, because I think they are just so bored. We'll pop by her classroom on our walk through the school." Max supported my thinking and said to give Human Resources a heads-up about the unsatisfactory and they'd let the union know. He volunteered to attend the meeting where I would give Harriet the results of the TPA and the required improvement plan.

Usually we would walk through and visit a number of classrooms, but Max asked that we start in Harriet's. On the way there, I pointed out Sarah's math class and Max chuckled at Chloe's room of bouncing balls, but we didn't get into details, as he needed specific information about parent concerns with Harriet. We found Harriet's classroom door was closed even though the teachers knew Max would be in the school that day visiting. I opened the door—thankfully it wasn't locked this time—and we stood at the back. A number of students raised their heads from their desks and sat up. A few students continued to scribble in their notebooks. The young girl directly in front of us was drawing hearts and flowers. Harriet glanced up from the book she was reading aloud. That certainly wasn't what we had planned together for the unit on persuasive writing. Perhaps she had found a different text to illustrate persuasive writing techniques? I waited for her to pause and conduct a lesson, but she continued with the text. It was a short story by William Faulkner and while a classic, it was not overly engaging for grade 7. I noticed Max take in the room: the mess on Harriet's desk, the lack of charts on the walls, the disengaged students. We observed Harriet reading for a very long five minutes, with no break in the monotony. Even the students who had sat up straighter soon returned their heads to their desks. I glanced at Max and he nodded towards the door.

"Just curious, Kristin. Did you inform the staff I was visiting today?"

I laughed a bit at that. "I did." Max understood. Harriet was a conundrum. She had to know I was concerned. I would have thought she might have made some sort of halfhearted effort to impress Max, but no. "It is like this all the time," I explained. "You didn't get any special treatment."

After observing Harriet, we discussed the holes in the parking lot, my support for Adam applying to the principalship, and a review of our budget, but there was no time left for a more robust tour of the school or a discussion of the school improvement plans.

"Kristin, you are doing a great job. Parent calls from this school are way down from last year. In fact, I don't think I have had any, even about Harriet. Haven't had any calls from the union, either, so the teachers must be happy. I don't know what you're doing, but keep at it. I've got to run. Feel free to call me anytime and let me know how it goes with Harriet." And he was gone.

I flopped down into my chair, deflated. Max was supportive and kind. But I wanted him to be interested in the things we were doing, all the stuff that I thought was really going to make a difference. Despite my occasional cynicism towards the conservative nature of education, I still was excited about the possibilities and longed to share my thinking, get feedback, and engage in the discussions that I thought would move us forward. These meetings, no matter how positive, often left me disillusioned. Our educational system is good. It ranks high in international assessments, but it could be better. I wanted to be part of something bigger; systemic change in education was needed.

Change at the school level, I had learned over three schools, was possible. I was already seeing the teachers here more engaged and trying new ideas. But I was weary of the isolation I felt. Systemic sustainable change in education is not well documented in the research. Most research studies are about individual classrooms, schools, or, occasionally, clusters of schools working together. And even when there are examples of district-level change, they do not appear to be sustainable—once the key driver leaves, the system reverts to how it had been. I'd seen this at the schools I'd been principal at as well. While I was there I could develop a sense of urgency and enthusiasm towards teaching and supporting students, but teachers often returned to old practices once I'd gone.

Classrooms and schools are very private places despite being funded with public money. There is little accountability, both within and to the larger community, and little uniformity between schools. While the research is very clear about which teaching practices will support students best, teachers are not required to adopt them. For example, it is well documented that lecturing the whole class is not as effective as a balanced approach, mixing in work with small groups of students who have a similar learning need. Yet my initial observation at this school was that the majority of the teachers gave whole-class lessons for most of the teaching time. We were making progress, though, and the desks weren't in rows anymore in most classrooms. But what I wanted was to talk about my efforts within a system perspective. I felt I was flying blind in leading the school—trying things and seeing what worked, but it wasn't part of any grander scheme within the board or the province. There were many discussions about board improvement plans and ministry initiatives, but mostly I felt like I was on my own. I worked hard to get the teachers in my school collaborating and it made a difference. I wished I had the same rich conversations at the system level. Even when principals did get together a few times per year, I felt it was without direction and the discussions rarely went beyond a surface level.

I looked at the clock and it was past recess. No time for lamenting today; I'd better check on Myles. As I opened my office door there were at least six kids sitting in the office still dressed in winter attire, boots forming slushy puddles below their chairs. "Busy recess," Joan said, tilting her head towards the group. I remembered that Adam, too, was absent that day with two small sick kids at home. I ascertained that all six kids belonged to the same problem, gathered their names, and sent them off to class. I didn't need Myles melting down again, so I'd visit with him first and then tackle the recess kerfuffle.

Arriving at the kindergarten room, I could tell that Myles was out of sorts. He was in the block center building and knocking down towers and the other kids were giving him a wide berth. I made my way to the blocks, stopping to admire a drawing of a snowman and exclaim amazement at a science experiment involving food colouring and water. "Hey, Myles. How's your day going?" I asked. The blocks went tumbling to the floor in response. "I am so sorry about this morning, but I have time for a visit now." Another tower crashed to the floor. "It's hard when our days don't go like we expected them to." He was tossing a few blocks halfheartedly. "I have some new markers you could use to decorate your spaceship." I was not above the occasional bribe. I got to my feet slowly to gauge what he would do. Finally, he tucked his small feet under himself and sprang up, running full speed through the classroom and down the hall. I could only hope he was headed to my office, not the schoolyard. It was slushy and rainy and I didn't want to end up outside in my high heels. Max's visit had required more professional business attire, which was not suited to chasing five-year-olds about the yard.

By the time I got to my office Myles was sitting in his spaceship. The sulkiness had left his face and he looked up in anticipation of new markers. I pulled them from my bottom drawer and he got to work. Although Myles was clearly more settled than he had been at the beginning of the year, it was the routines we'd put in place that were holding things together, not any internal sense of self-control. After half an hour of colouring, chatter, and three readings of *Mortimer*, Myles was ready to return to class. I stuck a big note to myself on my computer screen: MYLES. I would not forget tomorrow.

Heading down the hall, spiral notebook in hand, to begin my investigation of the recess altercation, I passed Jonathan, whose dad had complained earlier in the year about Harriet. I hadn't heard anything more, although I doubted that the parent was any happier, since I knew things hadn't improved. Parents rarely continue to complain when they are unhappy, since schools create cultures of invincibility: the teacher knows best. Plus, I think that most parents ultimately remember that they had lousy teachers and accept that their kids will, too. Part of me wished parents would complain more, but my more pragmatic side was thankful Jonathan's father had let it go, since I knew I couldn't make it better. I'd complained myself this year about Joey's English teacher, who was showing an inordinate number of feature films that had no assignments attached. The principal was an acquaintance of mine and listened patiently. He thanked me for my input and said he would follow through. The movies hadn't stopped and I had given up.

"Hi, Jonathan," I said in passing. "How's school?"

"Yeah, it's good." There was a pause and then, "Hey, Mrs. Phillips. I was just wondering, you know, I got an A in English."

"That's terrific, Jonathan. Congratulations."

"Yeah, I guess, but I don't know how, since I never had to hand anything in all year yet." How I wanted to respond and how I was going to respond were two different things. I don't think you should lie to kids, but it wasn't going to help matters to have the principal throw a teacher under the bus.

"Well, Jonathan, you know teachers can get marks from lots of different ways besides assignments and tests. I suspect that Mrs. Davis had observed you in class or had some conversations with you about your learning that led her to give you the A." Would that suffice?

"Hmm. I don't really remember her talking to me ever about stuff. But maybe . . ." Jonathan and I both knew the grade was a farce. But he was a good enough kid to play along—plus no one is going to question an A too much. I wondered if it was part of Harriet's strategy.

"You can always speak to Mrs. Davis about it and ask her to explain how she arrived at your mark," I suggested. I doubted Jonathan would; the kids knew it wasn't worth it and not to rock the boat.

"Thanks, Mrs. Phillips. Have a good day!"

I continued down the hall, fuming about Harriet. It was not fair that there were so many good young teachers out there without a job and yet my chances of getting rid of Harriet anytime soon, if at all, were slim to none. And we wonder why kids become disengaged as the years of school go by? There are many factors, but years with a mediocre or poor teacher can't help. I knew that the kids in Jim's class and Mac's class, even Bryce's class, were excited about their learning. It wasn't right that a kid like Jonathan had to endure a teacher who was incompetent and there was nothing I could do. This wasn't what I'd imagined when I had signed up for this job!

Two hours later I had thoroughly investigated the recess situation of the six boys in grades 5 and 6. The problem was Rafi Nader. The boys, it turned out, had come to the office on their own. Rafi had been tormenting them for weeks: pushing, name-calling, body-checking them in the hallways. Today had been the last straw, when he had threatened to beat up two of them after school if they didn't bring him money. Rafi still showed up in my office regularly both of his own accord and when he was kicked out of class for being disruptive. I hadn't had any other complaints of bullying since the TJ incident. Adam and I had avoided formal out-of-school suspensions. I didn't want Rafi on the streets during the day, nor did I know how his uncle would react. He'd served many in-school suspension days but there comes a point when you have to try something new. Plus, it had been a crappy day. Max's visit had gone well, and he'd been supportive and pleased, but I wished we'd had time to talk about the learning that was happening. Harriet wasn't going to improve and was Myles going backwards? Add slush and absent teachers and I was in a foul mood. I grabbed the paperwork to suspend Rafi for three days. I then called his uncle, who was gruff but supportive, and made phone calls to the parents of the six boys, none of whom were happy. But I could say Rafi had been suspended.

Dragging myself home, I contemplated if this was really the job for me. I missed the camaraderie of being a teacher; I wasn't sure we could make a difference with the most needy students; I hated the bureaucracy and the unionized environment that stopped me from doing what was right and allowed teachers like Harriet to continue teaching; I felt guilty about suspending Rafi since I didn't think that was going to solve anything.

After parking the car in the garage, I just sat there. Going inside meant dealing with supper and who knew what kind of mood Frankie would be in—she'd been spending more time in her room these days, refusing to talk to any of us. I was having a "terrible, horrible, no good, very bad day," I quoted to myself from the popular picture book. Like the titular character, Alexander, I wanted to move to Australia. Certainly there would not be these problems in Australia. I moped for a few more minutes, then gathered my courage and walked into the house. Joey had decided to make pancakes for supper and Frankie was lounging, uncommunicative but present, on the couch. Maybe I'd take my kids with me to Australia—maybe.

# Spring

# TWENTY-ONE

# Better Days

ADAM AND I WERE SITTING IN HIS office the Friday before spring break, which in Ontario falls in mid-March. Spring break signals the end of the dreariness of winter even though we could still get a big enough snow or ice storm in April to warrant a snow day. We had five teachers away "sick"—certainly not unusual right before or after a planned break. Officially I could have questioned these teachers, but it wasn't worth the fuss. With excitement for the end of school for a week, we knew we'd likely see more kids in the office for misbehaving, but we also knew that with five supply teachers for the day there wouldn't be a lot of solid teaching going on, either.

"I hate all the movies that I know will be shown today," I railed at Adam.

"Calm down, Kristin. It's just one day and it will make our lives easier." Adam was good at putting things in perspective for me when my desire for perfection clashed with real life. I sighed. "Besides," he added, "I think you have to look at all the good stuff that is happening around here. Just yesterday I was walking around and didn't see a single teacher talking in front of the class. I must have been to six classrooms and in each one the teacher was working with a small group of kids and the rest were working independently on meaningful tasks. Remember how many worksheets and word searches we used to see being photocopied?"

"You think? There does seem to be a general enthusiasm for teaching in the building—I've noticed it in the staff room while having lunch."

Adam smiled, remembering, I'm sure, how reluctant I'd been earlier in the year to join the teachers in the staff room. "You know, so many principals complain that they can't move their staff but I think we've done pretty well. Of course there is Harriet and Bryce. But even Leanne, who was so hesitant, is slowly moving."

"Maybe the difference is that you never tell them they have to do something, but you give them the time to try new things and experiment. Sarah stopped me in the hall the other day bubbling over about this new math thing that group of teachers is going to try. Spiraling?"

I then explained to Adam how they were going to return to math concepts multiple times over the course of the year—spiraling through the curriculum. "Try something new; no one will die," I said laughing. "Best phrase I ever came up with." We chatted some more about the positive changes we had been seeing: teachers eager to talk about their starfish, the collaboration happening among students, and Adam mentioned he'd even seen a good math lesson from Bryce—borrowed from Sarah but good nonetheless. Miraculously, we weren't interrupted by student behaviour at all. We moved on to a topic I knew was foremost in his mind.

"Tell me about the leadership activity you are going to highlight in your interview for the principal pool," I said. Adam's interview would be after the break. I had no doubt he was ready to lead his own school but selfishly I didn't want him to get a position for September. We worked well as a team and that wasn't always the case with principals and vice-principals. He thought about things a bit differently than I did and was good at reminding me that I couldn't be all business. The staff trusted him and a new VP would mean a period of getting to know someone new. There was no guarantee I'd be assigned someone with whom I could form such a strong working relationship.

Adam went over the work he'd been doing with the primary team this year to change how they approached teaching reading and writing. The first three years are critical to students learning to read and write yet our data showed a number of students not reading at the standard by the end of grade 3.

"What do you think is happening differently this year?" I asked.

"Like I said, there is more small-group instruction happening. Plus, the teachers all agreed to do more reading assessments so that they really knew what level each student was at." He proudly displayed the spreadsheets of data he had collected with the teachers. It was impressive. I remembered when in my first year of being principal one of the grade 1 teachers had approached me in May and exclaimed with glee that ten of her twenty students were reading at the board standard. I had been shocked: first that it was May and she'd only just figured this out, and second that she didn't seem concerned about the other ten who were not reading at the standard. Teaching can't be a wait-and-see-if-they-get-it game—teachers need to know every step of the way how their students are doing.

Joan knocked on the door. "Sarah is on the phone, Kristin, and she wants you to come down right away."

Standing up, I asked, "Do you know what's going on? Who is it?" It was unlike Sarah to make such a demand. She usually handled problems on her own.

"I don't know," Joan replied. "She didn't really sound panicky." I looked at Adam, shrugged my shoulders, and headed down the hall. I stopped in the doorway to Sarah's classroom. The students were all working on a math problem in groups of two or three. I peeked back in the hall—no kids sitting there in trouble. All seemed good. Had Joan gotten the wrong classroom? It seemed unlikely. Sarah spotted me and came over.

"Well?" she said in expectation. I looked around again. Nothing.

"What's up? I don't see any problems."

"Look at Sawyer," she exclaimed, grinning from ear to ear and indicating his table with a nod of her head. I looked and there was Sawyer animatedly talking with Paul about their math question. Then I noticed what had Sarah so pleased—Sawyer's hood was not up.

"The hood?"

"Yes! I can't believe it. He came in this morning with it down and it has stayed down all day. Even some of the kids have come up and whispered to me about it."

"You are doing something right here. What a milestone! And he seems relaxed working with Paul."

"The two of them hang around all the time now. Sometimes I have to tell him to be quiet and stop talking! I love those moments. He has come such a long way from the little boy huddled in the corner hiding under his hood."

He truly had. We watched in silence and then Sarah wandered over to work with a group. Just last week at the end of February, Sawyer's psychological assessment had arrived and we'd met as a group with his parents. Sawyer was found to have a learning disability in writing and in processing. Sarah had already begun to give Sawyer shorter tasks and break down the larger ones. She had introduced using a text-to-speech function on the Chromebooks and Sawyer had taken to it easily. Now, with the psychological assessment done, we would be able to apply to the special education department at the board level for a Chromebook for him to use exclusively. But more than all of those things, Sawyer felt safe and secure in Sarah's class. She'd ignored the hoodie and the sulking and found ways for him to succeed. And she'd found him a friend. At the meeting in February, Sawyer's dad told us that Sawyer had asked for Paul to come to their house to play—it was the first time he'd ever had a friend over. He hadn't mentioned any more bullying, but did say it wasn't a fight to get him out the door now. As I was leaving, I passed Sarah's desk, and there on the bulletin board behind her was a starfish.

Walking back to my office, I met my own starfish, Rafi, in the hall, but he was returning from the washroom, not sitting in the hall in trouble. I realized then that since the three-day suspension a few weeks before, I hadn't seen him in my office at all. Or sitting in the hall outside a classroom.

"Hey, Rafi. Long time no see," I greeted him in passing. He stopped, hiking up the jeans he was always at risk of losing.

"Yeah. I guess."

"Things going well? Keeping out of trouble?"

"Yeah." I didn't really expect him to share any great personal insights. He was a fourteen-year-old boy, after all.

"Stop by for lunch one day after the break," I said. "You don't have to be in trouble to have a visit, you know?"

"Yeah, maybe," he said, looking down with a slight grin. "See ya."

I was puzzled. I had been sure that the suspension would have a negative effect on his behaviour. Perhaps I had been wrong. He seemed more settled. I was reminded of my childhood favourite book character, Anne of Green Gables. When Anne became a teacher, on her "Jonah Day"—her "terrible, horrible, no good, very bad day"—she had whipped the classroom troublemaker and felt bad about it, but had garnered his respect. Was this the same? I remembered Dawson, from my first vice-principal experience; the suspensions had been detrimental, or at least not positive. But Rafi seemed to be toeing the line better. Kids never ceased to amaze me. One approach doesn't fit all.

On the way back to my office I popped into a few classrooms. I only saw one movie playing and there was a notoriously poor supply teacher in that classroom. I recalled Adam's words of wisdom. I'd let it go. Bryce had his students doing a word search and *that* I would address with him next time we met. There is no academic benefit to doing a word search at all and it was a pet peeve of mine. Kids will do them happily—I liked doing them, too, on occasion—but they didn't promote learning or even review. I always said to the teachers that I could give them a word search in German to do, and even if they didn't speak the language they could eventually find the words. It was simply a matching game.

I stopped at Harriet's classroom and peeked in. She was talking, again. She was lecturing the students about video game addiction. What that had to do with grade 7 English was beyond me. It certainly had nothing to do with the unit she told me she was doing on biography. Our meeting with the union was scheduled for the day after the break. I had written both her unsatisfactory performance appraisal and the five-page improvement plan and put them in her mailbox for review the day before. She hadn't come to see me. But the other classrooms were engaging and busy places. Jim and Mac both had discussion groups going, Maggie's grade 1s were writing stories and rushed to the door to share them with me, Kate's class was building ramps and measuring how far the toy cars went, and Mike's grade 6s, in comparison to Bryce's, were engaged in a role-play about the novel they were reading.

The year before at this time I had approached the head of Human Resources to discuss the possibility of returning to the classroom. I had been disillusioned with the principalship. As a teacher I'd enjoyed the difference I made with individual students, the camaraderie of the other teachers, and the leadership roles I had taken. Being a principal was lonely. I hadn't figured out how to be part of the school community, I hated the board politics, and I felt that at every turn something was holding me back from moving forward. Although we met as principals, I didn't always find the meetings engaging and it wasn't the same as working as a teacher, where there was daily interaction with your peers. In the end I had decided not to make the move. It felt like giving up and I wasn't sure how I would fit in as a "returned" principal to the classroom. Walking around today after my discussion with Adam in the morning, I was glad I hadn't. I felt comfortable here and we were moving forward. There was a palpable feeling of renewal in the school. The teachers were, for the most part, engaged and learning. When you are a principal the teachers become your "class" and I as their "teacher" was happy. Some of the changes I'd made in my approach to leadership had made me feel more included in the school community. The kids still sat up straighter when I entered the room, but the teachers were beginning to see me as one of the gang.

Reaching my office, I called Sawyer's dad. "John, it's Kristin Phillips calling."

"Oh, no, what's happened now?" John asked dispiritedly.

"Nothing at all!" I laughed. "I'm just calling to tell you that I was in Sawyer's class this morning and he is doing so well."

"What? I've never had a principal call with good news."

"Sarah actually called me to see. When I got there, he was engaged, working with his friend Paul, and his hood was down! Such a change from the beginning of the year." John and I had talked about the hoodie before, since John had tried unsuccessfully to have Sawyer wear something else to school.

"Thanks for calling, Kristin. This made my day. He's certainly happier about school these days. And he doesn't come home so much saying that the kids are bugging him."

"He has found a friend in Paul, for sure. Sarah was instrumental in finding another student that had similar interests. When he comes on Tuesdays to play backgammon, he talks to me now about how he plays with the other boys at recess time."

"Sawyer really likes his time to play backgammon with you," John remarked.

"He's a very good player," I said. "Might be better than me."

"Sawyer's mentioned that to me." John chuckled. "I thought maybe you were throwing the games."

"Nope. He is really very strategic and thoughtful. Well, I hope you both have a good break. Just wanted to let you know that Sawyer was doing well and we've begun to see changes. He is more confident and engaged at school and that's what we like to see."

"Thanks again for calling. You have a good break, too, Kristin." It had been a good day. I was looking forward to the break. We didn't have any plans but it would be nice to have lazy days at home with the kids.

# TWENTY-TWO

# Downward Spiral

LAZY MORNINGS WITH MY COFFEE WERE LUXURIOUS. By Wednesday of the break, I'd relaxed into holiday routines. Today the sun was shining and there was a hint of spring. Despite the still chilly temperature outside, I'd opened the window a crack to let in the fresh air. With three teenagers I had the house to myself until noon, when they would drag themselves downstairs and fix breakfast. By early afternoon, Joey was fixing pancakes and Lily was watching TV but there was no sign of Frankie yet today. Last night she'd gone out with friends, but I'd heard her come in by her midnight curfew.

"Anyone seen Frankie yet today?" I asked.

"She got up to pee," Lily remarked, "but she didn't talk to me." That wasn't unusual. Joey was making pancakes into hearts and trees and a blob he insisted was a dog. We enjoyed our brunch. When I hadn't seen Frankie by 2 p.m. I went upstairs, knocked on her door, and opened it a crack. She was hidden under the covers. Stepping over the mess that covered her bedroom floor, I sat down on the edge of the bed.

"Frankie, want to get up? It's already the middle of the afternoon."

"No," she sniffled. "I'm having a bad day."

"I see that. Want to talk about it?" I offered.

"No. I just want to lie here."

"It might be better to get up, have something to eat. Joey made some pancakes and there are a few left. I can warm them up."

"I'm not hungry. Leave me alone." Frankie did better, sometimes, with routine. I suspected something had happened last night with her friends that she was upset about. What I did know was that she could move with lightning speed from a slight upset to a full-blown tantrum.

I tried empathizing. "I see you are having a bad day, but you don't want to spiral downwards. Why don't you just come downstairs with us and watch a movie?"

"Go away. I hate it when you say that. You don't understand. I hate my life. I'm not getting up." She was right. I didn't understand, but I also knew this wasn't good. I was at a loss.

"Are you taking your medication?"

"Go away. Stop bugging me. I hate those pills. Nothing is going to ever work to make me feel better. Stop trying." She was sobbing now. The covers were still over her head. I didn't know what to do. Force her out of bed? Let her wallow? The pleasant calm of the morning had dissipated into worry. Obviously, all my attempts at empathy and gentle advice were not working.

"Okay. You have some alone time and I will come check on you later." I left her room, closing the door behind me only to find Lily and Joey standing in the upstairs hallway.

"Is she okay?" Lily whispered. "Should I try talking to her?"

"Does she want to hang out with us? We could watch a movie with her." Joey was concerned. He liked people to be happy.

They looked to me to have answers. I had none. "Let's leave her be a bit and I'll come check on her in an hour. Did either of you talk to her when she came home last night?" They shook their heads. I wasn't sure leaving her in her room was the right approach, but I could see that further discussion would lead us to an out-and-out fight. Those never solved anything, either. There seemed no way to reach her when she was like this. We were all tense now. Some days, most days, we never knew what would set Frankie off, never knew how to react to her moods. The ease of breakfast was gone and the kids plopped in front of the TV to watch a movie while I busied myself cleaning the kitchen and mopping the floor. Anything to keep me busy while I kept an ear to Frankie's room. It was quiet. I watched the clock, hoping to see her amble grumpily down the stairs, but I heard nothing. After an hour I ventured upstairs again, heart heavy.

When I knocked and opened the door, Frankie was sitting on her bed. There were fresh cut marks on her arms, blood trickling down onto white sheets. She looked up, tears pooling in her eyes. *I can't fall apart. She needs me.*

"Are you safe?" The social worker had said this was a good phrase to use.

"I don't know," she choked out. "I don't want to be here. I hate my life. I want it to be over." I sat down beside her and gently removed the razor blade from her fingers, grabbing a tissue to blot the blood. Her arms were a maze of old and new scars. I didn't know what to do with the razor blade and spied a shoebox next to her. She had a new box. I dropped it in and put my arms around her. Frankie stiffened but then relaxed into me, sobs racking her body. We sat like that for fifteen minutes but instead of it calming her she became more and more agitated, eventually pulling away and reaching for the box again. I knew that the physical pain could help distract from the emotional pain, but I couldn't let her cut. I could see Lily and Joey hovering outside her door. The knots in my stomach tightened. I wanted to run from the room and hide under my own covers, but I was the mother here. I had to hold this family together.

"Find Frankie's coat and shoes," I said to Lily. Turning to Frankie, I said, "Let's put on your sweatpants. I think we need to go to the hospital. You are not safe." I hated this. She allowed me to get her dressed and Lily brought her coat and shoes, tears streaming down her face. I gave her a quick hug and whispered that I'd ask Dad to come over and be with them. She sniffed and said they were okay and to call from the hospital. I'd call their dad anyway. Pouring Frankie into the car, I could tell she was spiraling down quickly. Should I have gotten her up earlier? Could this have been avoided? I was racked with guilt and worry as we drove the fifteen minutes to the emergency department. I knew the drill by now. We entered and waited an hour for triage. The public waiting room calmed Frankie to an extent and she sat with her head in her hands, silent but not crying. Her name was called and we went in to talk to the nurse.

"What brings you here today?" she asked as we settled into the small cubicle. Frankie did not answer. I hated saying the words.

"Frankie is feeling suicidal. She has been cutting and feels unsafe. She has been admitted to the Child and Adolescent Psychiatric Ward before." The nurse looked at Frankie for affirmation but Frankie said nothing. She was crying again.

"She will need to be evaluated by a doctor in the emerg." I gave the nurse the intake information and we were escorted to an examination room in the emergency department. There was a gurney and two plastic chairs in a partially curtained-off room. The lights were glaringly bright and doctors and nurses scurried about paying no attention to us. As we waited, Frankie became more and more agitated again, scratching at her arms, rocking in her chair, and crying loudly.

"Shhh. I know you feel bad," I said. "The doctor should be here soon." I tried to comfort her and she pushed me away.

"I hate this. I hate my life. Why did you bring me here? This is fucking stupid. No one can help."

"We need some help, Frankie. We do. You are not safe." Although she continued to scream at me and cry, she did not try to leave. Paradoxically, Frankie knew she needed help even though she didn't believe it would make a difference. We continued in this state of distress for at least an hour. Me trying to offer solace, Frankie alternating between bouts of silence and screaming. The doctor arrived during a screaming fit with me sitting beside her but I'd given up trying to say anything. Dr. Jensen, as he introduced himself, maybe about forty, had a kind face but he looked tired. This was probably the end of his shift, as it was close to 7 p.m. by now. His attempts to talk to Frankie were met with a tirade of screams.

"She is very agitated today. I can't seem to quiet her." I explained her history and the latest probable diagnosis of borderline personality disorder. I had done some research and didn't like the diagnosis—mostly because it didn't have a very positive prognosis. Frankie certainly exhibited some signs consistent with BPD, but not all of them. Most days I felt the medical community was as confused as I was. "We've been here before. Last time she spent ten days on the Child and Adolescent floor but things haven't really improved."

"I'm going to give her something to calm her down, since you say this has been going on for four hours now. And I'm going to admit her on a Form One." I knew now that meant a seventy-two-hour stay. "She's an adult now so she will be admitted to the adult mental health floor. It's on the first floor."

An adult? This was new. But then I remembered she'd had her eighteenth birthday in February. I wasn't familiar with that floor. It sounded more ominous. She wasn't an adult with psych problems—she was my baby, a kid still.

"I'm just giving her an injection of haloperidol. It will make her drowsy. I'll get an orderly to take you to the floor. You can go with her and get her settled." With the injection Frankie immediately calmed down and was transferred to a wheelchair. She was now so drowsy that she doubled over and laid her head on her knees. An orderly accompanied by a security guard came to escort her to the floor.

"Why do we need a security guard?" I asked, looking at Frankie, who was unresponsive and doubled over in her chair.

"Procedure for mental health admissions" was the terse response. The orderly guided her chair to the unit, with the security guard walking beside her and me trailing behind carrying our coats. The ward was locked and we were buzzed through. Unlike the children's ward, the hallway was bleak, painted an institutional mint green with dirty smudge marks. The air smelled stale and there were grates on all the windows. There were adults of all ages walking the halls or sitting in chairs. An elderly woman with a walker shuffled past us murmuring to herself. A television blared, interrupted by an occasional loud laugh. There were no rainbows painted on the walls or posters of koalas. A bulletin board had tattered notices of group meetings, meditation sessions, and work experience programs.

Frankie was wheeled into a ward with four beds. In the children's ward she'd always had her own room. Two of the beds were occupied. Remnants of hospital suppers were congealing on deserted trays. A younger woman of maybe thirty was sitting cross-legged on one bed. She was dressed in an orange sweatshirt and gray sweatpants. Her brown hair was pulled up into a ponytail and she sported big gold hoop earrings. A colourful nonhospital comforter covered her bed. She was flicking through a pile of *People* magazines. As Frankie entered, the woman glanced up and said, "Hey. Welcome to room six. I'm Louise. Crazy name. Everyone calls me Lou. What's your name?" Frankie was too out of it to respond but I smiled weakly. I didn't respond, either. The second bed was occupied by an older woman but her age was difficult to ascertain. She could have been forty or sixty. Her hair was going gray and was clipped close to her scalp. Her face looked worn-out. She was sitting in a chair by her bed, slouched and staring off into space. Lou continued to talk, asking Frankie what her name was and commenting on the magazines. Thankfully the orderly pulled the curtain as the floor nurse entered.

"So this is Frankie. I'm Sandy. I'm one of the nurses on the floor." Frankie stayed slumped in the wheelchair.

"They gave her something to calm her. I'm her mother, Kristin." I held out my hand. The nurse was young. Her name tag said she was a student nurse. She looked at me for a long second.

"You're Mrs. Phillips? Did you teach math at the high school?" I had taught math one summer many years before. "I think you were my teacher. At E. J. Johnson Collegiate? It was a summer school course." This happened from time to time as a teacher—kids or parents from years ago recognizing me and I had little or no recognition of them. I had taught hundreds of kids by this point in my career. Usually I enjoyed these moments, feeling pleased that I was remembered and hearing what they were up to. But this was not the moment. I didn't want to be recognized at all.

"Oh, yes. I did teach there one summer. Maybe ten years ago. You're a nurse now, I see. That's terrific." I was on autopilot.

"This is your daughter? Okay, then." Sandy returned to her professional role and asked me a series of questions about allergies and food preferences and past experiences in the hospital. She reminded me that Frankie's phone wouldn't be allowed unless approved by a doctor, so I put it in my bag. Frankie would be devastated to wake without it, I knew. Sandy handed me a hospital gown, given that I hadn't packed a bag for Frankie, and said I could help her into bed. With the medication she wouldn't wake until morning. She handed me a plastic bag and asked me to put Frankie's shoelaces and scarf in it. I knew by now why. Sandy left me to help Frankie into her gown and into the bed, which was covered by a scratchy brown blanket. I made a note to bring in the quilt her grandma had made her, although hopefully this would be a short stay. Tucking her in, I sat on the edge of the bed smoothing the hair from her face, using my thumb to try to wash away the tear stains, painfully aware of the bright lights, the hospital antiseptic mixed with old-food smell, Lou in the next bed humming as she flicked through the magazines. Was this a better place for Frankie? Would this help her to heal? Find peace? Reluctantly I got up, carrying my coat since the ward was unbearably warm, and left, whispering I'd see her in the morning. I heard the unit door click behind me as it locked.

It was nearing 9 p.m. by the time I got back home. I felt as though I had been run over by a truck. I was physically and emotionally drained. The morning with the breath of spring in the air seemed so long ago. The remains of a large pizza sat on the coffee table while the kids and their dad lounged in the family room. I plopped down next to my ex and he pulled me in for a hug. We were still friends and still family. I grabbed the last piece of pizza and explained what had happened, leaving out the long wait and the terrifying effects of the medication. The other two kids didn't need to know everything. Stu left an hour later and the kids went to bed. I poured a glass of wine and cried.

Stu and I were at the hospital by nine in the morning the following day. As we walked down the hall, he whispered, "This place is depressing." I had a bag of clothes and toiletries for Frankie and we found her alone in her room, picking at an unappetizing breakfast. She had dark circles under her eyes and her hair hung long and oily.

"Why am I here? Why can't I be on the sixth floor like always? I don't like it here. The people are creepy." The reality was that Frankie had always enjoyed her stays on the Child and Adolescent ward. She had felt safe there. It was an escape from real life. The nurses and social workers were friendly and she had related well to the other patients. She had had her own room, and the common room was a place to have social interaction without feeling inferior or anxious—all the kids there had issues. The adult unit had a different atmosphere to it—institutional, sadder.

"Do you remember yesterday? You were pretty unhappy and cutting. You weren't safe, remember? We came to the hospital."

"I remember, but then I don't remember. I just woke up here and I didn't know where I was. I feel really bad and groggy. This nurse came in and told me but I don't understand why I can't be on the sixth floor like before."

"You turned eighteen. Now you are an adult."

"Being an adult sucks."

I laughed. "I agree. Sometimes it does." The three of us spoke of other things for a few minutes before a social worker came in to talk to us. Felix was his name. An older man with graying hair and a bushy beard, he was wearing baggy jeans and a plaid shirt. He asked Frankie's permission before he spoke in front of us. Frankie was surprised and looked at us in a new light. Maybe her parents weren't omnipotent after all.

Addressing Frankie, he explained that all the patients were encouraged to take part in group therapy every day; it would begin at 1 p.m. He asked her about past therapy and any medication. Frankie was honest about not liking therapy and not sticking to the medication. He asked about things at home and she said they were fine. Fine was not how I would have described it.

"On a scale of one to ten, with ten being fantastic, how would you rate your mood today?" he asked next.

Clearly exasperated, Frankie answered, "Two. Why does everyone keep asking me that?"

"Sorry that bothers you," Felix replied calmly. "We are trying to gauge how you are feeling and if you are unsafe. Why would you say you are a two today?"

"'Cause I'm stuck here. And that medication they gave me yesterday has given me a hangover. How would you feel?" she retorted. "I thought when we were coming to the hospital that I'd be back on the sixth floor. I like it there." Felix explained hospital policy and Frankie turned her head. The doctor would be in to see her before group therapy and we were welcome to stay and visit but couldn't take her off the floor. She was given permission to have her phone. Felix left and Frankie held out her hand for her phone. Stu and I sat there saying little while Frankie fixated on her phone for the next hour. Any attempt by either of us to talk was met with an exasperated sigh and a curt response. When the doctor arrived we were asked to leave, so we made our way to the hospital coffee shop. Together again in response to Frankie, it was both easy and awkward. We were still new to being divorced. We avoided talking about Frankie and concentrated on the other two—far safer. As we returned to Frankie's room the doctor was just leaving.

"I'm Dr. Ramusdun," he said, shaking our hands. "Frankie has given me permission to talk to you. She seems much calmer now than she was upon presentation and tells me that she is no longer feeling suicidal. I'd like her to stay today and if by tomorrow she is still feeling stable, then she can go home. She says she lives with you, Kristin?" I nodded. "And you feel comfortable having her at home?"

"Yes. But I'd like her to have ongoing support once she leaves. We keep doing this. In and out of the hospital. She will be fine for a while and then spirals down again. The cutting continues. She needs help." I was desperate. I was tired and discouraged. I felt the tears stream down my cheeks.

"Of course, we all recognize that, but until Frankie is willing to seek therapy and stick with it, and the medication . . ." I knew that, too, but I wanted there to be a different answer. "I'm going to make a referral to a psychiatrist who does very good work with teenage girls. Dr. Candice Larson. And I'm going to give Frankie a different prescription—something that won't have quite the weight gain that risperidone did. Frankie indicated that was a problem for her." I was thrilled we were actually going to get a psychiatric referral instead of the same list of psychiatrists.

"Can't I just go home now?" Frankie pleaded. "I'm not going to hurt myself. I promise."

"I'd feel more comfortable if you stayed one more day, Frankie," responded Dr. Ramusdun. "We can keep you by law for seventy-two hours. I won't keep you that long if I feel that you are stable and safe tomorrow." Frankie sulked and turned her head.

"Let's see how you are tomorrow, sweetie, and then you can come home," I said.

"I hate it here. I'm not going to group," she stated adamantly.

"I think you could find it beneficial, Frankie," Dr. Ramusdun stated calmly. He was certainly unflappable. "But it is your choice."

"Maybe you could go but you don't have to talk," suggested Stu, always the peacemaker. Frankie shrugged.

"Maybe."

We stayed through her lunch and then left her heading towards group therapy, no spring in her step. Stu and I said an uneasy goodbye in the parking lot and I went home. Part of me wanted to ask him to come home with me, but we weren't together anymore. When I walked in the door, the other two came to give me a hug. I knew that Joey and Lily had lots of questions, but they didn't ask them. Besides the bare minimum, I didn't say much to them. Joey had made some eggs for dinner and we all pretended to watch a movie. I left them early and went up to soak in the tub with a glass of wine. Despite having begun to confide in a few close friends and my parents about Frankie's difficulties, I didn't call anyone. It wasn't in my nature to reach out for support and I couldn't bear to relive the past twenty-four hours. Would this ever end? Would she actually succeed in killing herself one day? Is that what she wanted? The tub water turned cold before I crawled into bed, the glasses of wine lulling me into a fitful sleep.

The following morning, Stu and I met again at the hospital entrance. We'd left Frankie her phone and we'd both received texts that group therapy hadn't been so bad but she still hated it there. Upon arrival in her room, Frankie was dressed and chatting with Lou, or rather Lou was talking and Frankie was listening. But Frankie's face was less haggard and her affect was better.

"How would you rate your mood today, Frankie?" I smiled at her, teasing.

"Mom! Stop that." But then she relaxed and said it was a 6. The nurse, a new one, not Sandy, thankfully, came in and said Frankie was being discharged. She also handed us an appointment slip with Dr. Larson for the end of the month. In the world of psychiatry that was a fast appointment. Dr. Ramusdun went up in my estimation for arranging something so quickly.

Frankie came home and the weekend before the end of spring break passed quietly. Frankie was a bit calmer and had agreed to try the new medication. We did a family bowling night where she was cheerful and engaged. For me, the roller-coaster ride continued. When would everything fall apart next?

# TWENTY-THREE

# The Hard Stuff

ON MONDAY MORNING AFTER THE BREAK, THE normal routine resumed. Lunches were packed, my coffee was rushed, there was no time for opening windows and letting in the spring air. Frankie, dressed in long black sleeves and leggings, got into the car without a word or a glance and we all headed to school. It seemed surreal to me that five days earlier I was admitting Frankie to the psych ward and now we were going to school as if nothing had happened. I dreaded the "How was your spring break?" question that I'd soon face. How could I respond? Would I tell people, maybe just a bit? Or keep it quiet as I had been doing?

I didn't like sharing so much. I was very cautious, keeping some separation between my home and school life. On the other hand, I was also trying to fit in more with the staff and move away from my position of power. Although in my head I knew that sharing was good, I had not been raised to be overly emotional. But as I was getting older, I wasn't sure that was working so well for me anymore. You'd think by this point in my life I would have more figured out! I gathered my courage and walked into the building. I still hadn't decided how I would handle the question about my break.

In the office Joan immediately motioned that the phone was for me, mouthing "Olivia." I wrinkled my brow and entered my office. The piles of papers were right where I'd left them. I sat down without removing my coat and grabbed my notebook.

"Good morning. Kristin Phillips here."

"Kristin, it's Caroline. Olivia's mom."

"Caroline. Hi. How are you? How was your break?" I asked the question I was dreading myself. I was met with a short silence. "Caroline? Is everything okay?"

"Not really. Olivia's in the hospital. We weren't having a very good break at all. You know any disruption to her routine is hard. On Thursday she got so upset that she had completely trashed her room and was banging her head repeatedly against her wall. We tried to stop her, but she kept hitting us. So I did what you said: I called the crisis team and she was admitted. She is on the children's mental health ward. Do you know it? What do we do now?"

*Did I know it?* Had Frankie not been admitted to the adult ward we would have crossed paths there. But this was not the time to share. Caroline needed support. I could offer her what I so desperately wanted myself.

"Oh, Caroline. That's rough. Yes, I know about the unit at the hospital. They will be in touch with us to support Olivia's schooling while she is there. I suspect you signed papers for us to talk to them?"

"I think so. It's all a blur. I told them everything . . . About being on the wait list for Dr. Samson, about the troubles at school and home. It was a bad day, you know, so I cried. Like you said."

"You've had a hard time but maybe Olivia will get the help she needs now." I wasn't sure that was true, but it was the right thing to say. I was on the other side of the table now. "I think Dr. Samson is part of the medical team on that floor?"

"He is. He will see her and us today. Could you come, too? You know her so well and can talk about all her difficulties. I'm afraid I will miss something." I took a deep breath. I did not want to go back to the hospital today.

"Sure. I will be there. How are you and Lucas doing? This isn't easy for parents, either."

Caroline's voice was barely above a whisper. "It's so hard. I feel like such a failure as a mother." I knew that feeling.

"You aren't. Olivia needs some help. You and Lucas are doing all the right things," I assured her. And they were. While sometimes you could point to family dysfunction as the cause of the child's difficulties, often you could not. Some kids were difficult. But, as I knew, that didn't make it easier and the shame as a parent was intense. "I know this is hard, but you did the right thing calling the Crisis Unit. Olivia was in crisis. And maybe you've been able to skip the queue to Dr. Samson. I've worked with him with other students." I had, and he was reasonable and listened. Fortunately, we hadn't run into him for Frankie all the times she'd been admitted. Even though he was good, I didn't want to mix my professional and personal lives, particularly in this arena.

Caroline and I agreed to meet in the hospital lobby at 12:50 p.m. for their 1 p.m. appointment. I hung up the phone and sat in my office with the door closed. "O Canada" played over the loudspeaker. The day was only beginning.

I opened the door and as I was hanging up my coat there was Myles, grinning ear to ear.

"Myles, how are you? How was your break?" I knew he wouldn't ask about mine, so it was a safe question.

"Good. Jalal asked me to come to his house and play. My mom said yes. We had pizza pops for lunch. We played Lego. We are going to play blocks today in class." Myles was wandering about my office. He looked at his spaceship, got in, and then got out again right away, talking to me nonstop about playing with Jalal. Before the break I had introduced

Tiffany to our social worker Bridget. I knew that Bridget was working on some parenting support with Tiffany and maybe it had worked.

"Did you want to read a book?" I asked.

"Nah. I'm going back now to play with Jalal." With a quick wave and a smile he was off. Kim beamed at me from the doorway and followed him out of the office. I was smiling as Adam entered.

"Hey, Kristin. Welcome back! How was your break?" There it was. The conversation with Olivia's mom had thrown me and I was just holding on. I wished he was coming to tell me about a problem that needed solving.

I closed my eyes briefly. *Breathe.* "Not so great. Frankie ended up in the hospital again." I had disclosed to the staff a bit about Frankie at our January staff meeting, then I had told Adam the whole story one night over drinks after a school council meeting. "She's out now. She was admitted to the adult ward and I don't think she liked that as well. We have yet a new psychiatrist appointment."

"Ahh. I'm sorry, Kristin. That sucks." Adam knew me well enough not to press for details. "Is she at school today? Do you have to call and tell them?" I thought of Caroline calling me right away and yet I hadn't thought about calling Frankie's guidance counselor. Now that she was an "adult" the hospital might not have the same relationship with the schools that the Child and Adolescent ward did. I hadn't found Frankie's school overly supportive in the past, but I supposed I should call them.

"Yeah. I guess so," I conceded. "Have a seat." I explained about Olivia and that I was heading to the hospital later that day to meet with the family and Dr. Samson. It was easier for me to focus on Olivia than Frankie.

"Then I will head directly to the board office for four p.m. We have the meeting with the union about Harriet," I reminded Adam. I looked at the clock. It was 9:30 a.m. and already the day was stressful. I needed something that would remind me why I liked this job. "I'm going to classrooms for the rest of the morning. See what's going on and do some real teaching maybe. Remind myself why being a principal might be a good job."

"I'll hold the fort here. And I'll go to the staff room for lunch today if you want." Adam knew that I wouldn't want to talk about my break in the staff room but that would be the topic of conversation. I smiled gratefully and headed out, stopping to ask Joan about her break. She had been south with her husband, daughter, and the new grandchild so she had lots to talk about and I was able to sidestep my own break easily enough.

As I walked into Maggie's grade 1 class, Ana came running up to me. No tears today. She gave me a hug and then pointed to her sweatshirt.

"See my shirt?"

"You went to Niagara Falls?" I asked.

"Yes. With my family. We goed to the falls and seed the whales!" For a girl who spoke no English at the beginning of the year, Ana had made remarkable progress. She pulled my hand and led me over to her desk. "See. Write story." In her notebook there was a family standing next to a whale. She had written five sentences about her trip to Niagara Falls, with very inventive but readable spelling. She dropped into her chair and grabbed a blue crayon to add the falls to her picture. Maggie and I exchanged a smile across the room and I joined a table of other writers to read and exclaim over their spring break adventures.

Kate's students were sitting in groups with math blocks of various shapes and colours. I joined a group and asked what we had to do.

"We have to make a shape where one-third of the blocks are red," Aiden volunteered, busy making a shape that looked vaguely like a truck.

"Oh?" I replied. "How are you going to do that?" His shape of ten blocks had only one red block.

Concentrating on making his truck, Aiden replied, "I'm not sure. You like my space truck?"

"I do," I answered. I waited for him to come to a pause in his building. I was pleased with Kate's problem. There was a lot of thinking and creativity involved but it might be a challenge for Aiden to move beyond building and into math. "Can you show me what one-third looks like with some other blocks?"

"Yup! I can!" He grabbed two yellow blocks and a red one and placed them in front of me. Good. He had the concept.

"So, if you have three blocks, then one of them has to be red for it to be one-third?"

"Yup!"

"What if I made a design with six blocks?" I asked, grabbing some blocks, none of them red. "How many would have to be red?" I had purposely grabbed one larger yellow block that I knew could be substituted by two red blocks.

"Hmmm." Aiden leaned over, abandoning his space truck for the moment. Touching each block, he counted out six. He added a red one and counted again. "Seven."

"Yeah. But I only want to make a shape with six blocks. And you said that Miss Wiarton said that one-third had to be red." Aiden counted the blocks again. I moved our design of three blocks closer to him. He counted the three blocks and then recounted the seven blocks and took away the red one. He looked up at me, eyes squinting. This was the hard part about teaching. I didn't want to tell him the answer but rather to help him figure it out himself. The questions you ask are so important.

"In this design you made with three blocks there are two not red and one red. And that's one-third?"

"Yup. Two not red and one red." He concentrated on this design.

"I wonder if we could make this one bigger but still have two not red and one red?" I asked. I watched. Aiden grabbed two blue blocks and another red and added them to the design.

"There!" His tongue was sticking out in concentration. "Always two not red and one red. Right?"

"I think you've got it." I smiled. "Can you help me with my six blocks?" I pushed my original design towards him, omitting the red block he had added. Aiden counted them again.

"There are six but no red ones. Two not red and one red is one-third." He looked at the big yellow one and took it away, replacing it with two red ones. He counted again, touching each block as he counted. "Not red, not red, red! Not red, not red, red!" He looked up expectantly.

"That's it. Two not red and one red is one-third." I gave him a high five. "Thanks for helping me with my design. How many blocks are in your space truck? Do you have two not red and one red?" I got up to leave. I thought that Aiden was ready to work on his own now. Sarah had given me some good advice about teaching math—she'd said that she always left before the kid had the right answer. It showed trust that the student could do it. As I moved on to another table, I could hear Aiden saying "not red, not red, red!" as he looked at his space truck.

I passed by Kate and whispered, "I love your math problem," before leaving the room. I continued to pop into classrooms. I loved teaching. I made a mental note to ask Kate to share her problem at the next staff meeting—maybe guide everyone in trying it. Sarah should share her walk-away strategy, too. This was the part of being a principal that kept me going. Connecting ideas. Seeing good teaching and creating opportunities to share it with everyone.

I stopped into Jim's class and talked to a group about the book they were reading. I went out for recess and played foursquare with a group of grade 5s. Afterward, I stopped at Myles's class and noted he was indeed playing with Jalal.

By 11:30 I had enough courage to call Frankie's school and let them know what was happening. I reached Mr. Wright, her guidance counselor, and briefly explained the situation. He said all the right things and agreed to check in with her later. Frankie didn't have a bad relationship with him, but she didn't have a great one, either. I asked if he would let Ms. O'Grady know since I was sure she would want to check in on Frankie. I didn't like to interfere with Frankie's relationship with her, but I knew Ms. O'Grady was Frankie's go-to at school.

As I reached the hospital for the meeting with Olivia's parents and Dr. Samson, my heart was racing and my stomach was upset. It would be years before I could pass the hospital without a flood of emotion. I knew I could have declined the meeting and saved myself the anguish, but I didn't. Olivia was important, too.

The hospital is old. The lobby dingy and brown, with a busy hush blanketing it. A few patients in wheelchairs with IVs hanging. A happy couple carrying a new baby in a car seat. Doctors and nurses waiting in the coffee shop line. And there were Caroline and Lucas huddled together next to the information desk, coats unbuttoned, as the heat blasts you the minute you enter.

I smiled wanly as I approached. They looked like I felt. Would it help them for me to share that I had been here, too, the week before? That I understood their feelings? But I was here as the principal. In the end my upbringing kicked in and I kept my personal life to myself.

"Caroline, Lucas. Hi? How are you holding up?" They smiled but didn't answer. "Are we on the sixth floor?" Of course I knew that was the floor.

"Yes," Caroline whispered. I knew the way to the elevators. I wondered if they questioned my familiarity with the hospital. We crowded into the elevator, not making eye contact, and pushed 6. Even that was difficult. *Does everyone in this elevator know what floor that is?* Caroline and Lucas kept looking down. We were buzzed through the locked doors and waited in a consultation room.

"Thanks, Kristin, for coming," Caroline said. "It has been such a difficult weekend. I don't know if this is the right thing to do."

"Caroline, it was. We had no choice. Olivia was aggressive. She was hurting herself and wouldn't calm down," Lucas maintained, although he, too, didn't sound convinced.

"Let's see what Dr. Samson says," I replied. "I have had positive interactions with him before and he may have suggestions."

The room was small and stiflingly warm. We removed our coats and tried to make small talk. Fifteen minutes later Dr. Samson entered. He was tall and lanky, his just-graying hair still styled in a longer boyish cut. His white coat covered brown corduroy pants and a denim button-up.

Introductions were made and although his eyebrows rose as I intro-duced myself as the principal, there was then a glimmer of recognition from our previous case a few years ago. He had been the psychiatrist who was working with an adolescent boy who was so anxious he could not leave his house to come to school. I'd been impressed with how well Dr. Samson communicated with both the boy and his parents. As a team we had been able to slowly get the boy back to school for a few hours every morning.

Dr. Samson reviewed Olivia's presentation during his meeting with us and then asked for past history. Again, he listened well and did not rush the conversation or come to quick conclusions. I could see Caro-line and Lucas relax as he spoke.

"I see that you have tried a number of medications from your family doctor but nothing seems to have made much difference. It sounds from the school and home as if Olivia's difficulties forming relationships, fol-lowing routines, and just being happy in herself are not improving."

"No," stated Caroline.

"We hate to say this, but we think it is getting worse," Lucas added. I nodded in agreement.

"Sometimes in these situations the best solution is a residential pro-gram where we can do a full assessment and really try to figure her out." Dr. Samson let that sit and I could see Olivia's parents deflate. "The best program is in London, Ontario." That was a good hour-and-a-half drive away. "It would be a four-week assessment program." I thought this might be the right move for Olivia, as I knew there was nothing available at the school board level in town until at least the following September. Caroline and Lucas were aware of that, too, but sending your child to a program so far away was a difficult decision to make. Dr. Sam-son continued to describe the program: there would be an assessment, family involvement, schooling, ongoing treatment, and a reintegration program. He patiently answered their questions and it was agreed that an outreach worker would be in touch with them within a few days. Olivia was able to go home with them and return to school until the residential placement was secured.

Leaving them to gather Olivia, I suggested they go home and think about it. "It's a tough decision to make, but honestly, I don't think the school system can offer you anything comparable. We are happy to have Olivia at school, but I think she needs more than we can offer her. I know it doesn't seem like a good thing but maybe it is." Then I added, because I knew they needed to hear it, "You are good parents."

Driving back to school, I thought about Frankie some more. Would an intensive treatment program work for her? I didn't like the thought of it any more than Olivia's parents did, but I would google it this evening at home—maybe. I stopped at the drive-through for a coffee even though it was midafternoon. There was still the meeting with Human Resources and the union and Harriet. I had suggested we meet at the board office instead of the school. As much as possible I wanted to avoid the staff gossip that would ensue should such a meeting take place at school. At school nothing was a secret.

The room booked at the board office was antiseptic: a table, six swivel chairs that looked more comfortable than they were, a whiteboard, no windows. Marianne, the head of the union for our district, was sitting there when I arrived. Her tan set against a pale yellow suit revealed a spring break trip south. Holding out my hand, I introduced myself. "Marianne, hello. It looks like you had a good spring break. Go somewhere sunny?" She launched into the tennis holiday she'd gone on to Arizona with her husband and her son, who happened to be on a tennis scholarship at a university there. I smiled and nodded. She was still expounding when Max arrived with Norm, the head of Human Resources, and we all sat down, opening the folders I handed out.

They began to peruse the copies and I doubted they'd read them ahead of time (I'd sent digital copies in advance). "I gave Harriet her copy before the break. I'm not sure where she is. School ended forty-five minutes ago. It's only a ten-minute drive." We all glanced at the clock above the whiteboard and sat in uncomfortable silence. Marianne wouldn't talk about Harriet ahead of the meeting, nor would we. Although it wasn't a battle, it wasn't a friendly meeting, either. Harriet arrived five minutes later, pulling off her ski cap—her hair was flattened by the cap and tangled. She wore a bright green baggy sweater that was misbuttoned, and unfitted beige pants. One would have thought she'd want to make a good impression.

"Oh, hi, everyone. Took me a while to get out of the school." She didn't elaborate and no one asked what she had been doing. I didn't want to know. Max provided context and introductions.

"Harriet, I assume you have had an opportunity to read the performance appraisal. Any thoughts?" Max asked.

"Oh, well, um . . . yeah, I've had a quick perusal but haven't really read it in depth." Max, Marianne, and I all looked at the table. Eye contact at this incredulous statement would not have been a good idea. She knew it was an unsatisfactory TPA. I had told her so and you only had to look at the last page to see the unsatisfactory box checked. We then went through the appraisal, with me paraphrasing each paragraph so that the concerns were on the table. I kept talking. Marianne, Norm, and Max were each taking copious notes. Harriet did not say anything or take notes. We then went through the improvement plan. I had outlined exactly what needed to change, what evidence I would look for to know it had changed, and what supports would be offered to Harriet in order to make the changes. I tried to engage her in the plan, but she simply nodded and said everything looked fine.

"Thank you, Kristin. Harriet and I will discuss this together," said Marianne. Max, Norm, and I were dismissed.

"Thanks, everyone," Norm said as he headed off towards his office. "If I hear anything from Marianne, I will let you know." Meetings with the union about teacher performance were always stressful and they were not conversations. Throughout my career I had had a few such meetings and each time they struck me as businesslike and impersonal. Usually, the union representative knew the situation was dire but protected the façade. Any real discussion wouldn't happen at my level.

"Thanks, Kristin, for being so thorough." Max and I walked together to the parking lot.

"That went as well as could be expected," Max said with a smile.

"I wonder if Marianne gets how significant the issues are," I said.

"Probably, but she can't say anything. And you should be prepared for them to grieve the improvement plan."

"Really? It is fair, I think."

"Doesn't matter. They will grieve it. We will fight it and make a few changes but nothing major, and then it will go through. Norm will handle all of that. You won't be involved. I suggest you just move forward with things. Do you think Mrs. Davis can make the changes?"

"I'd like to say yes, but I really don't think so. We have already tried this year. I've been working with her, offering suggestions. I even taught a lesson for her and then all she had to do was repeat it for her next class the following period and she couldn't even do that." Max looked at me and raised his eyebrows. "Honestly, she started to, but then she got sidetracked and wasn't able to finish the lesson at all. And it was an easy lesson that we had planned together." Well, officially we had planned it together, but she wasn't very involved. Was that the issue? Honestly, I was at a loss as to how to help this teacher.

"Well, Kristin. I know this is a lot of work on your part but it's the right thing to do." I appreciated Max's support. "Keep me posted with how it goes."

The day had turned gray and cold, matching my mood. I arrived home to kids slouched on the sofa watching music videos. My "how was school?" was met with silence. At least Frankie was there with the others and not ensconced in her room. Small blessings. I wouldn't look at residential treatment for her. We would see how it worked out with Dr. Larson.

## TWENTY-FOUR

# Principal Wins Day

"HEY, MRS. PHILLIPS!" I WAS ON THE elliptical machine at the gym, hair in a ponytail, in slightly sweaty workout clothes, earbuds in, listening to music. I looked up and two young men were standing there, grinning. I searched my memory. Nothing.

"Know who we are?" I grimaced a smile, eyebrows lifting.

"Umm, you are . . ." I was beginning to remember those faces, now much older than when I knew these two boys. "Abdul and Tyler? Right?"

"Yeah!" they exclaimed. "How are you? Didn't know you worked out here."

"I'm great. What are you two up to?" I remembered now. Abdul and Tyler had been students at the school where I was first principal. Abdul had been a refugee from Somalia and Tyler came from a family of six kids. We had spent lots of time together, since both boys were a handful. Abdul had fought a lot with everyone—an angry young boy who'd already had more challenges than a seven-year-old should. Tyler was energetic, but felt ashamed every day about being held back a year. Eventually when they were in grade 4 I had reversed the retention and moved Tyler forward a grade to be with his friends. There is no research that suggests retention has positive outcomes. In fact, one study revealed that 30 percent of students who are retained one grade do not finish high school and 100 percent of students who are retained twice do not graduate. Those are sobering statistics.

Years ago, I was teaching grade 1 and ended up starting the year with three boys who were repeating the grade. In one case the student had transferred to our school, having failed grade 1 in his previous school. Another had been retained because the parents insisted! "I was held back," said the dad, "and it worked fine for me. My son is just slower." For the third, the school had decided to retain him, as he was still performing at a pre-kindergarten level. I was apprehensive about the retentions, but throughout September and October I wondered if I was wrong. The three boys were doing well and were actually performing in the top half of the class. However, by November their difficulties with learning were apparent. By the end of the year the three were still experiencing significant difficulties, although they had made some gains. All three were still at the bottom of the class.

The truth is, they would have made the same gains had they been promoted to grade 2 and put on an Individual Education Plan. All three had learning challenges and required a great deal of individual support. The social and emotional implications of being held back are huge. Tyler had repeated grade 2 and it had devastated him. He was rebellious and frustrated and acutely aware that he had been retained. He felt that everyone knew, although I suspect most of the kids paid no attention to that fact. When I moved him directly from grade 4 to grade 6, most of the behaviour problems disappeared. He was able to catch up and finished grade 6 in the middle of his class.

"I am studying social work at college," said Tyler.

"I have a scholarship to the University of South Dakota for

basketball," Abdul said, beaming. "I'm just in town for a few days to visit my family."

"Wow! That's terrific, guys. I guess you are staying out of trouble," I teased with a smile.

They went on reminiscing about the toys in my office and how we used to go for donuts if they were on time for school for a whole week. If I had had to guess back then, I wouldn't have thought they would finish high school, and yet here they were, confident young men with futures ahead of them. There were teachers at that first school who thought I was crazy to waste time, as they saw it, trying to get them to school. Many thought they should have been suspended more. Those two boys were frequent visitors to my office, mostly for minor infractions, but also for physical aggression at times. And I admit that over those few years, I despaired many times. Yet I kept trying to make a connection, let them know I liked them, and believe they could do better.

I had an idea. Grabbing my phone, I asked, "Mind if I take your picture and use it at a staff meeting next week?" They looked at me, confused. "I want to tell the story of two boys who used to be in trouble who made it good. I want teachers to know that we can't give up on kids just because sometimes school is tough for them."

Abdul looked at Tyler. "Hey, we'll be famous!" I laughed and took the picture. They were my original starfish. For sure, I hadn't made the only difference. I knew that the principal at their junior high school had also taken an interest in them, because he used to call me. There had been other teachers along the way who had searched for the diamonds in the rough. I knew their parents cared about them and were also responsible for their success. But I wanted to tell their story to my staff as we reviewed our starfish to show how important it was to make the extra effort. Clearly Abdul and Tyler remembered me as someone who cared. They hadn't mentioned the suspensions or recess detentions. They remembered how I used to try to get them to come to school on time. They recognized me more than a decade later.

Abdul met me again as I was walking to my car. "So do you like South Dakota? What's school like there?" I asked. He talked to me about the basketball team and how he loved playing the game. "Yeah," I said, "but how's school? You know, your courses."

"Oh! You were always about the learning," Abdul replied, smirking. "I have a 3.3 grade average."

"Congratulations. You are doing well. It was great to see you two."

"You too, Mrs. Phillips. You were my favourite principal." Slinging his gym bag over his shoulder, he departed with long, lanky strides. I beamed as I got into my car. That kid had done good.

The following Tuesday was my weekly time with Sawyer. The backgammon board was set up and he was hunched over it, elbows on the table, chin resting on his hands, concentrating. The hoodie was still conspicuously absent. As usual Sawyer was moving his pieces across the board with more ease than I was.

"Would you really announce it to the whole office if you won?" Sawyer asked, not looking up from the board. A few weeks previously I had been joking again that it should be "Let the Principal Win Day" and had said that if that ever happened I was going to announce it to the whole office and put up a sign on my office door: Champion Principal Backgammon Player!

"I would," I confirmed. He continued to study the board. I looked at it as well and realized that I had myself in a precarious position and I was about to lose a checker to the bar. Today would not be the day I won. He looked up at me and smiled and then moved his checker so that I could move forward. I looked at him, my brow furrowed, but he was looking back at the board. Was Sawyer purposefully throwing the game? His sloppy playing continued through the next few moves. The room was silent. He pondered the board and made another silly move.

I was certain now that he was letting me win but I said nothing. Three more moves and I had won. Sawyer looked up, grinning ear to ear.

"I win!" I shouted. "Finally!" Sawyer just kept grinning. I went to my office door, "Hey, Mrs. Johnson," I said to Joan, "I just beat Sawyer at backgammon. Finally, it is 'Let the Principal Win Day'! Where is some paper? I'm making a sign for my door!"

"You won? No way! Sawyer, what happened?" Joan played along.

"I don't know," Sawyer said, grinning. "She won today and now she is going to tell everybody!" He looked expectantly at Adam's office. I knocked on the door and he came out.

"Guess what? I won at backgammon today! I finally beat Sawyer!" I said, smiling widely.

Adam, too, played along, stifling his laughter. "No way. Sawyer must be sick today. Sawyer, are you feverish? Feeling all right?" Sawyer grinned even more.

Vince, carrying a box of lightbulbs, happened by at this point and we repeated the conversation. I made the sign for my office door and put it up. I also wrote a note about my victory for him to give to his teacher. Sawyer, standing up prouder than I'd ever seen, left my office.

For principals, April and May are all about staffing for the following year. In fact, once April hits, the focus for everyone shifts from this year to the next. Staff assignments are determined and teachers who want to move schools go through transfer and interview procedures. Principals with openings spend hours interviewing teachers, educational assistants, child and youth workers, and secretaries as everyone finds a home for the following year. There are complex union rules to follow so the workload to principals increases, since all interviews must be done before or after school hours and not on weekends. One principal friend calculated that he spent sixty hours more per month working in the spring. My days were becoming more about student numbers and registrations than they were about learning or kids.

For kids the spring brings the freedom of the outdoors. Mud covers the hallway floors and we provide loaner clothes every day for kids who come in from recess having "slipped" into a puddle. The older students feel the spring fever of young love and all the drama that entails. Girls cry in bathrooms; furtive hand-holding happens under the desks; social media issues abound as secrets are told. Adam was busy.

Teachers, too, can begin to disengage in the spring as well. There is the rush to finish any curriculum not done. The end is in sight. As staffing decisions are made, some teachers are leaving, some are changing grade assignments, but everyone is looking to either the summer vacation or the following September. Part of my job at this time was to keep up the momentum for learning and caring about our students. We still had three months left. This was on my mind as we began the April staff meeting.

As the teachers entered, the picture of Tyler and Abdul smiling, arms draped about each other's shoulders, was projected on the screen. I began the meeting with their story. "These were my first starfish as a principal." The best way to get people to care is by tugging at heartstrings. I could see that the teachers were anxious now to tell their own starfish stories and I gave them the opportunity to talk about their successes and challenges. As I wandered about listening in on conversations, the names were often familiar to me: Sawyer, Myles, Olivia, Rafi. But some were not.

Maggie talked about a shy young girl in grade 1 who had barely said a few words at the beginning of the year but was now talking a blue streak to her. Jim spoke about Andy, a boy who was reluctant to write although he was an avid reader. Jim was reading a poem Andy had written. Debra was showing a video she had taken of Mateo. Everyone knew Mateo as a grade 7 boy who was always dressed in the latest fashion and had a gaggle of followers—he was "too cool for school" and didn't engage beyond the minimum. The video showed his excitement as he explained the bridge he'd built in science. Vanessa was excited about a grade 2 girl, Samantha, who hadn't been able to read at the beginning of the year but was now reading Dr. Seuss. There was no one disengaged. The activity had worked. Everyone cared about their starfish. We finished with everyone committing to a next step for the remainder of the year for their starfish. We needed the momentum to continue.

Vanessa and Sarah next provided an overview of our thinking about spiraling the math curriculum. We had been working on a template and they were excited to try it out next year. I could see some excited faces but many more dubious ones. Change is difficult and why would a teacher go through the struggle of something new if they felt that the old way was good enough? It's the perennial problem in teacher professional development. I didn't want Vanessa and Sarah to be deflated with their efforts and the spiraling was a good idea. I quickly prompted Chloe to tell her story about division. Chloe had a good sense of humour and everyone knew about her bouncy-ball class of boys. There was laughter and a bit more interest as she relayed her adventures with her class this year. A quick look at the clock pressed me to wrap up.

"April is the best time to try something new," I stated to a group that could see the end of the school year within their grasp. Often in education we think about doing new things in September. I have found that it is a terrible time to try new things. "You know your kids now and they will forgive you if you mess up. Remember they have already built the shrine to you." Laughter. "Plus, you know their academic abilities really well. Although you won't, because you have more curriculum to teach, you could probably write their final report cards now." This was a bit riskier to say. It was true, but not professional to voice. "September is usually when we try new things, but it is a lousy time. A group of new kids. Maybe a new grade or new classroom. Maybe even for a few of you a new school." A few teachers had indicated they would be looking at the postings for next year and I encouraged movement among schools. After five to seven years in a school, some teachers become stagnant. Movement creates growth. "In the fall you've got IEPs to write and routines to develop." I saw Kate smile and nod. She would be setting those routines much earlier next year. "So, September is not the time to try new things in your teaching—April is. We have been working on engaging students in their own learning more this year and all of you have tried new things. I see students working in groups more often. I see purposeful use of technology. I see fewer worksheets and no word searches."

"We only do word searches when you are out of the building, Kristin!" Mac joked, and everyone laughed.

"Lots of you have tried book clubs to get kids reading more, or writer's workshops to get kids to love writing. Jim was talking about that earlier. And then today, too, Vanessa and Sarah talked about a different way to approach math so that you are returning to key concepts many times throughout the year. Even if you took fifteen minutes every day to come back to a previously taught concept, would that make a difference, I wonder? We have three months left of school. That's almost one-third of the year. It's the most exciting time for you to try some new ideas and see if they make a difference. You can work out the kinks with this group of kids who love you so that you can start with it in September without worrying."

I paused and looked at my audience. They were attentive. It was probably a new idea for most of them. It had been a new idea for me, too, a few years ago. But I had been frustrated with all the new ideas that never got off the ground in September despite planning for them. Planning didn't equate with doing. It works better when teachers try out the new ideas in a safe environment. April was a safe environment.

"I'm not going to ask you to commit to a specific thing. I know you all have new things you've been trying this year. But if you've got that strategy figured out and you are pretty sure you are going to do it with your class next year, then see if there's something else you are curious about and try it out now. Come and chat with Adam and me about your new ideas. And, if you are interested in exploring spiraling more, watch in the weekly memo for that group's next meeting later this month. Remember, try something new; no one will die." A few laughed and some rolled their eyes.

I could hear the chatter as teachers left. A few were talking to Vanessa and Sarah. That was promising. I was curious to see how many teachers would pick up the challenge to try something new. Usually when I wanted change, I asked for a commitment, but I was nervous about that in April. Standardized testing was on the minds of the grade 3 and 6 teachers. Report cards would come soon enough. Track-and-field events, which disrupted all classes, loomed. Staffing decisions created stress as teachers worried where they would be next year. I was trying to change my leadership style to be more invitational. Earlier in my career I would have just said we were all doing something, but that hadn't worked too well. I was hoping that the motivation of how they had worked with their starfish might inspire them to try something else. My next moves would be important. I needed to be interested without being authoritative.

Relationships were important, I thought on my drive home. That was something I'd learned over the years. Developing them didn't come easy to me. I'd much rather just tell people what to do. But telling people what to do—be they kids or adults—doesn't really work. It didn't help Frankie for me to tell her how to be happy. She needed someone to support her in making her own decisions. I hoped Dr. Larson would be able to do that. It was hard realizing that I couldn't be the one to help my kid. It didn't help Sawyer to tell him to take off his hoodie. He needed to feel safe to do so. It didn't help Myles to tell him not to have tantrums, when that was the only response he knew. He needed to feel that school would be predictable. The teachers needed to feel safe enough to try new things, too. They didn't need me telling them what to do, but they did need my support. The sun was shining and there was the hope of spring. A robin was on the front lawn. I smiled. Today I liked being a principal. And today I had beaten Sawyer at backgammon.

# TWENTY-FIVE

# You Win Some . . .

THE AIR WAS STIFLING AND IT WAS hot. Late April was supposed to be temperate, but a heat wave was blanketing the city and despite the open windows there was not a breeze to be found. While I was only a few steps away from my air-conditioned office (the only room in the building that had an A/C unit), my blouse was sticking to my back and I could feel rivulets of sweat dripping down the backs of my legs. Thank goodness I'd remembered to remove the sweater I needed to wear in the office. It didn't do for the teachers to see that I could wear a sweater on a day when they would suffer.

I was roaming the halls, phone in hand, taking pictures. I'd been asked to give a presentation to the trustees about the use of technology in classrooms. Max was responsible for May's trustee meeting and had invited me to speak about how the teachers were engaging students with technology. I wasn't convinced we were anywhere near ready to show off, but you did not say no to your superintendent.

But, peeking into classrooms, I was excited by what I was seeing.

Unlike my walk-throughs in September where I saw teachers talking or students engaged in individual tasks, today there was very little of that. I took pictures of students working together on math problems, discussing books, writing poetry, building structures to determine how they could be stronger, looking through microscopes, and working with papier-mâché. Kids of all ages were reading books, not even looking up when I snapped a photo. I noticed teachers working with small groups of students or one-on-one. There were few lectures or teachers sitting at desks. Even Bryce was sitting with a group of students, discussing their writing, his phone nowhere to be seen.

There is a palpable feeling in a school when there is student engagement. Some schools are noisy and chaotic and a visitor immediately feels on edge. In other schools kids are busy but there is little sense of purpose. Other schools are eerily quiet. No one is talking and heads are down. Tasks are being completed and the teachers are in control. But it differs from schools where there is a hum of engagement. Lev Vygotsky, a famous cognitive psychologist, called this heightened engagement *flow*—when there is such focus that nothing else matters. That's what I could feel this spring day. I was excitedly snapping photos until I remembered that I was supposed to be documenting our use of technology. Where was the technology?

Thankful I had opted for low heels today, I started my tour of the school again. Surely we were using technology. Jim had provided workshops to the teachers about Google Classroom. Adam had ordered projectors. We had lots of Chromebooks and the teachers seemed to be sharing them, since I often heard them talking about them in the staff room. Why had I not noticed it? When I peeked into Mr. Crewson's grade 5 class the students were working on a social studies project. I could see a question on the whiteboard: How were ancient civilizations both the same as and different from ours? That was a good question. I remembered back to our fall conversation on what Siri couldn't do. She couldn't answer that question, for sure. The students were in groups. There were books on each table, and Chromebooks. I hadn't noticed them before but clearly students were doing internet searches.

In Maggie's grade 1 class the students were at centres building structures. There was a centre for building with straws, one for building with blocks, one for building with cubes, and one where the students were on the Chromebooks using an app to explore structures. In Tara's language class the students were in groups talking about their books. Some students were recording their comments on paper and some on Chromebooks. As I looped again past Bryce's class, I realized that a number of students were writing on the Chromebooks. Some were not. However, unlike earlier in the year, no one was simply typing a "good copy" into the Chromebook—they were using the technology to write and edit their stories. As I continued through the school, peering into classrooms, stopping to chat with students, it became apparent that the technology was no longer an event—it was simply another tool for the students to use. I remembered back to just a few years before, when all the computers were in one room and students would walk in orderly lines down the hall to "do computers." Most of the teachers in my school had spent their teaching careers using computers as glorified typewriters or devices on which to play games. So although technology in the "real world" had become an integral part of how we do business, the leap to the classroom was slower.

For many years there has been a belief that technology itself will improve education. It does not. In fact just the other day I'd been at a meeting where a group of principals was lamenting the fact that none of their teachers were using the Chromebooks they'd purchased. Another principal had presented an elaborate scheme of how her teachers had to sign up to use the Chromebooks once a week. I had no idea how my teachers were sharing the Chromebooks at our school. I knew that we didn't have enough for each student to have their own, but they seemed to share easily. At least I was blissfully unaware of any infighting.

Two things were apparent, though. One, the teachers had shifted how they used technology to teach. Second, technology seemed to be part of the equation but not the whole thing. During lunch I decided to bring up the conversation in the staff room. We had one long table in the staff room and there was already a line for the two not particularly clean microwaves. I squeezed in towards the middle of the table with my yogurt and fruit. Since my kids no longer ate their lunches, I no longer made them. That resulted in my own packed lunch being a rather sorry affair consisting of whatever I could grab quickly out of the fridge in the morning.

"Hey, Kristin. How come all the pictures this morning? Were you spying on us?" Mike joked. A perfect segue.

"You are all going to be famous," I replied with a smile. A few more teachers looked my way. "Max asked me to showcase how you are using technology at the next trustee seminar."

"Tell them we need more money!" Mac said. "I could use another fifteen Chromebooks."

"I will definitely have a slide. I was curious, though, how you all share the Chromebooks we do have."

Debra looked up. "Oh, each grade group has a set and we just talk among ourselves on how to use them." There were nods about the table. "But more would be better."

"Got it." I paused. "I was at a meeting the other day and a number of principals mentioned reluctance to use the technology in their schools. . . ."

Sarah joined the conversation at this point. "I think as I have changed how I teach my students—you know, more student talking and less from me—more choice in how the students do things, and all that stuff about what Siri can't do, the technology just fits in. Before I thought I needed a device for every kid so that everyone would be doing the same thing, so it would be fair. Now I don't worry about that."

"Yeah, at the beginning of the year I always wanted all my students to use the Chromebooks at the same time for writing their good copies," Bryce piped in. He was in the staff room? He was joining in? I was shocked. "Now some kids use them to write but some kids prefer paper and pen."

"You know, the kids we have now are pretty used to technology," Maggie added. "It's not such a big deal for them. I think it was a bigger deal for me. I don't worry anymore about giving every kid an equal chance every day. In the end it is just another way of getting the work done."

"The other day I was using the Chromebooks for the kids to collaborate on a play they were writing for history," Tara chimed in. "It was interesting that kids who normally wouldn't participate in a group discussion were right in there like a dirty sock."

The conversation continued this way, them sharing how they were using the technology. But it seemed to me that they were more excited about the teaching and learning that was happening, not the technology itself. I had my story for the trustees. It wasn't going to be so much about technology as about changing teaching. With a plug, of course, for more money for technology.

I returned to my office, happy with how things were going, only to be met by Adam looking grim. He followed me into my office and shut the door. I looked at him expectantly as he plopped down into the chair by my desk.

"Just had a call from HR. Harriet has applied for a leave of absence for the remainder of the year. Has a doctor's note for stress." I laughed and sighed at the same time. I was sure the performance appraisal was stressful—it's meant to be a wake-up call. But this is what would happen sometimes in these cases. Now she would be off for the rest of the year and because the TPA had been completed while she was "ill," it wouldn't be valid. I'd have to start again in September. I had to play in the union sandbox but I didn't have to like it.

"When's her last day? She's off sick today anyway, isn't she?"

"Yup. Leave begins tomorrow," Adam answered. There was nothing left to say. But I was thinking that it would be good to have Harriet out of the building. "Amanda is in for her. She's a good young teacher. Kids seem to respect her. Think we could hire her for the remainder of the year?"

"We can try," I said. "But because of contractual obligations, you know we will have to hire one of the five most senior applicants. Let her know we will be posting and keep her there until the job goes through."

"Don't you think we could get HR to make an exception? Those kids in her class have had a lousy year," Adam pleaded.

"You make the call. Go ahead and try. But my bet is that contractual obligations trump having something make sense. Let me know." Adam got up to make the call. A few minutes later he stuck his head in. "You were right. Let's hope Amanda is one of the five most senior applicants. Can you interview next Tuesday after school? That will be five days and the posting will have closed. Until then Amanda will be in the class." All of the research says that whom you hire is one of the most important decisions you make. But the union's contracts made good choices next to impossible. Our only hope was that because it was late in the year there was a chance that not too many would apply to the position and Amanda might be in our top five. I'd interview her anyway in case all of the top five were awful, but then if I went out on a limb and hired her I'd have to prove the others weren't suitable for the job and it would be grieved for sure. But maybe it would be June by then. Sometimes I felt like I was in a poker game, not running a school.

A knock on my door reminded me that Bryce and I were meeting about his final TPA. I'd put the final copy in his mailbox earlier in the week. Giving him a satisfactory rating had been a difficult decision. While he'd made a few improvements, as I had seen today, he was not a stellar teacher. The thing was, I wasn't sure he was ever going to be a stellar teacher, and the unionized system was made for mediocrity. Unlike

Harriet, he wasn't harming kids. His students loved him and I had had no parental complaints. If I had given him an unsatisfactory, he would not have been eligible for the staffing process. With any luck he'd see a posting he liked and move schools. He couldn't do that if we were in the midst of a negative performance appraisal. Was I selling my soul? Playing the odds, it felt like.

"Ready, Kristin?"

"Come on in, Bryce. Have a seat."

"Sure thing. How's your day going? I really appreciated you coming into my class today. Guess we will be in the presentation to the trustees, eh?"

I smiled and took a deep breath. "I got some great photos today of all the wonderful things that are happening here. I appreciated you sharing in the staff room today how you had changed your approach to writing this year."

"Oh, yeah. No prob."

"Do you find that the kids are writing differently at all now that they aren't all doing the same thing?" I asked.

"Well, they still do all the same thing but I couldn't get enough Chromebooks to do it the other way, so now we take turns. If we get more money after your presentation, then that would be great and each kid could have a Chromebook." He wasn't getting it after all.

"I really liked that you weren't having students use the Chromebooks as a glorified typewriter for their good copies," I ventured.

"Thanks. I changed that after you said so. The kids who do pen and paper, though, they do good copies. Sometimes they use the Chromebooks." We weren't quite where I had hoped.

"I wonder if perhaps when kids are using pen and paper they might not have to always do a good copy? It seems like a lot of time spent copying. Do you ever have students pick only one or two writing pieces per term to bring to the final 'good copy' stage?"

Bryce looked at me with a slight frown. I think he thought this was a trick question. "Uhhh, no . . . they always do a good copy."

"You might want to chat with Mike about how he handles good copies," I said. "Current pedagogy suggests that the process of writing and editing is probably more informative for both students and teachers than the final 'good copy' stage." I was beginning to wonder about my choices for his TPA. I knew that his grade group had had this very discussion many times during grade team planning. "Anyway, let's move on to your TPA. Did you have a chance to read it over?"

"I did. Thanks, Kristin. It's great. Very fair. I signed it already."

It wasn't great at all. Despite there being a satisfactory checked off, the comments suggested quite a number of improvements.

"It is a satisfactory TPA for a beginning teacher," I began. "I do hope you noticed, however, that there are a number of areas for improvement."

"Oh. Of course, Kristin. For sure. Always room for improvement," he said as he began to rise from the table.

"I just want to make sure that you understand the process for staffing moves, in case that is of interest to you." I had interrupted his leaving and he reluctantly sat back down. "As you begin your career, it is always good to find a great fit between you and the school. As you know from practice teaching and your long-term occasional assignments, all schools have their own unique culture." I was trying to say that the culture of this school wasn't a good fit for him, but of course I couldn't. "The first posting for openings comes out next week and if you have any questions, let me know. As I said at the last staff meeting, it is always good for everyone to have their résumé up-to-date in case your dream job is posted."

"Oh, for sure, Kristin. Maybe I will look but I like it here. My plan is to apply for the vice-principal pool in five years. Maybe I should stick to one spot before I apply." I guess I wasn't winning this bet.

"Well, let me know if you decide to apply somewhere. I will make a copy of the TPA for your records and send a copy to HR. If you feel next year that you've really addressed some of the suggestions and want me to redo it, I'd be more than happy to."

"Hmmm. Of course. I'll let you know, Kristin. And thanks again." This time when he got up, I let him go.

# TWENTY-SIX

# Welcome to Kindergarten

THE SCHOOL LIBRARY IS PACKED WITH ANXIOUS young moms and dads sitting in chairs that are too small. It's late May and already uncomfortably warm in here. Some of the parents are chatting animatedly but many are silent and nervous or talking in whispers to their partner. A few have brought children with them and there are a few babies—some sleeping and some fussing, as they'd rather be at home in bed.

It is New Kindergarten Parent Night. Next September these parents will be sending their precious children off to school for the first time. They have come to find out what to expect. Is this place going to be a safe spot for their bundle of joy and hopes? Some come excited, remembering school experiences that were filled with learning and new friendships. Some arrive cautious and wary, having had the opposite experience. It is the school event that brings out the greatest number of both mothers and fathers—almost as many as the annual holiday celebration in December.

At 7:00 p.m. I begin. "Welcome to kindergarten. My name is

Mrs. Phillips and I am the principal. I am thrilled that so many of you could join us this evening. There are some toys at the back if you have brought your child and they are getting antsy. You will have to supervise them there and listen with your other ear but as parents you are experts in that!" Laughter follows. Good—it helps cut down the anxiousness in the room. "And in case you were wondering, the air-conditioning is not broken. We don't have air-conditioning except in the office." The tension is relieved a bit more as everyone has another small laugh, although I can see some parents glance at each other, already concerned their children will not be comfortable at school.

"How many of you already have children in school?" Only a handful of hands go up. "You experienced parents are thrilled to have another one leave the nest," I joke, "but the rest of you are sending off your bundle of joy to school for the first time and that can be scary. This evening we will go through what the kindergarten program is like, what your child should bring to school and what to leave at home, talk about the first day of school, and answer your questions."

I'd given the "new to kindergarten" speech many times, always in late May and almost always (somehow) on the hottest evening. My feet were tired from high heels and I knew my cheeks would hurt from smiling when the hour was done. I scanned the audience, looking at the faces, hoping that I wouldn't have a parent dominate the question-and-answer period, although Adam and I had agreed earlier that should that happen, he would swoop in and invite them to his office to answer all their questions. Definitely a VP job. Smiling and ignoring my left big toe, I took a breath and commenced in earnest.

"I want to begin by assuring you that we here at school love kids. All kids. That's why we are teachers. And we will do everything we can to make sure that your child is safe, happy, and learning." The tension eases a little bit more as I begin my slides. I review that kindergarten is a play-based program for 3–5-year-olds. Through that play the students are introduced to early literacy and numeracy, and encouraged to explore and learn about topics of interest. A hand goes up.

"My child is entering junior kindergarten but she doesn't know how to write her name yet. Do we have to work on that all summer before she gets to school?"

"No," I say with a smile. "All children develop at different rates. Your child doesn't need to know how to do anything in particular in order to enter kindergarten. Please do not spend the summer doing worksheets or drilling your child with numbers or letters or words." I can see a few puzzled faces, and a few parents look down at the floor. They have probably just been to the store and purchased the pre-kindergarten workbook. "Certainly, if your child is interested in writing, or pretend writing—you know, all those squiggles your child writes and then reads back to you as if it were Shakespeare—you can encourage that. The best preparation you can give your child for kindergarten is to talk to them about the world around them, encourage their curiosity, model reading and writing at home, and read to your child daily. For example, you might show your child how you write your grocery list down. If they want to try, then let them add things to the list even if it doesn't make sense. For years I had corn 'flacks' on my grocery list!"

Another hand. "Really? I heard that kids who knew all the letters before they entered kindergarten were at an advantage."

"All your children will learn their letters. I promise. They will learn to read and add and subtract and know their shapes. Some may know those things coming into kindergarten and your child's teacher will move them forward. Some may not learn those skills until senior kindergarten or even grade one. But the teachers here are experts in teaching young children. That's what we love to do. I suggest that you do activities that are 'by the way.' Like counting out the forks and knives as your child helps to set the table or the stairs in your house as you head up to bed. Reading books together and looking at the pictures and the words. Talking about what they wonder about and answering all those 'Why?' questions that drive you crazy sometimes!"

I glance around. This conversation comes up every year. I hope that my reassurances will stop those who may be feeling pressured to drill their four-year-olds with worksheets all summer. I know parents are doing what they think is right, but for some it is stressful. They feel pressure to make sure their child has every advantage and it is exhausting for them. I hear of battles between parents and kindergarten students because the kid wants to play but the parent has bought the workbook. I scan the audience and there are no more questions. A few faces of relief. A few of guilt. And a few who clearly don't believe me.

The next few slides are about what to bring to school: a small backpack, shoes the child knows how to do up since we don't teach laces anymore in kindergarten, a lunch, and the communication book that will go back and forth. I stress the importance of parents checking for notes from the teacher daily and emphasize that the teacher will do likewise if the parent has something to communicate. I suggest extra clothes in case of an accident and extra socks because of puddles. A hand goes up. It's an older mother, over thirty-five, I would guess, and she looks embarrassed.

"What about toilet training? What if there is that kind of accident?"

This question comes up every year, too. "We do like it if your child is toilet trained," I begin. "However, let's remember that school is still three and a half months away. So if you are still working on it, you've got time. Remember your child in February? They have all grown so much in just that short time. The child you will kiss goodbye on the first day of school is not the same one that is living with you today." I see some shoulders relax and parents look at each other and smile. "If in September toileting is still a problem, just give me a call for a heads-up and we will figure it out. Your child can still come to school. And for all children, accidents are common in kindergarten. That's why we suggest the extra clothing. If the accident can't be dealt with at school we will give you a call. Don't worry."

Another hand goes up. "I am worried my daughter won't eat her lunch at school. I always have to remind her to finish up. Will the teacher do that?"

It's another common concern, one we hear every year. "We certainly encourage the kids to eat their lunches and provide a number of times throughout the day when they can have either lunch or a snack. However, we do not make the children eat their lunch and you may find that your child comes home with very little eaten at first." Immediately heads tilt up and eyes fasten on me.

"School is an exciting place and there are friends to talk to during lunch. It is our experience that after a few days, kids figure out to eat when they are hungry. It is also our experience that some parents do pack very large lunches." Some laughter. "Your child is going to school, not overnight camp. If your child tends to eat half a sandwich and a yogurt at home, chances are that's what they will eat here. Also, we do discourage a lot of sugary snacks and junk food. Like anyone, your child will choose that first and then not be hungry for the healthy food you sent. In the end, I have never had a student starve themselves. Kids will eat when they are hungry. Again, if after a few weeks you are really worried, then give the teacher or me a call."

There are a few more questions about backpack size and shoes. Many parents are taking notes. I remind myself that it is a big deal to send your kid off to school and trust someone else to take care of them.

"Let's talk about the first day of school." I explain about the buses and drop-off points. "Now, you and your child are going to be excited and scared. I have some rules about the first day of school . . . for you." I pause and look around. "You don't get to cry." I see a number of mothers, and a few fathers, quickly look down. "When it is time for your child to come inside, you can give them one kiss, not forty-seven, a quick hug that lasts four seconds, not five minutes." There is some tittering, as they all know they could be guilty of this. "You are going to say goodbye with a small hug and it is going to be sweet and short. You are *not* going to cry, even if your child does. You are not going to fol-low your child into the building, even if they are crying. We are very experienced in taking care of crying children. You are not going to sneak around the building and look in the windows." There is nervous laugh-ter now. It is a bit funny, but I'm actually being serious. I have found that I need to be explicit about these things. "If you feel the need to cry, you can do it on the way home. I did. And if after a little while we can-not get your child happy about joining in—which, I have to say, almost never happens—then I will call you. I promise. Remember, we love kids here. We want them to be happy."

It has been my experience that many parents need as much support as their children do in entering school. Ironically, I give pretty much the same speech to parents before the grade 5 camp trip evening: you can kiss your child goodbye once, hugs last four seconds, you may not look in the bus windows, you may not follow the bus in your car, you may not call your child at camp. We will take good care of your loved one.

And so begins the complicated relationship that schools have with par-ents. Parents entrust teachers with their most precious possessions. I once heard a saying that having a child is like having your heart walk around outside your body. The relationship needs to be one of trust. On the parents' part, beginning this relationship means letting go and allowing your child to become independent—hence my rules about the first day of school or going off to camp. Parents who are too clingy are subconsciously telling their child that they do not trust them to cope in this new situation. Plus, the first day of school in kindergarten can be challenging enough with up to sixty three- and four-year-olds in a new situation. Children that age are understandably needy and prone to crying. It only makes things harder for them if their parents are, too.

Today's parents are often accused of being "helicopter"—hovering over their children to manage every moment—or, the latest, "lawn mower" or "snowplow" parents who pave the way ahead and remove all obstacles, challenges, and hazards. Somewhere along the way in the last twenty to thirty years, the collective parent group decided that children should not suffer—ever. Parents spend countless hours ensuring that their children are constantly supervised, constantly entertained, constantly mollified. The result is a generation of young adults who have very few coping skills.

Universities and colleges lament that students arrive who have never had to make a single decision on their own. Many postsecondary institutions now send parents of new students a very politely worded back-off letter. Parents, it states, are not allowed to call profs and ask for an extension or their child's marks. Nor can they call to ask the dean to watch out for their child. My own parents did not receive such a letter when I went off to university, I am sure. Psychologists today are working with a new set of young patients who have no experience with the ups and downs of life or being able to cope with disappointment. Heightened anxiety is rampant, too. Students get anxious when they have a test. They get anxious when there is a school trip. They get anxious if they forgot to do an assignment. They get anxious if they aren't invited to a birthday party.

Schools provide numerous opportunities for children to experience "cope-able" problems. My job was to help parents recognize these as opportunities, not as catastrophes.

It is a challenging navigation to help a parent see that rescuing their child from new or stressful situations is actually more harmful than good. The parent's sole motivation is to make the crying stop, the unhappiness go away. Over the course of a school year I will help parents see that forgetting one's lunch and getting food from the school supply of yogurts, apples, and granola bars will be fine and they don't need to rush over with McDonald's. I will counsel parents to let their child solve problems with their best friend without my interference and that I am not going to tell a student they can't play with another student. Parents will call me because their child is unhappy with a teacher, a friend, or an assignment. I will try to determine whether the concern is one that needs grown-up interference or not. Sometimes a teacher is unfair or a student is being bullied and my interjection is required and necessary. But often I have to convince parents to let go and trust that their child can figure it out.

Mrs. Lopez was one such parent this year. Willie, her son, was in grade 5. He had hit his growth spurt early and was noticeably larger than the other boys. Despite his more mature appearance, he was fearful of everything and needed many reassurances to get through the day. Mrs. Lopez called me all the time: to help him find his snow pants, to make sure he ate his lunch, to see if he had his homework with him. I felt that his anxieties were caused, at least in part, by her. Willie didn't know how to cope without his mom checking in on him. She arrived in my office the day after the grade 5 camp trip meeting.

"Mrs. Phillips, I don't think this is a good idea for Willie. He says he wants to go but it is two nights away from home. What if he gets homesick? You know how forgetful he is."

"Willie is growing up," I said. "He needs to learn how to get along without you helping all the time. You are a good mom and you really love him, but I think camp would be a good idea."

"I don't know. You know when you talked about saying goodbye to the kids going to camp? I think you were talking directly to me. I know I would do those things."

I smiled. "You would. But so would other parents. My job is to help you let go for just a short period of time. Willie will have a great time at camp and you know the teachers will be there to help him if he needs it. I always go up for a day and I will touch base with him, too."

"But can't he take a phone and call me whenever he needs to?"

"No. We ask that kids enjoy camp without cell phones. If he really needs to talk to you, then the teachers will let him use their phone."

"Oh, then I could call his teacher?"

Mrs. Lopez wasn't giving up easily. "No. The teachers can't be getting phone calls from all the parents all the time. If you are really worried, you can call me at school." Mrs. Lopez and I had formed a relationship over the course of the year and I had worked to help her let Willie have a few difficult problems to solve on his own, like looking for his snow pants in the lost-and-found himself (he found them) or dealing with his teacher when he forgot his homework (she let him bring it the next day).

With a few more reassurances, Mrs. Lopez decided to let Willie go to camp. She followed the rules and didn't fuss too much as he was leaving, although he did have the largest overnight bag for two nights that I've ever seen. In the end, Willie loved camp. He didn't ask to call his mother once, although she called me at school both days! She called me the day after he came home and told me he had a great time, made some friends, and even swam in a lake!

John, Sawyer's dad, had called me about grade 5 camp as well. He wanted to check in and see what I thought about sending Sawyer to camp.

"You know," John began, "he is so much happier now at school and you haven't called me in a while about problems. And he tells me about playing with friends during recess. He loves his teacher."

"He is doing much better. He even cancelled coming to play backgammon with me a few times because he didn't want to miss what his class was doing. I think he would do fine at camp. And if there was a problem, you know we would call." Sawyer still lost his temper occasionally but got back on track much faster. He was doing well at school and Sarah had figured out how to work around his learning disability. But, most important, I wasn't his only friend anymore.

The relationship with parents starts on Welcome to Kindergarten night. Parents have to be seen as partners in their child's education. They need to be supported and feel welcomed. Cathy, the school council chair, had organized a Spring Fair this year and the parents had done all the work. It was a roaring success. It had also been an opportunity to show the teachers that we could work with the parents, not against them. Mr. Byun had brought in spicy noodles that he made himself and he shared them with the staff. Occasionally he popped by to ask for my help but not often. Sawyer's dad didn't call at every incident complaining that he had been bullied but rather was more willing to support Sawyer in forming relationships at school. Even Tiffany had been more trustful as she began to work with the school social worker.

The school's primary job is teaching kids. But alongside the kids come the parents, partners in their child's education. The relationship is complex because just as every kid has different needs, so does every parent. Just as every kid needs to feel welcomed, so does every parent. Schools are places where kids can learn independence. But these are also places where parents learn independence as well—how to let their children solve their own problems, how to trust that their children can survive without them, how to grow apart so their children can become healthy and productive adults.

The question period of the new-to-kindergarten night went off without a hitch. There were the usual questions about peanut allergies and EpiPens (yes, we had a policy), homework (only reading in kindergarten), and could they know who their child's teacher would be right now (not yet). As the night was winding down, a young couple with a new baby in tow cornered me with a myriad of questions about how their little girl would do in kindergarten and I finally suggested they book an appointment to see me at the end of August. Maybe they'd be calmer by then, but I doubted it. Another parent approached me privately and asked if she should be concerned that her three-year-old wasn't talking yet. Without letting my surprise show, I made an appointment for her to meet with me tomorrow and would make a referral to preschool speech services.

As the last of the parents made their way out, I took off my heels and walked with Adam on our way to our respective cars. "You going to cry on the first day of kindergarten for your little Sam next year?"

"Not now." We laughed. I would miss Adam.

# TWENTY-SEVEN

# Last Day of School

"MY MOM SIGNED ME UP TO GO to day camp. Jalal is going, too. And my sister, I think. My baby brother is too little."

Myles is kneeling in the chair by the table, his feet tucked up under his bottom. His hair is tousled as always and the June sun has already brought out more freckles. He fiddles with some Legos as he chats with me this morning, but he isn't building anything. Kim is leaning in the doorway smiling as she observes our interaction. A few minutes before, he had skipped into my office with a cheery "Good morning, Mrs. Phillips" and plopped down. He'd been chatting nonstop ever since.

What a difference. Was this the same boy I used to chase after every morning? With Sondra's and Kim's patience and willingness to work with him, Bridget working with Tiffany on parenting, and all of us creating a predictable environment, Myles had flourished. I was wearing different clothes, but I was always the same.

"And today we are having a picnic lunch outside 'cause it's the last day of school. Next year I will be in grade one."

275

"I know. That's a pretty big deal, grade one."

"Yeah. Jalal will be in grade one, too." Myles paused, scrunching his eyebrows together. "Will you be here in grade one?"

"I will." I smiled. "Right here in this office. You can come and visit anytime."

"Okay." Myles looked up at Kim. "I gotta go now." And off he scampered. Had I been expecting a heartfelt hug and words of gratitude for all the morning visits? Maybe a bit. But Myles was five. He lived in the moment. He probably didn't even remember all the times in September when he entered my office screaming and swearing. My phone was ringing; no time to be sappy and reflective on this last day of school.

There is a hum to the school on the last day. The halls are strewn with overflowing trash cans as students empty lockers and desks. Doors and windows are open to let in a hint of a breeze on the early summer morning. The smell of recently discovered gym clothes and long-forgotten lunches mingles with the freshness of the recently bloomed flowers of June. There are stray shoes, boots, sports equipment, and even snow pants that no one is inclined to claim. Next week Vince will gather it all and we will put it on a table in the foyer to see if any parents come by to claim the items, but most likely it will all go to charity. The staff room table is layered with all sorts of treats baked by parents as thank-yous and I grab a butter tart on a detour before making my walk down the hall.

Maggie's class is sitting on the carpet, engrossed in a read-aloud. Ana is sitting right up in the front, hand waving in the air so she can voice her opinion about the story. Kate's class is busy working on one last math problem. Kate will be teaching in the same grade and classroom next year. There are traditions in education, like anything else, and in many schools the newest teachers are the ones who move around the grades each year as enrolments and classes change. But I keep my new teachers in the same grade and classroom as much as possible and have the more experienced teachers switch grades when changes are needed.

Chloe's class is bouncing up and down on their balls-instead-of-chairs and a lively debate is going on. Peeking into Sarah's class I see Sawyer standing at the front reading a story he's written. I catch Sarah's eye and she gives me a thumbs-up. Heading towards the intermediate wing of the school I nearly trip on a pair of legs sprawled in the hallway. Rafi. I give him a look.

"Yeah, yeah. I know." He looks down, guilty as charged.

"Come have lunch with me today if you want," I say, casually stepping over his untied running shoes. We haven't had any more instances of out-and-out bullying since the suspension and he doesn't stop by my office every day anymore. But Rafi still causes his fair share of disturbances in the classroom and I worry how he will fare in high school next year.

Bryce's classroom is quiet. The students are doing a word search again and a pin could drop. Bryce is sitting at his desk, feet up, phone out. Is he chewing gum? *Really?* He hadn't applied for any of the openings and he would be teaching grade 6 in the same classroom next year. It had meant that Mike needed to change grades for September, being the more experienced teacher. It killed me to do it. I had wanted to give Bryce a terrible assignment in the hopes it would nudge him towards applying to the postings, but that wasn't fair. Bryce doesn't look up and I decide to move on.

Then the fire alarm goes off. I stop in my tracks. We had done our regulation 3 fire drills for the spring. Adam had not mentioned a drill today and I certainly hadn't planned it. As I head towards the office the students are efficiently and quietly exiting the building. Teachers are looking at me puzzled and I can only return the look.

Joan is gathering her binders for a fire drill and Adam is closing the office windows and doors.

"What's going on?" he asks. "You trying to test me on the last day?"

"I was going to ask you the same thing. Do you smell smoke?"

"Nope."

Vince comes running in. "Is this a drill?"

"Nope," we both respond. All of us shrug our shoulders and exit the building to the back. The classes are all in lines waiting quietly and then we hear the fire trucks. The students go wild with shouts and pointing and excitement. During a drill the trucks do not arrive. I can hear Peter's special education class beginning to wail and Adam immediately heads in their direction. I head towards the fire truck.

"Hi, I'm Kristin Phillips, the principal. We are not having a drill."

"We'll go in and check it out." I return to the students and staff and raise my hand for silence. It takes a minute but eventually all eyes turn to me for answers.

"Thank you to everyone for exiting the building safely and quietly. Right now, we are not sure what is happening, but the firefighters have gone in to check it out. I suggest that you sit down in your lines and wait patiently. I will let you know when I know more." Then I begin the checklist in my head. I call the emergency response number at the board but the person on the other end is already aware the fire trucks have arrived. Do I need them to send someone? I say I'll let them know when I know what the issue is. As of yet we do not see smoke or flames. I call Max's cell phone and leave a message. I call Cathy, the school parent council chair, to let her know what is going on in case she gets phone calls. I'm sure the phone calls have already started, as we have houses across the street. Managing the fallout will be as important as managing the event. The chief is approaching me.

"Well, looks like someone lit a fire in the boys' bathroom in the back wing. It was in a garbage can and went out on its own. No damage done."

"Terrific," I mumble under my breath. "Thanks for checking it out. Can we return to the building?"

"Yes, we're done." I ponder how much to say to the students. They will all know soon enough through the grapevine. Best they hear it from me. I raise my hand again for silence.

"The firefighters have said that it is safe to return to the school.

There was a small fire in a garbage can in the boys' bathroom in the intermediate hallway. It's out now and there was no damage. That washroom will be closed for the next hour for cleaning. If you have any information about the fire, you can let me or your teacher know. It is not tattling when you report something like this. The person who lit the fire was not keeping us all safe. It is important that we are all safe." I did not want to deal with this on the last day of school. Making my way back into the building, I notice the kindergarten and grade 1 classes gathering around the fire trucks. A number of grade 8 students surround me.

"It was Rafi, Mrs. Phillips."

"I saw him in the bathroom."

"I saw him in there when I went, too. He looked like he was hiding something."

"Rafi was laughing when you were talking."

"It was Rafi. I heard him talking about it at recess. He said he had matches."

"Thanks for the information," I say, scanning the faces so I'll know who to talk to later.

Adam sidles up beside me. "I hear it was Rafi," he says. "A bunch of kids surrounded me with information."

Jim joins us and says, "I am hearing the same thing."

"Well, at least we know where to start the investigation. Adam, can you ask Vince to make sure all the remnants are taken care of and the washroom is clean?" The bell for lunch rings as I settle into my office, picking up the phone to call the emergency response line at the board (no, we don't need you) and then leaving another message for Max. I send a quick text to Cathy. I make a note to myself that I will have to send a letter home with the students today to reassure parents. Then out of the corner of my eye I see Rafi plop down at the table, lunch in hand. I swivel in my chair to look at him.

"What?" He scowls. I look at him some more. "What?" I wait. Rafi looks down.

"Want to tell me what happened?"

"I didn't do it."

"Lots of people say you did."

"They are framing me."

"Really? That's a lot of people to be framing one person." Silence. Rafi toys with the edge of his lunch bag but doesn't take anything out. I'm disappointed. We have made great gains this year with Rafi and he hasn't been in serious trouble in at least two months. What is going on?

"Sometimes we do things we wish we hadn't," I say. I wait. "It doesn't mean all the good things that person has done don't count."

"Yeah."

"Yeah, what?"

"Yeah, it was me." His face is a mixture of bravado and tears. He doesn't know what to feel. I don't, either.

"Why? The school could have caught on fire."

"No, it couldn't. It was in the steel garbage can and the walls in there are concrete," Rafi counters, as if that made the act not so significant somehow.

"It was still a fire. You can't start fires in schools. It's against the law." I need to think. One, it is the last day of school and I don't want to deal with this. Two, it's Rafi. He's my starfish. I thought I'd saved him. "Wait here a minute." I go into Adam's office and plop down in his second chair. His office is packed up in boxes, as he has been promoted to principal and will have his own school in September. I am not happy about that, either.

"Rafi?"

"Yup. He confessed. Didn't even take long. He showed up in my office on his own for lunch!" I laugh, but I am not happy.

"What are you going to do? I guess a suspension isn't really worth it and is it an expellable offense? Police?"

A few months ago, I would have made Adam run through all the steps with me as practice, but we are beyond that now. "A suspension isn't going to be on the table. Makes no sense to have the high school implement it in September. We could start an expulsion process, but this just doesn't seem like part of an escalation of incidents. He was doing so well. I really thought we'd turned a corner."

"You have to do something. It was a fire. You can't let it go."

"I know." I text my school police resource officer to give me a call. "Rafi can deal with the police this summer," I tell Adam. "It's a logical consequence. And I will let the high school know personally, not just leave it in his record, so that if his behaviour escalates, they've got enough evidence to move towards expulsion."

The expulsion process is long and time consuming and students who end up being expelled are offered, if available, a spot in a behaviour program for a year. If they do well there, they return to the regular system. It was the best the board could do but it didn't have a high success rate. Usually by the time a student ended up there, the problems were numerous and complex. Most likely the student had spent years already in and out of suspensions and in and out of behaviour programs. I didn't think it would be a good fit for Rafi.

I went by the staff room for another butter tart and to update the teachers who were there. The reaction was mixed. Some felt he should be taken out in handcuffs and expelled. Some felt sorry for him. Everyone was angry that the last day of school had been marred.

Dragging my high heels back to my office, I sat down to talk to Rafi. His head was in his arms on the table, his lunch untouched.

"It is a serious thing to start a fire. It disrupted the last day for the whole school. It is against the law. If it weren't the last day of school, you would be suspended for a long time."

"I know. So, what are you going to do?"

"Well, first I'm calling your uncle. I have left a message for the school police officer to call me back. You have committed a crime and you are older than twelve so you could be charged. That will be up to Officer Bob." Rafi looked up, tears flowing.

"I could go to juvie?"

"I don't know." I would have been surprised if that happened, but I wouldn't let him know that. "That will be up to the police. The third thing I need to do is have the school board psychologist do an assessment to see if you are at risk of further dangerous situations. That will happen over the summer."

"What? I have to see a shrink?"

"She will talk to you and your aunt and uncle to see if you are at risk for more dangerous behaviour. This is serious, Rafi. I don't know why you would do such a thing."

Actually, I now had my suspicions. Rafi was scared of leaving and going to high school. Often the kids who show the most bravado are those with the least self-confidence. At the beginning of the year, Rafi had gotten in trouble and bullied other students to show his "social power." Over the course of the year he had discovered that he didn't have to make a big show to feel like he belonged—we'd worked hard to make school feel safe for him. Now he was leaving and didn't know how to feel about it. Starting the fire was reverting to previous behaviours, although he had certainly upped the ante. I was worried.

"I'm going to call the high school as well and give them a heads-up. I want to make sure there is someone there to connect with you in September."

"I don't need to connect with anyone."

"Hmmm. Are you excited to be going to high school?"

"I don't know. I like it here."

"I know. You have really turned things around here since March break. I've hardly seen you. Maybe you are feeling scared about going to high school?" Silence. His head was down on the table again. "This is not a good way to end the year, but I still like you." I could hear Officer Bob in the main office, so I left Rafi to update him on the situation.

"Hey, Bob. Nice of you to come right away."

"What's up on the last day of school, Kristin? What a day for a problem." I escorted him into Adam's office, where I explained the situation.

"I'm torn on this one, Bob. He's a kid with problems, for sure. He's been doing so much better, I just don't want to believe this is the tip of the iceberg, but I can't say for sure. Fires are no small potatoes."

"Well, let me go talk to him." I sat there with Adam. We talked of his plans for tomorrow, when he would go to his new school for the first time. Tomorrow was the last day of school for the teachers, a Professional Development Day, and new principals had a meeting with their new staff. My new VP would join our staff meeting. Bob returned after five minutes.

"He's an unhappy kid. Surly."

Bob relayed his conversation, or lack thereof, with Rafi. I knew only too well how difficult it was for Rafi to communicate. Rafi was sticking with his story of it being a joke, but both Bob and I knew that kids didn't "joke" by lighting fires. "What's next?" I asked.

"Have you called the parents yet? I think I will drive him home and chat with them. We will have to charge him in this one. But I'll do it from his house, not here. I don't want to walk him out in handcuffs if he will come with me."

"Adam, why don't you escort Rafi to his locker to grab his stuff and I will call his uncle." Looking at Bob, I said, "Rafi lives with his aunt and uncle. No mom in the picture and dad is just out of prison." Bob looked at me knowingly. I knew Rafi had to be charged. Like being a mom, being a principal meant that you sometimes had to do the right thing even when you didn't want to.

The call went as well as could be expected. After a few choice words, his uncle seemed resigned to the situation. I felt for him. It wouldn't be an easy summer. I explained about the threat risk assessment the psychologist would do and suggested that it might be a way to get Rafi some counseling, which might help.

"Thanks for all your support this year," I said, ending the call. "Rafi really did make some improvements. I hope this is just a glitch and that he gets back on track."

"I hope so, too, Mrs. Phillips. You've been good to him. I know he likes you and that school. I'm sorry he's been so much trouble. We just don't know what to do with him, you know?"

"Officer Bob is ready to drive him home, so he should be there soon. I'll touch base with you as soon as I know about the assessment."

I walked with Rafi and Bob out to the parking lot. Bob and I walked together, with Rafi shuffling behind us, dragging his backpack along the ground, head down.

"Rafi, you can be a good person. I know it. This was a lousy day and there will be consequences. But you can still choose to be a good person." I put my hand on his shoulder and gave it a squeeze as he got into the back of the cruiser. He didn't say anything. He didn't say good-bye. I watched him ride away, and just as they were about to turn out of the parking lot, he turned his head and looked back at me through the rear window.

The bell rang—the end of the last day. Parents were milling about in the yard. Kids came bursting out of the doors laden with bags, backpacks, and lunchboxes. They were moving out. As I made my way to the buses to wave goodbye, I received hugs from the little ones, high fives from the bigger ones, and thanks from the parents. The buses lined up out front were full, kids waving and shouting out of the open windows. The teachers were gathered on the sidewalk to wave goodbye. It was a school tradition. I spotted Sawyer heading home burdened with two backpacks and a plastic bag of belongings.

"Hey, Sawyer, have a great summer." He ignored me and kept walking. Sarah was standing next to me.

"He certainly had a great year," she said. "Thanks for your help with him. He loved the backgammon days. Glad you finally beat him."

I laughed. "He did have a good year. You were the perfect teacher for him," I said as I watched him turn the corner. I chatted with a few parents and said goodbye to the straggling students. I scooted the circles of grade 7 students off the property since they didn't want to leave. Jim, a grade 7 teacher, was kibitzing with the students as well.

"Crazy last day, eh?"

"Never a dull moment," I said. "Despite the fire alarm, did your last day go well?"

"Always hard to say goodbye to the students at the end of the year." Jim paused, shuffled his feet, and looked down. "I just wanted to say that this has been a great year for me. We've learned so much that I feel the same excitement I did at the beginning of my career. After fifteen years I thought I'd figured it all out, but I tried things this year that really changed how I thought about teaching. Thank you."

"Thank *you*. Your team really worked hard this year. I've been thrilled with what I've seen and I brag about how wonderful you all are to anyone who will listen. I'm so glad you've had a great year. Rest up this summer and next year will be even better. That's the best thing about teaching. Every year is a new opportunity." I smiled.

My hand was on the front door when I heard "Mrs. Phillips!" I turned. It was Sawyer running back to school, dropping his bags on the sidewalk. He ran right into me and gave me a hug. He turned and left before I could say anything.

"Have a great summer, Sawyer. I'm going to practice my backgammon game!" I yelled after him. He glanced back and grinned and then he was gone.

# Summer

TWENTY-EIGHT

# August Dreams

LAUGHTER MIXED WITH THE SOUND OF THE cicadas. A brilliant blue sky. Lily and Joey were pushing each other off the swimming dock and Frankie was lounging nearby, not partaking but not hiding out in the cottage, either. There was just one week left before I would head back to school and the summer pause would end. I looked up from my book, a romance mystery, not one of the books on education that I'd brought with me and hadn't yet cracked open. Frankie, bikini clad despite the scars crisscrossing her arms, seemed calmer. While the sulkiness wasn't gone, she was more present and joined in playing Hearts in the evenings and kayaking during the day. She had been taking a new antidepressant daily and seeing Dr. Larson weekly for the past four months and hadn't given up. Although she didn't confide about their sessions, she had mentioned the day before that maybe I could join them one time. I smiled and agreed but inside worried how that would go. Would Frankie be angry with me? I racked my brain for any interaction that might have contributed to her distress. But I would go. She would begin university in the fall, choosing to stay in town and live at home. I had mixed feelings about that, remembering how I had enjoyed leaving home for university, the friends I had made. I worried that she would miss out on the whole university experience, but, on the other hand, I would worry about her living away as well. She was nervous but not talking to me about it.

Joey had worked as a junior ranger this past summer and he seemed more grown-up—plus there were strict rules about alcohol and drugs and that had been good for him. He wasn't worried about school beginning again; he rarely worried about anything. He had a part-time job lined up and had decided to form a band with his friends. Apparently the rock star career was still Plan A in his mind. He had decided to live with his dad every other week, starting in September. I supported this but I would miss him.

In her last year of high school, Lily had plans to go and live with my brother's family in Germany for six months. This had been a surprise to me, but she said she wanted to learn German. I think she also wanted a break from the challenging family dynamic but she didn't want to say so. I knew that Lily worked hard to be "perfect." She would leave in January. When your kids are little you think it will last forever: the swimming lessons, the playdates, toys all over the house, apple juice and Kraft dinners. But life was changing now and they were going off on their own. I would have to think about my own personal life now. Dating? I'd think about that later.

The previous night, I'd had the "August Dream." Ask any teacher and they will know what you are talking about. Mine is always on the same theme and I always have it a couple of weeks before school begins. I have a class of students who are completely unruly and won't listen to a thing I say. This time there was a food fight in the middle of the math lesson I was teaching. Never mind that I have never had problems with classroom management; the effects of the dream lingered and I was thinking more about school starting up. I opened my email after ignoring it for the last four weeks.

Harriet was returning to school part-time, under doctor's orders. She'd start with 20 percent teaching for September and gradually increase it until she was full-time by December. It didn't matter that this would mess up my timetabling or that it wasn't good for kids. When she'd gone on leave in the spring, we had been able to hire Amanda and the kids had learned more in three months than they had all year. I had been able to hire her for Harriet's leave for the fall, too, but would now have to let her know that it wasn't as full-time as I had hoped. I wasn't sure that she would take the job, given that she might be able to get something better at another school. Plus, she was so good that I anticipated a flurry of parent calls as the students moved from her teaching to Harriet's. Norm had also reminded me that the negative performance appraisal couldn't continue and that I would have to start again.

But as I scrolled through more back-to-school messages, I began to smile. The dates of the system meetings and when the enrolment updates were due, reminders about fire and tornado drills, a warning to make sure you have a health and safety team who has their first aid training, updates about students, questions from parents, teachers requesting assignment changes—it was all starting again. For me, New Year's Day is September 1.

The first year as principal at a new school is always the hardest, as you figure out the culture and form the relationships. Teachers are usually wary of a new principal, wondering what will change and if they will be left alone. All principals come with their own ideas and philosophies. That's both a good thing and a bad thing. All organizations need fresh ideas and a principal can imbue a school with renewed enthusiasm. I hoped I had managed to do that, remembering Jim's comment about having learned so much it felt like he was a new teacher again. However, principals can change frequently and for teachers there is sometimes a sense of "waiting it out." It can be challenging to implement change when teachers feel it won't be long-lasting. Also, when two principals have very different ideas on how a school should run, meaningful changes may not have the opportunity to take hold if they are replaced with something new within three years. But I wasn't going to worry about all that now as I entered year two at my school.

My walks around the school and my conversations with teachers throughout the year had pointed to an enthusiasm for teaching and learning. Teachers had connected with their starfish and had changed how they approached teaching to help students learn. We were increasingly using a twenty-first-century lens and beginning to focus less on rote learning and more on critical thinking skills. I was eager to see how the experiment with spiraling math would work. About half the staff had shown some interest. I'd have liked there to be more but perhaps the excitement of those trying it would spill over to the others. When, in the past, I had tried to impose all of my ideas, I had received lip service but little real change. I was trying a new style of leadership (and no one had died, yet). Like Jim, I felt a renewed sense of purpose moving into year two. Maybe I really did like this principal thing.

I loved teaching. I always had, ever since I played school with my dolls as a kid. I felt I was teaching again, only this time I was teaching teachers, not kids. Education is always about the "what-ifs." This past year I had wondered, What if I change how I lead? What if I work on forming better relationships? What if we can get those students learning who hadn't? The myriad administrative tasks that make up September loomed, but I was thinking about the learning. What if the teachers continue to grow in their practice? What if Kimoni approaches me with a new staff activity? What if we collaborated in grade teams even more? I was having the best-principal-ever feeling.

"Mom!" Joey yelled from the dock. "What's for supper?"

# *Epilogue*

## COVID-19

### MAY 2021

CAMDEN'S DAD WAS ON THE PHONE, AGAIN. For the third time in just over a year, Covid-19 had locked down the schools and the students were learning remotely. He was a single father of two boys, eleven and thirteen years old, and he couldn't afford to hire anyone to stay at home during the day while his sons were "at school" looking at a computer screen for five hours.

"I'm a bad dad. I don't know why Camden won't go to school. Every morning I wake him up and get him to eat. He promises me that he will log on, but you are saying he is not."

"You are not a bad dad. You get him up, you make his breakfast, you call me back even when I bet you don't want to. These are difficult times for everyone. I will have the special education teacher call Camden and see if we can reduce his course load so he feels he can get some work done." This was the fifth parent I'd called and it was only 10:00 a.m.

Remote learning was not working for many students, who found they missed the social interaction of school. Many years ago a student had told me, "All teachers think their subject is the most important. Lunch is." Kids go to school to be with their friends. And kids were missing that. Even when we had in-person learning, the masks, the desks in rows, and the myriad rules all had contributed to a school environment that was challenging for student engagement. I'd never walked down halls that were so quiet or worked in a school office that wasn't a revolving door of parents, teachers, and students. A lot of the fun stuff was gone.

I am now retired. The last three years of my career had been at the board office. I'd never have thought I would work at the system level, but I was at a point where I was seeking a challenge. I had discovered that school change was possible, but could we make system change? I learned that it is very, very hard to do. The educational system has lots of innovative ideas, but implementation at a large scale is no easy task. Working at the board office was enlightening and gave me a greater sympathy for the system as a whole, but I missed the autonomy of being a school principal. As I was entering my fourth year at the board office (already four years past my official retirement date), I was weary of meetings and the slow pace of change. The excitement I'd felt for learning as a teacher and a principal had become mired in memos (cc everyone you know), policy, and meetings. By Labour Day weekend, two weeks into the school year, I was already searching for new jobs.

"Wanted: Math Teacher in Tanzania." Where exactly was Tanzania? I looked it up (east coast of Africa) and then read the position more carefully. A paid volunteer position, teaching math to girls who had been rescued from forced early marriage. I read about the NGO. I googled pictures of Tanzania—wild animals, lush mountains, incredible reefs off Zanzibar. This would be a new adventure and I could find my passion for learning again. I applied and two weeks later I was offered the position, which would start November 1. In a whirlwind, I retired from the board, rented my house, got my inoculations, and left with a backpack full of math books and long skirts. Shinyanga, the town where I lived for the next five months, was not the Tanzania of the photos I'd seen. It was flat and rural and dusty. There were animals roaming around, but they were cows, goats, and chickens. The school was four rooms with concrete walls, window openings but no glass, and dirt floors with the occasional rat or snake. I had a makeshift blackboard and chalk—most days. There were no Chromebooks, no projectors, no textbooks, no photocopier, and limited paper and pencils. I loved it. Teaching there reminded me why I started this career so many years ago.

I ultimately came home because of the pandemic, returning to a much quieter life than I was used to. Frankie, Lily, and Joe (we call him that now) were all grown up and living on their own and my days were only punctuated by the weekly trip to the grocery store and Zoom calls with friends and family. Frankie, with years of therapy and support, is a successful businesswoman. She speaks openly about the mental health challenges, and I have learned to as well. I don't cry when I drive by the hospital anymore. Lily has just begun her practice as a midwife but lives a few hours away. Joe, ever joyful, lives in the mountains out west and makes a living doing a variety of outdoor contracts. But he reads books now. He still asks me to make pizza when he comes to visit.

The pandemic found the school system desperate for retired principals to work and it was a chance to go back to the job I had loved the most. While I miss lunches in the staff room (staff can't gather) and playing foursquare at recess time (no recess allowed), many things at school are the same. Teachers are still looking for that best-teacher-ever feeling, parents get their kids (now masked and screened for Covid) to school every day, and kids still love coming to school.

There are significantly more mental health challenges for both staff and students. In one week, I had three staff members request a leave. The rules say that students must stay in their cohort, so I ended up scooting one young girl back to her own class every lunch hour as she so desperately wanted to visit her friend down the hall. The learning gaps are huge—we have grade 3 students reading at an early grade 1 level and grade 7 students trying to cope with algebra who haven't mastered basic math concepts. Unfortunately, the Ministry of Education has not offered any solutions to this problem and they are the only governing body that has the authority to streamline the curriculum while students get caught up. In fact, in our jurisdiction, in the middle of this pandemic, a new math curriculum was introduced! I worry that there is not a plan to address the significant learning gaps in two years of disrupted education.

The job was both the same and different. Some of the people had retired but I had a chance to reconnect with others. At a Zoom meeting I ran into Bryce's principal and she raved about his ability to connect with kids during the pandemic and how the other teachers looked up to him at her school. He was teaching them about book clubs! Maybe I should have taken him under my wing more. As a teacher you soon realize that you aren't the best match for all kids. I guess it is the same with being a principal.

Now that I'm retired, I wish school didn't start at eight thirty—I've gotten used to drinking my morning coffee leisurely. But I feel at home at these schools when I am filling in. Teachers still want to make it work for kids. Some of the problems are Covid-related. How do we have story time if the students can't gather? Do I have to sanitize the calculators after we use them? Should we send a coughing student home?

What has struck me the most, however, is the resilience of teachers in being able to adapt to the "rules" and still find ways to engage students. There is a greater use of technology and *all* teachers are now comfortable with it. Roger, a grade 5 teacher, is curious about how to engage his students by having them write letters about the books they are reading. Suzanne uses French video clips to give her students frequent movement breaks, since recess isn't possible right now. And Tom is curious about how to integrate subjects so that he can find more time in the day to address reading gaps.

The kids are resilient, too. When I had heard of all the new rules, I wondered how students would cope. But they do. Students sanitize their hands as a matter of course. The masks might slip down but no one fusses when you remind them it needs to cover their mouth and nose. But they are still kids, dealing with kid-type problems. Alana, in grade 8, thinks the boy she has a crush on likes her best friend better and believes that's why she can't concentrate on her history project. Harrison, a grade 1 student who needs more wiggle time than he is getting, goes for a walk with me at breaks. Samar had to go home early because he vomited and those are the Covid rules. But I don't think he was too sick, because when his mom came to pick him up, he said, "I only puked because my gummy bears tasted like broccoli. Don't put my gummy bears next to my broccoli in my lunch!"

It is still the best job I ever had.

# Acknowledgments

THIS BOOK IS REALLY THE COMBINED STORY of all the students, teachers, colleagues, and parents who shared their hopes and dreams, joys and sorrows with me over my career. Each and every one taught me something about learning and schools and myself. It is their story and I thank them for sharing their tales. I wrote the words, but they provided the guidance, the content, the memories.

Simon & Schuster Canada made publishing a first book easy, and they were supportive through all the steps of writing it. Who knew there would be so many steps! In particular, thanks to Justin Stoller for guiding me through the editing process (he didn't even use a red pen), Nita Pronovost for overseeing everything, and Kevin Hanson for believing I could write the book in the first place.

My family (brothers, parents, and my three kids) have supported me throughout. I appreciate their humour and patience and wise words of advice. In particular, I'd like to thank Joey for his joy and exuberance, Lily for always being there, and Frankie for the courage to let me tell her story. Being a principal was a wonderful career; being a parent to such amazing people has been my greatest joy.